War

War

War

Other books in the Current Controversies series:

War

John Woodward, *Book Editor*

Bruce Glassman, *Vice President*
Bonnie Szumski, *Publisher*
Helen Cothran, *Managing Editor*

GREENHAVEN PRESS
An imprint of Thomson Gale, a part of The Thomson Corporation

THOMSON
———✳———™
GALE

Detroit • New York • San Francisco • San Diego • New Haven, Conn.
Waterville, Maine • London • Munich

LIBRARY OF CONGRESS CATALOGING-IN-PUBLICATION DATA

War / John Woodward, book editor.
    p. cm. — (Current controversies)
  Includes bibliographical references and index.
  ISBN 0-7377-3236-9 (lib. bdg. : alk. paper) —
  ISBN 0-7377-3237-7 (pbk. : alk. paper)
    1. War—Causes. 2. War—Prevention. 3. War on Terrorism, 2001– . I. Woodward, John, 1958– . II. Series.
  JZ6385.W365 2006
  303.6'6—dc22   2005046261

Printed in the United States of America

Contents

Chapter 1: What Causes War?

Chapter 2: Is the War on Terror Justified?

Chapter 3: How Should Wars Be Conducted?

Chapter 4: Can War Be Prevented?

Yes: War Can Be Prevented

No: War Cannot Be Prevented

Foreword

By definition, controversies are "discussions of questions in which opposing opinions clash" (Webster's Twentieth Century Dictionary Unabridged). Few would deny that controversies are a pervasive part of the human condition and exist on virtually every level of human enterprise. Controversies transpire between individuals and among groups, within nations and between nations. Controversies supply the grist necessary for progress by providing challenges and challengers to the status quo. They also create atmospheres where strife and warfare can flourish. A world without controversies would be a peaceful world; but it also would be, by and large, static and prosaic.

The Series' Purpose

The purpose of the Current Controversies series is to explore many of the social, political, and economic controversies dominating the national and international scenes today. Titles selected for inclusion in the series are highly focused and specific. For example, from the larger category of criminal justice, Current Controversies deals with specific topics such as police brutality, gun control, white collar crime, and others. The debates in Current Controversies also are presented in a useful, timeless fashion. Articles and book excerpts included in each title are selected if they contribute valuable, long-range ideas to the overall debate. And wherever possible, current information is enhanced with historical documents and other relevant materials. Thus, while individual titles are current in focus, every effort is made to ensure that they will not become quickly outdated. Books in the Current Controversies series will remain important resources for librarians, teachers, and students for many years.

In addition to keeping the titles focused and specific, great care is taken in the editorial format of each book in the series. Book introductions and chapter prefaces are offered to provide background material for readers. Chapters are organized around several key questions that are answered with diverse opinions representing all points on the political spectrum. Materials in each chapter include opinions in which authors clearly disagree as well as alternative opinions in which authors may agree on a broader issue but disagree on the possible solutions. In this way, the content of each volume in Current Controversies mirrors the mosaic of opinions encountered in society. Readers will quickly realize that there are many viable answers to these complex issues. By questioning each author's conclusions, students and casual readers can begin to develop the critical thinking skills so important to evaluating opinionated material.

Current Controversies is also ideal for controlled research. Each anthology in the series is composed of primary sources taken from a wide gamut of informational categories including periodicals, newspapers, books, United States and foreign government documents, and the publications of private and public organizations. Readers will find factual support for reports, debates, and research papers covering all areas of important issues. In addition, an annotated table of contents, an index, a book and periodical bibliography, and a list of organizations to contact are included in each book to expedite further research.

Perhaps more than ever before in history, people are confronted with diverse and contradictory information. During the Persian Gulf War, for example, the public was not only treated to minute-to-minute coverage of the war, it was also inundated with critiques of the coverage and countless analyses of the factors motivating U.S. involvement. Being able to sort through the plethora of opinions accompanying today's major issues, and to draw one's own conclusions, can be a complicated and frustrating struggle. It is the editors' hope that Current Controversies will help readers with this struggle.

"The weapons of war will most certainly look different in the years ahead, even if the causes of armed conflict remain familiar."

Introduction

During Operation Enduring Freedom, America's 2001 war to topple the Taliban regime in Afghanistan, observers frequently witnessed a striking combination of ancient and modern war technologies, such as elite U.S. Special Forces commandos calling in satellite-controlled precision air strikes while on horseback. This was a visual reminder that war looks very different today than it did many decades ago. What will war be like in the future? The weapons of war will most certainly look different in the years ahead, even if the causes of armed conflict remain familiar. In fact, some military experts believe that the development of new weapons technologies will eventually result in the elimination of soldiers and armies altogether and the emergence of the "postheroic" war, in which machines and organisms do battle on behalf of people.

The most feared weapons today are nuclear, chemical, and biological—those commonly referred to as weapons of mass destruction (WMDs). Ironically, the development of these extremely powerful weapons, particularly nuclear weapons, was largely responsible for preventing wars between large nation-states in the latter half of the twentieth century. After World War II the United States, China, and the Soviet Union engaged only in proxy conflicts in places such as Korea, Vietnam, and Nicaragua, rather than engage each other directly using weapons that could lead to global catastrophe. As long as WMDs were closely controlled by a handful of responsible nations, the risk of their use was low. Today, however, technological advances and the proliferation of the materials used to make WMDs have made their use by asymmetrical fighters—guerrillas or insurgents—more likely. Many analysts believe it is likely that WMDs will be used by a rogue state or terrorist group in the coming years.

Major nations may use these weapons, too, although in slightly altered form. The United States, in a controversial move, has recently invested considerable sums of money on the development of low-yield nuclear weapons designed to penetrate subterranean bunkers that are impervious to conventional explosives. Supporters contend that these "bunker busters" would generate much less radioactive fallout. Critics argue that bunker busters are not as safe as many advocates assert, however. They contend that the weapons would not penetrate far enough to eliminate dangerous fallout.

Biological weapons are being transformed as well. In the future, advances in biotechnology may lead to the development of more dangerous and disturbing

13

biological weapons. Some military analysts believe that advanced countries may develop powerful antidote-resistant pathogens that target specific ethnic groups. Such "genetic bombs" could contain anthrax or plague and be tailored to activate only when they recognize the genes that identify a member of a particular ethnic group. In addition, smallpox, anthrax, or other viruses might be genetically modified using new DNA-manipulation technologies so they are more virulent or resistant to treatment. As is the case with nuclear weapons, many experts contend, the greatest danger is that such bioweapons will fall into the hands of terrorist groups lacking the self-restraint of responsible nation-states.

As the world becomes more dependent on computers, an enemy's information technology infrastructure may become a more valuable and tempting target to its enemies than its army or civilian populace. One potential future weapon that could be used to attack this infrastructure is the radio frequency (RF), or high-power microwave, weapon. The RF waves created by these weapons are similar to FM radio waves, but with an important difference—they cause the targeted material or device to generate heat and burn itself up. This simple but powerful technology could be used to essentially fry the electrical components of a target. According to General Robert Schweitzer, RF weapons would have a crippling impact on a country: "They can affect the national power grid, anything that has got an electronic chip in it, a circuit board, any piece of electronic gear that is touched by one of these weapons. And, they come either as narrow beam over long distances, or ultra-high beam, ultra-wide beam, ultra-wide band weapons that can project greater rates of power."

Looking decades ahead, future weapons currently in the concept stage are even more fantastic. Some target human senses or are designed to manipulate fundamental forces of nature. For example, sound may one day be used as a weapon that could stop an entire army. Certain sound frequencies can greatly affect the human body, and it is believed that a sonic weapon could be developed that could produce uncontrollable bowel movements, unconsciousness, and perhaps even death. It is possible "sonic bullets" might replace conventional ordnance. Other weapons would use sunlight. Today, sunlight is used to generate electricity, but a very different application of solar power is now being envisioned. Called the Solar Energy Optical Weapon, it would consist of a collection of space-based mirrors that could focus and direct solar radiation on targets on the ground, in the air, or in space itself. Other potential weapons of the future seem to come straight out of science fiction. For example, military planners envision something called an airborne holographic projector, which could project a realistic three-dimensional image as part of psychological warfare. The holographs could be used to frighten, trick, and distract the enemy, particularly an unsophisticated one.

Perhaps the most spectacular weapon envisioned involves robots almost too small to see with the naked eye. These attack microbots, perhaps only an eighth of an inch in size, could be deployed in huge numbers and used to attack facilities, weapons, and even people with chemical or electromagnetic energy. They may eventually be so small that they could be dispersed in aerosol form. Scientists believe that by the year 2020 it may be possible to construct robots small enough to penetrate the skin and enter the human body without making an incision. According to Professor Paul Hirst, the microbots may eventually replace chemical and biological arms as the ultimate weapon. As he puts it, "these microbots would be deadly bio-machines of finite life that could be released by sub-munitions, showering opponents in millions of nanobots . . . that could literally eat humans alive."

With such deadly new weapons on the drawing board, future wars may become more catastrophic. Whether or not war—including wars using these horrific weapons—can be prevented in the future is one of the issues debated in *War: Current Controversies*, in the following chapters: What Causes War? Is the War on Terror Justified? How Should Wars Be Conducted? Can War Be Prevented? How the nations of the world attempt to resolve their differences will determine the direction of weapons technology development in the years to come.

Chapter 1

What Causes War?

Current
CONTROVERSIES

The Causes of War: An Overview

by John Avery

About the author: *John Avery is the chairman of the Danish Peace Academy.*

Humans are unique among living organisms on earth in having two modes of evolution—genetic and cultural. During the last ten millennia, cultural evolution has changed our way of life so rapidly that genetic evolution, which proceeds very slowly, has not been able to keep up. Therefore human nature is not necessarily appropriate for the way of life which cultural evolution has given to us. Fortunately, humans are able to substitute learned behavior for instincts to an extent which is unparalleled by any other species. Ethical education is able to overwrite those parts of human nature which are inappropriate for civilized life.

It is interesting that many of the greatest ethical innovators and teachers in history lived at approximately the same time: For example, Socrates, Plato, Aristotle, Buddha, Lao-tzu, and Confucius all were approximate contemporaries of each other. All of them lived at the time when humans were making a transition from a life as tribal hunter-gatherers or herdsmen to a more settled, agricultural way of life, with large permanent settlements, cities and nations. The transition from tribalism to life in larger groups required a new ethic. Similarly, in our own time, the transition from nationalism to globalism will require a new ethic.

One aspect of human nature which is certainly inappropriate and dangerous in our own time is related to intergroup conflicts: This is what might be called the "communal defense mechanism". In the 1930's, J.B.S. Haldane and R.S. Fisher attempted to understand on the basis of the Darwinian theory of natural selection why humans are willing to die in battle. One would think at first sight that by sacrificing themselves in battle, humans would reduce their chance of producing progeny, and hence it was difficult at first for Haldane and Fisher to understand how natural selection could have acted to produce this aspect of human nature. They solved the problem by introducing the idea of group-selection. Haldane and Fisher pointed out that our early ancestors lived in small tribes, competing for territory on the grasslands of Africa. Since marriage within the tribe was much more frequent than marriage outside it, each tribe was genetically very homogeneous. In Haldane and Fisher's model of human evolution, the tribe as a whole was the unit upon which the forces of natural selection acted. The tribe either survived or perished; and its survival was more likely if it was composed of individuals who were extremely loyal, protective, kind and altruistic within the group, but willing to kill or be killed in defense of the tribe. If an individual sacrificed himself or herself in battle for the group, the genes for self-sacrifice were carried into the future by the surviving members of the tribe.

The communal defense mechanism seems to be part of human nature, and it can easily be understood on the basis of Haldane and Fisher's group selection model; but it is totally different from ordinary aggression of the type which appears in conflicts between individuals. In Konrad Lorenz's much praised and much-criticized book, *On Aggression*, he says: "An impartial observer from another planet, looking at man as he is today—in his hand the atom bomb, the product of his intelligence—in his heart the aggression drive, inherited from his anthropoid ancestors, which the same intelligence cannot control—such an observer would not give mankind much chance of survival". One problem with Lorenz's statement is that the word "aggression" is used here to denote a behavior pattern associated with intergroup conflicts, but the same word is often used to denote behavior in conflicts between individuals; and the two types of emotion and behavior are fundamentally different. So let us remove the words "aggression drive" from Lorenz's statement, and let us substitute "communal defense mechanism". Can we then agree with it? Certainly it is a strong warning that space-age science and stone-age politics form a highly dangerous mixture. We must be aware of the danger; but Lorenz does not sufficiently take into account the possibility of modifying human behavior through ethical education.

The fact that the institution of war has been eliminated locally within very large regions of the world shows that it is possible to eliminate war globally. What is needed is a new global system of governance, and a new ethic, whose core will be the loyalty of each individual to humanity as a whole. In a large, multi-ethnic nation such as the United States, within which war has been eliminated locally, the group or tribe to which all owe loyalty is taken to be the whole nation; and this perception is reinforced by education and by the mass media. The fact that wider loyalty can be produced within such a large geographic area makes it extremely probable that a similar wider loyalty can be created globally, given the

> *"Despite the end of the Cold War, the world still spends roughly a trillion US dollars per year on armaments."*

support of educational systems, religions, legal systems and the mass media. All these forces must be mobilized to support a new ethic, according to which individual humans will owe their primary loyalty to humanity as a whole.

Chapter 1

Political and Economic Aspects

It is extremely important that research funds be used to develop renewable energy sources and to solve other urgent problems now facing humankind, rather than for developing new and more dangerous weapons systems. Despite the end of the Cold War, the world still spends roughly a trillion US dollars per year on armaments, i.e. 10^{12} dollars—a million million. While this is going on, approximately 40,000 children die every day from starvation and from diseases related to malnutrition. The World Health Organization [WHO] lacks funds to carry through an antimalarial program on as large a scale as would be desirable; but the entire program could be financed for less than the world spends on armaments in a single day. Five hours of world arms spending is equivalent to the total cost of thee 20-year WHO program which resulted, in 1979, in the eradication of smallpox. With the diversion of funds consumed by three weeks of military expenditures, the world could create a safe water supply for all its people, thus eliminating the cause of more than half of all human illness. Diversion of funds from military expenditures could also support programs for family planning. It is vital for these programs to receive adequate financial support if ecological catastrophe and widespread famine are to be avoided throughout the 21st century.

It is often said that we are economically dependent on war-related industries, but if this is so, it is a most

> *"At the most primitive level, religions are tribal in character."*

unhealthy dependence, analogous to alcoholism or drug addiction. From a purely economic point of view, it is clearly better to invest in education, roads, railways, reforestation, retooling of factories, development of disease-resistant high-yield wheat varieties, industrial research, research on utilization of solar, geothermal and wind energy, and other elements of future-oriented economic infrastructure, rather than building enormously costly warplanes and other weapons. At worst, the weapons will contribute to the destruction of civilization. At best, they will become obsolete in a few years and will be scrapped. By contrast, investment in future-oriented infrastructure can be expected to yield economic benefits over a long period of time.

It is instructive to consider the examples of Germany and Japan, whose military expenditures were severely restricted after World War II. The impressive post-war development of these two nations can at least partly be attributed to the restrictions on military spending which were imposed on them by the peace treaty.

Besides swallowing vast amounts of money which could much better be used for constructive purposes, the enormous global weapons industry has some directly negative economic effects. For example, during the Cold War, both sides poured small arms and land mines into Africa. These weapons are still there, causing great suffering as well as political instability. This political instability, in turn, hinders development.

19

The almost unimaginably large amounts of money devoted to weapons and to military activity imply that war can be regarded as an institution. We might inquire to what extent this institution influences our other social structures—science, education, our political system, and the mass media. For example, looking at the "Discovery" television channel, one sees disproportionately many programs devoted to weapons and to war, almost as though weapons and war were being advertised. Are

> *"The most bitter interethnic conflicts take place between groups which are competing for the same territory."*

these programs somehow encouraged and aided by the military? It would be interesting to know; and it would also be interesting to know to what extent the campaigns of our politicians are supported by war-related industries. Science itself is not free from the stigma of accepting money from war-related sources. For example, NATO [North Atlantic Treaty Organization] has become a patron of science. The extent to which the institution of war has infiltrated all of our institutions makes the eradication of war a difficult task; but if civilization is to survive in the long run, we must carry through this great social reform.

Ethnicity and Religion as Causes of War

Humans have a tendency to be kind and protective towards members of their own group; but if they perceive the group to be threatened by outsiders, they are willing to kill or be killed to defend it. Undoubtedly this characteristic of human nature has its roots in prehistory, when our hunter-gatherer ancestors lived in small, genetically homogeneous tribes, competing for territory on the grasslands of Africa. The evolutionary success or failure of a tribe depended on the "team spirit" of its members—on their loyalty and altruism towards each other, and their willingness to use violence in defense of their community.

At the most primitive level, religions are tribal in character. They reenforce tribal cohesion, and mark tribal boundaries, making intermarriage across these boundaries difficult and infrequent. On the other hand, the most widespread religions of our own time emphasize the universal brotherhood of humankind, so one would at first expect religion to be a unifying force in the world. However, in practice, religion has often sharpened the boundaries between ethnic groups and has acted to make marriage across these boundaries more difficult than it otherwise would be. Thus, in practice, religion has often proved to be a divisive force rather than a unifying one.

In his book entitled *The Biology of Peace and War*, Irenäus Eibl-Eibesfeldt introduces the concept of "pseudospeciation". He points out that humankind is a single species in the biological sense: Marriage is fertile across all known racial boundaries. However, humans have a tendency to divide themselves into groups, sharpening the boundaries of these groups by means of cultural and religious markings which are analogous to the scars by which some African tribes mark their own members. When marriage across the boundaries of such a group becomes very infrequent, the group becomes, according to Eibl-Eibesfeldt, a pseudospecies. It is not a real species, since marriage would be fertile if it took place across the ethnic boundaries. But since strong cultural and religious barriers hinder such marriages, the group might be thought of as a pseudospecies.

One can notice that the most bitter interethnic conflicts take place between groups which are competing for the same territory, especially when marriage across the ethnic and religious boundary between the groups is infrequent. For example, one can think of the bitter conflicts between the Catholic and Protestant communities in Northern Ireland, the struggle between Arabs and Jews in the Middle East, between Hindus and Muslims in South-East Asia, and so on. To the extent that religion has hindered intermarriage across the boundaries between ethnic groups, it can be blamed for these conflicts.

If the human race is to survive, it must have a new ethic, whose central theme will be that each individual owes his or her primary loyalty to humanity as a whole, rather than to a particular nation or ethnic group. Intermarriage across racial, ethnic, and national boundaries can do much to aid the process of welding all of humanity into a single family.

Relationships Between Human Rights and Peace

Modern weapons have become so destructive that, in the long run, civilization cannot survive unless we succeed in abolishing the institution of war; but if we are ever to do this, we must provide the peoples of the world with a global system of security to replace national armies. This will necessarily involve reforming and strengthening the United Nations [UN]. The fact that war has been eliminated locally within a number of large regions of the world demonstrates that it is possible to abolish war globally; and such regions can provide us with models as we work to build an effective system of global governance. Among the most successful of the political structures which have achieved local peace within large regions are federations; and examples of federations include the United States, Canada, Brazil, Germany, Switzerland and Australia. The European Federation also provides an interesting example, although it does not yet have sufficient powers to be classified as a true federation.

"We must provide the peoples of the world with a global system of security to replace national armies."

The federal form of government is attractive because it has shown itself to be strong enough to abolish war locally within large multi-ethnic regions of the world; but at the same time, federations allow as much as possible to be decided locally. Federations have several key powers which the present United Nations lacks—the power of taxation, the power to make laws which are binding on individuals, and a monopoly on heavy weapons within the region over which their authority ex-

21

tends. At the same time, the states which join together to form a federation retain a considerable degree of autonomy.

For example, the Constitution of the United States declares that "all powers not expressly delegated to the federal government are retained by the several states". The success or failure of a federation depends on how well the line is drawn between the issues which ought to be decided locally, and those which require central decisions. In most federations, basic human rights are guaranteed by the central government, and the poorest sections of the federation are given economic aid.

The question of human rights is treated ambiguously by the present United Nations Charter. On the one hand, the Universal Declaration of Human Rights seems to guarantee these rights to all the peoples of the world. On the other hand, the Charter states that national sovereignty must not be violated; and the Charter provides no mechanism for the defense of human rights. Furthermore, action by the United Nations to prevent persecution of minorities within nations can be paralyzed by a veto in the Security Council.

These ambiguities regarding human rights need to be clarified, and the possibility of effective action by the UN must be increased. Ideally, the UN ought to have the power to arrest and try individuals for gross violations of human rights. The establishment of a Permanent World Court with jurisdiction over war crimes and genocide is an important step in the right direction. As we move towards a true system of world law and world government, under which basic human rights and reasonable living conditions will be guaranteed to all the peoples of the world, existing federations can serve as valuable guides.

> *"Ideally, the UN ought to have the power to arrest and try individuals for gross violations of human rights."*

Resources and Environmental Degradation as Sources of Conflict

The famous book on population by T. Robert Malthus grew out of his conversations with his father, Daniel, who was an enthusiastic believer in the optimistic philosophy of the Enlightenment. Daniel Malthus believed that the application of scientific progress to agriculture and industry would inevitably lead humanity forward to a golden age. His son, Robert, was more pessimistic. He pointed out that the benefits of scientific progress would probably be eaten up by a growing population.

At his father's urging, Robert Malthus developed his ideas into a book [*Essay on the Principle of Population*], the first edition of which was published anonymously in 1798. In this classic book, Malthus pointed out that under optimum conditions, every biological population, including that of humans, is capable of increasing exponentially. For humans under optimum conditions, the population can double every twenty-five years, quadruple every fifty years and increase by a factor of 8 every seventy-five years. It can grow by a factor of 16 every century, and by a factor of 256 every two centuries, and so on.

Obviously, human populations cannot increase at this rate for very long, since if they did, the earth would be completely choked with people in a very few centuries. Therefore, Malthus pointed out, various forces must be operating to hold the population in check. Malthus listed first the "positive checks" to population growth—disease, famine, and war. In addition, he listed "preventive checks"—birth control (which he called "Vice"), late marriage, and "Moral Restraint". The positive checks raise the death rate, while the preventive checks lower fertility.

> *"The only possible way to eliminate poverty and war is to reduce the pressure of population by preventive checks."*

According to Malthus, a population need not outrun its food supply, provided that late marriage, birth control or moral restraint are practiced; but without these less painful checks, the population will quickly grow to the point where the grim Malthusian forces—famine, disease and war—will begin to act.

In the second edition of his *Essay*, published in 1803, Malthus showed in detail the mechanisms by which population is held at the level of sustenance in various cultures. He first discussed primitive hunter-gatherer societies, such as the inhabitants of Tierra del Fuego, Van Diemens Land and New Holland, and those tribes of North American Indians living predominantly by hunting. In hunting societies, he pointed out, the population is inevitably very sparse: "The great extent of territory required for the support of the hunter has been repeatedly stated and acknowledged", Malthus wrote,

> The tribes of hunters, like beasts of prey, whom they resemble in their mode of subsistence, will consequently be thinly scattered over the surface of the earth. Like beasts of prey, they must either drive away or fly from every rival, and be engaged in perpetual contests with each other . . . The neighboring nations live in a perpetual state of hostility with each other. The very act of increasing in one tribe must be an act of aggression against its neighbors, as a larger range of territory will be necessary to support its increased numbers.

> The contest will in this case continue, either till the equilibrium is restored by mutual losses, or till the weaker party is exterminated or driven from its country . . . Their object in battle is not conquest but destruction. The life of the victor depends on the death of the enemy.

Malthus concluded that among the American Indians of his time, war was the predominant check to population growth, although famine, disease and infanticide each played a part.

In later chapters on nomadic societies of the Near East and Asia, war again appears, not only as a consequence of the growth of human numbers, but also as one of the major mechanisms by which these numbers are reduced to the level of their food supply. The studies quoted by Malthus make it seem likely that the nomadic Tartar tribes of central Asia made no use of the preventive checks to population growth. In fact the Tartar tribes may have regarded growth of their own populations as useful in their wars with neighboring tribes.

In many of the societies which Malthus described, a causal link can be seen, not only between population pressure and poverty, but also between population pressure and war. As one reads his *Essay*, it becomes clear why both these terrible sources of human anguish saturate so much of history, and why efforts to eradicate them have so often met with failure: The only possible way to eliminate poverty and war is to reduce the pressure of population by preventive checks, since the increased food supply produced by occasional cultural advances can give only very temporary relief. Today, as the population of humans and the size of the global economy rapidly approach absolute limits set by the carrying capacity of the earth's environment, it is important to listen to the warning voice of Malthus.

What would Malthus tell us if he were alive today? Undoubtedly he would say that we have reached a period of human history where it is vital to stabilize the world's population if catastrophic environmental degradation and famine are to be avoided.

In Malthus' *Essay on the Principle of Population*, population pressure appears as one of the main causes of war; and Malthus also discusses many societies in which war is one of the principle means by which population is reduced to the level of the food supply. Thus, his *Essay* contains another important message for our own times: If he were alive today, Malthus would also say that there is a close link between the two most urgent tasks which history has given to the 21st century—stabilization of the global population, and abolition of the institution of war.

Islam Causes War

by Don Feder

About the author: *Columnist Don Feder is the author of* A Jewish Conservative Looks at Pagan America.

People keep asking me what we learned from [the terrorist attacks of] September 11, 2001 and the deaths of 3,000 of our fellow citizens, I'm tempted to say: Absolutely nothing. (Who was it who remarked that the lessons of history are the last things we ever learn?)

Among the many unlearned lessons of Day-Which-Will-Live-In-Infamy-II— the necessity to control our borders, the need for a patriotic renewal and the importance of combatting multiculturalism—the most significant is the nature of Islam. You will note that I do not say militant Islam, or radical Islam, or Islamic extremism or other such weasel words—but Islam, period.

Every one of the hijackers who flew airliners into the World Trade Center and Pentagon were professing and practicing Moslems, as is [terrorist leader] Osama bin Laden. The Al Qaeda [terrorist] network is based in Moslem countries and supported financially by pious Moslems in Saudi Arabia.

The overwhelming majority of Moslem religious authorities who've spoken out on the subject, including those at the main mosque in Mecca and Egypt's prestigious Al Azar University, either endorse or rationalize acts of terrorism. On a day when Americans were incinerated or buried under tons of rubble, from Nigeria to Indonesia, Moslems celebrated in the streets.

A 1400-Year Jihad

Sept. 11 was one chapter in a 1400-year jihad [holy war]. Every day, the World Trade Center massacre is reenacted on a smaller scale somewhere in the Third World—Jewish women and children are burned alive in a bus on the West Bank, a missionary is beheaded in the Philippines, gunmen shoot up a church in Pakistan (deliberately firing into the prostrate bodies of women trying to shield their children), ancient monasteries and convents are destroyed in Kosovo, a woman is sentenced to death for adultery in Nigeria, Hindus are murdered in the Kashmir, a nun is found beheaded in Baghdad—and the beat goes on.

Genocide in the Sudan, ethnic cleansing in the Balkans, religious persecution in Saudi Arabia, calls for another holocaust in mosques from Mecca to Gaza, the imposition of Islamic law in Nigeria, forced conversions in Indonesia, synagogues burned in France, Jews attacked across Europe—these are everyday events, as Third World and much of the First slowly turns Islamic green.

A Religion of Peace?

And still our leaders, from President [George W.] Bush on down, insist on peddling the absurdity that Islam is a religion of peace—a creed of kindness and benevolence tragically and inexplicably corrupted by fanatics.

At a conference, I recently had an exchange with Tom Ridge, the Director of Homeland Security, wherein I questioned the governor on Islam a la Hans Christian Andersen. Ridge replied that Islam was indeed a pacific faith corrupted by a handful of heretics: I replied that the "handful"

> *"Of 22 conflicts in the Third World, 20 involve Moslems versus someone else."*

is in the hundreds of millions and—as far as I can see—it's the Moslems who aren't trying to kill us who've misinterpreted their religion.

Why this reluctance to confront manifest reality? The reason lies partly with our absurd foreign policy. We've declared certain Moslem nations to be our loyal allies—including Saudi Arabia, Egypt and Jordan. We wouldn't want to offend these dear friends by saying something unflattering about their bloody, butcherly, dark ages faith.

Then too, Americans are naturally benevolent. Most of us are taught from childhood that religion is good (and it doesn't matter which religion). As long as little Johnny believes in God and goodness, it's inconsequential whether he lights candles, wears a skull cap to services or prays in the direction of Mecca.

This works with every religion except Islam.

The Reality of Islam

Consider the following: Of the three major monotheistic religions, one was started by a lawgiver, one by a man of peace (try to imagine Mohammed telling his followers to turn the other cheek) and one by a warrior. Mohammed led men into battle. The essence of his message is holy war—slaughtering your enemies for the glory of Allah. He even advised his followers to negotiate phony truces to lull their enemies.

For almost 1,400 years, that has been the reality of Islam. Within a century after the death of Mohammed, Islam spread throughout the Middle East and across North Africa. It overran the Iberian peninsula and was finally stopped in southern France. It spread eastward as far as the southern Philippines. It was not propagated by fresh-faced young men knocking on doors and announcing: "Hello. I'm from your local mosque. Have you considered the Koran?" It was spread by force—conversion by the sword. To a large extent, it still is.

Islam's Bloody Borders

Some will respond that all religions go through periods of violence, usually in their infancy. Christianity had its crusades and Inquisition, its forced conversions and expulsions. But the evil committed in the name of Christ happened centuries ago. The evil committed in the name of the Prophet is going on now, as you read these words. Of 22 conflicts in the Third World, 20 involve Moslems versus someone else. Coincidence? In his brilliant book, "Clash of Cultures and the Remaking of World Order," Samuel Huntington speaks of Islam's "bloody borders."

There is no Methodist Jihad, no Hasidic holy warriors, no Southern Baptist suicide bombers, no Mormon elders preaching the annihilation of members of other faiths.

Islam is a warrior religion—the perfect vessel for fanatics, the violence-prone, the envious and haters of all stripes. This is one reason why Islam is making so many converts among the peaceable denizens of our prison system.

Still, much of the West is addicted to a fairy-tale version of Islam. Christian and Jewish clergy fall all over themselves to have interfaith services with imams. Representatives of Moslem groups are invited to the White House. The president signs a Ramadan declaration. In California, public schools ask children to role-play at being Moslems. Our universities take carefully selected verses from the Koran and present them as the essence of the faith. All that's needed is a Moslem character on "Sesame Street." Look—it's the Jihad Monster!

> *"Islam is a warrior religion."*

This perspective engenders a fatally false sense of security. Imagine, in 1940, Winston Churchill taking to the airwaves to announce that Nazism was an ideology of peace which, regrettably, had been perverted by a few fanatics like Hitler and Goebbels. But most storm troopers and SS men are fine follows—your friends and neighbors.

An Expansionist Force

For the first thousand years of its history—from the death of Mohammad to the 17th century decline of the Ottoman empire, Islam was an expansionist force. For the next 300 years, as the West rose to preeminence, Islam receded. For the past four decades—fueled by Arab oil wealth, a surplus population in the Middle East, the waning of the West and the rise of more virulent strains of the faith (Shiism, Wahhabism, Sunni fundamentalism)—Islam is expanding once more. Round and round she goes and where she stops nobody knows.

Due to Moslem immigration and aggressive proselytizing among the underclass, Islam is being exported to the West. Moslem populations are burgeoning throughout Western Europe. (In southern France, there are said to be more mosques than churches.) In Judeo-Christian America, Islam is the fastest growing religion. It's also spreading down the coast of West Africa, through the Balkans (after Serbia, Macedonia is the next target) and up from Mindanao in the Philippines.

Wherever it comes, Islam brings its delightful customs—child marriages, female circumcisions, rabid anti-Semitism, terrorism and support for terrorism and a virulent intolerance of other faiths.

Islam Has Declared War on Us

Am I suggesting we declare war on 900 million Moslems? The question is irrelevant—many of them have declared war on us. When one side knows it's at war and the other thinks peace and brotherhood prevail, guess who wins?

Ultimately, it's not about Jews in the West Bank, or Orthodox Serbs in Kosovo, or Hindus in Kashmir, or Maronite Catholics in Lebanon, or Christians in Sudan and Nigeria but all of us. As Ben Franklin would have it—Either we will hang together, or surely we shall all hang separately.

Islam Does Not Cause War

by Javeed Akhter

About the author: *Javeed Akhter is executive director of the International Strategy and Policy Institute, an organization that publishes books and conducts public discussions on issues relating to Islam in America.*

The evangelist Franklin Graham and the conservative Christian commentator, Pat Robertson's assertion that Islam exhorts its followers to be violent against non-Muslims, are only two of the most prominent voices that are part of a rising cacophony of vicious criticism of the Qur'an. One can read and hear a whole range of negative opinions about this issue in the media. Few have taken an in-depth look at the issue. What does the Qur'an actually say about violence against non-Muslims? Does it say what Robertson and Graham claim it does? Does it say that it is the religious duty of Muslims to kill infidels? But first some basic principles about reading and understanding the Qur'an. After all studying the Qur'an is not exactly like reading Harry Potter. Like any other scripture there are rules that may be followed for a proper understanding of the text.

Principles for Understanding the Qur'an

Muslim scholars suggest that those who read the Qur'an should keep at a minimum the following principles in mind. First the reader should have an awareness of the inner coherence in the Qur'an. As the verses are connected to each other the reader should study at the least the preceding and following verses for a sense of the immediate context. Also the reader should look at all of the verses that deal with the same subject in the book. These are frequently scattered all over the scripture. The indices provided in many of the exegeses of the Qur'an as well as the books of concordance allow the reader to get this information relatively easily. Often there is information available about the occasion of revelation, the historical context, of a particular verse. This requires at least a cursory knowledge of Prophet Muhammad's life. As Professor Fazlur Rahman of the University of Chicago would frequently point out, the Qur'an, in part at least, may be looked upon as a running commentary on the mission of

Prophet Muhammad. Finally Qur'anic scholars advise us to analyze the way Prophet implemented a particular directive in a verse of the Qur'an in his own life and ministry. For all Muslims Prophet Muhammad was the ultimate exemplar of the Qur'an and its living embodiment.

Let us examine the verses in question with these exegetical principles in mind. One of the verses says "put down the polytheists wherever you find them, and capture them and beleaguer them and lie in wait for them at every ambush" (Qur'an 9:5). The immediate context, as Muhammad Asad (*The Message Of The Qur'an*) points out, is that of a "war in progress" and not a general directive. It was an attempt to motivate Muslims in self-defense.

> *"The 'holy war' concept, for which many non-Muslims use the word 'Jihad,' is foreign to Islam."*

Muslims were given permission to defend themselves around the time of Prophet Muhammad's migration from Makkah, where he grew up, to the city of Madinah where he spent the rest of his life. This occurred in the 13th year of his 23-year mission. The danger to Muslims in Makkah at this time was extreme and there was a real possibility of their total eradication. They were permitted to fight back in self-defense against those who violently oppressed them. "Permission is given (to fight) those who have taken up arms against you wrongfully. And verily God (Allah) is well able to give you succor. To those who have been driven forth from their homes for no reason than this that say 'Our Lord is God.'" Qur'an goes on to add, "Hath not God repelled some men by others, cloisters and churches and synagogues and mosques, wherein the name of God is ever mentioned, would assuredly have been pulled down." (Qur'an 22: 39–42)

On another occasion Qur'an says, "Fight in the cause of God those who fight you, but don't transgress limits; for God loves not the transgressor."

The verse goes on to say "And fight them on until there is no more oppression, and there prevail justice and faith in God; but if they cease let there be no hostility except to those who practice oppression." (Qur'an 2:190–193)

Muslim scholars are of the opinion that war is permitted in self defense, when other nations have attacked an Islamic state, or if another state is oppressing a section of its own people. When Muslims were to fight a war they had to maintain great discipline, avoiding injury to the innocent and use only the minimum force needed. Striking a blow in anger, even in battle, was prohibited. The prisoners of war were to be treated in a humane fashion. However this is only a part of Jihad that Muslims are allowed to practice.

A greater Jihad is struggle against one's own inner self.

Jihad and Internal Struggle

The word Jihad comes from the root letters JHD, which means to struggle or to strive. It is understood by piety minded Muslims as a positive, noble and laudatory term. That is how most apply it in their personal, social, political and military lives. The history of the Muslim rulers, on the other hand, gives us examples of those who attempted to sanctify their wars of personal aggrandizement as wars for a noble cause by applying the label "Jihad" to them. A few even named their war departments as the departments of Jihad. This kind of behavior may be likened to a politician's attempt to wrap him in the flag. Such exploitation of the term should not be allowed to corrupt the original or the commonly understood meaning of the word, which is to strive for the highest possible goals, struggle against injustice and practice self denial and self control to achieve the moral purity to which all piety minded people aspire.

The "holy war" concept, for which many non-Muslims use the word "Jihad," is foreign to Islam. Rather, it comes from a concept first used to justify the Crusades by the Christian Church during the Middle Ages. The concept of "holy war" may even go back to the time when the emperor Constantine the Great allegedly saw a vision in the sky with the inscription on the cross, "in hoc signo vinces" (in this sign you will be the victor). The Arabic term, as has been pointed out by scholars, for "the holy war" would be al-harab al-muqaddas, which neither appears in the Qur'an or the sayings of the Prophet Muhammad (Hadith.) Prophet Muhammad's wars were defensive wars against groups who sought to eradicate Islam and the Muslims.

It is interesting and useful for social scientists or philologists to study how the meaning and usage of words differ in different communities. Ironically the word "crusade", because of its association with the crusades in the Middle Ages, should have had a pejorative sense to it and yet the word has acquired an ennobled meaning in the West. This in spite of the fact that the Church itself, along with most historians, acknowledge the injustice of the Crusades and the atrocities done in the name of faith. On the other hand, the word "Jihad" which means for Muslims, striving for the highest possible goal, has acquired the negative connotation of the holy war.

> *"It is clear from even a cursory study of the Qur'an that Islam does not permit, condone or promote violence."*

It is clear from even a cursory study of the Qur'an that Islam does not permit, condone or promote violence. Just the opposite, it abhors violence and allows it only in self defense. A claim to the contrary is no more than bad fiction.

The critics of the Qur'an should remember that if the Bible were similarly quoted out of context it would appear to be an extraordinarily violent scripture. I will leave Graham and Robertson to defend the violence in the Bible and the history of Christianity.

Religion Causes War

by Kenneth W. Phifer

About the author: *Kenneth W. Phifer is senior minister in the First Unitarian Universalist Congregation of Ann Arbor, Michigan.*

Is peace possible?

Does our survival as individuals or as a society require that we be prepared to kill?

Is non-violence an adequate response to violence?

Is there any human situation that gives us the right to slaughter others?

Is violence sometimes necessary in order to resolve intractable human conflict?

Are war and preparation for war an ineradicable part of human life?

Is peace possible?

These questions are usually answered in political, economic, or sociological terms. Each of these categories is, of course, important, but if we are to understand war and peace we must also address these questions from a religious standpoint.

Religion and War

The religions of the world deal with the ethical and spiritual dimensions of human life. The religions of the world are not centrally about tangible things like land and money. The religions of the world have to do with that which stirs our souls, fills our hearts, excites our minds. The religions of the world help to clarify what is special, unique, and precious about being human.

What do the religions of the world say about war and peace?

One thing they say is that sometimes war is good, that sometimes killing is moral, that sometimes violence is necessary.

It might almost be said that without religion there would be no war.

Religion is about meaning. Religion gives us a framework within which our lives make sense. Our lives can take on a larger, worthier significance because of the deities we embrace, the theologies we believe, and the moralities we act out.

We are made ready for the ultimate sacrifice of life or the disabling sacrifice of body or mind that war asks of its participants by believing that our way of life and thought is divinely sanctioned. Our faith then requires of us that from time to time we be prepared to defend it at the cost of life or limb. To die, to be wounded, to give up personal comfort is worth it if we are fighting for the right cause.

When [U.S. president] George W. Bush has spoken of [Iraqi president] Saddam Hussein, he has described him as being part of an "axis of evil." He has talked of all nations choosing to be for us or against us. He has spoken of our nation as divinely called to lead the world. He has used the presidency, as others before him have done, as a bully pulpit. If one believes the president's rhetoric, how could such a person not be on the front lines in Iraq right now?

Saddam Hussein has spoken in the same vein, though he is not noted for his religious convictions. He still uses the word, jihad, as a call to unite the Muslim community against America. A leading cleric in Baghdad . . . urged Muslims to kill Americans wherever they are as a sacred duty to protect the faith.

Religious justification for war is an ancient and ubiquitous phenomenon.

There were war gods like Ares among the Greeks and Mars among the Romans. The Scandinavians had Wotan and Thor and hosts of other militaristic deities, while the Yoruba had war-like Ogun. War among tribal peoples was a fact of life, which the gods themselves honored and joined in. In a majority of human societies, war has been held in reverence and the call to arms answered as readily as a call to nature.

The Zoroastrians even built a whole religion around the concept of war. Life, they contended, was a battle between light and darkness. Our task is to align ourselves with the forces of light and goodness against the forces of darkness and evil.

One of the most important sacred texts of Hinduism, the Bhagavad Gita, is the story of a battle in which one of the gods tells a reluctant warrior that "there exists no greater good for a warrior than war enjoined by duty." Dying in such a war is worthy and not to be avoided, not even when it means killing others.

> *"Without religion there would be no war."*

Buddhists justify war for self-protection and Confucianists as a last resort. The Israelites relied on "the Lord, mighty in battle . . . (who) will go with you to fight your enemy for you and give you the victory."

Christians were told by their leader, "Do not think that I have come to bring peace on earth; I have not come to bring peace, but a sword . . . let him who has no sword sell his mantle and buy one."

Muslim jihad, striving, is partly directed against unbelievers and enemies of the faith. It can involve the use of violence against threatening foes.

[Professor of philosophy] Gad Horowitz has written of the concept of blood sacrifice that is part of every religion and part of every war. He argues that what ancient peoples did in sacrificing humans to appease the gods, we have come to do in war.

Evil Impulses

We as much as the Moabites and the Aztecs need to rid ourselves of evil impulses. They did it with a scapegoat human being on whom all wickedness was symbolically laid. This sacrificial person was then consumed in flames on a high altar.

We do not sacrifice people on high altars now. We use the fields of battle for a similar purpose.

We send our children into war knowing that some of them will die and that some will be maimed. We do not blame ourselves for these deaths and injuries. We blame the Enemy.

One soldier in the Persian Gulf War of 12 years ago [1991] described the enemy as "cockroaches . . . as they come out of their holes we kill them."

Wickedness in us is replaced by righteous wrath against the Other, who is evil personified.

> *"Religious justification for war is an ancient and ubiquitous phenomenon."*

[Philosopher and historian] Norman O. Brown said of this psycho-theological transference that "the problem of war is the problem of idolatry."

Absolutism

The religions of the world give aid and comfort to war in their absolutism, in their fatalism, in their other-worldliness, in their idolatry. War would be much harder to justify without the aura of meaningfulness which religious support gives to it.

For the most part Unitarians and Universalists have not done this.

We have no absolute god or creed or text or guru that could give us the assurance that heaven is smiling on our murderous behaviour. Each of us as an individual chooses what stance to take, militaristic or pacifistic.

Yet even we have had our dark moments. Several months after this nation entered the First World War, former President William Howard Taft presented a resolution at the May Meeting of the American Unitarian Association that called on all ministers and all congregations to give full and open support to the war effort, on pain of being denied any help from the Association. Twenty-six ministers lost their jobs for standing against the war. An apology some 20 years later did not erase this stain on our heritage.

The religions of the world sometimes justify war.

The second thing that the religions of the world say about issues of war and peace is that peace begins in the inner life of the individual.

If we are frightened and insecure and lonely, if we are filled with bitterness and anger and hatred, we are more likely to be subject to the lure of war.

A hate letter I received in the wake of my interview with an Ann Arbor news reporter about the differing views on war and peace that my son, Karl, and I have clearly illustrates this. In a two page handwritten letter, the author was venomous in his condemnation

> *"The religions of the world sometimes justify war."*

of me for opposing the use of violence and thought my soldier son was a great hero. His language was vituperative and hostile, a man ready to be called to fight wickedness.

The Demonic Double

War makes things simple. War is Us against Them, Right against Wrong, the very language that the president has used frequently since [the September 11, 2001, terrorist attacks]. War gives us a transcendent cause that enables us to quit wallowing in our own woes and weaknesses. War enables us to feel good about ourselves, whether we ought to or not.

[French novelist and philosopher] Jean Paul Sartre has described this process as that of creating a Demonic Double. We cannot face ourselves, so we project onto some other person or group that which we most hate and fear in ourselves. Seeing that evil we most despise in ourselves out there in someone else, we can then relax our inner watchfulness and become the very thing we are most afraid of being and do the very things we are most fearful of doing.

War is the ultimate act of Demonic Doubling. Nothing is quite so satisfying to our psyches. As King David in Joseph Heller's *GOD KNOWS* puts it, "There is no palliative like war for the terrors . . . that our inner lives ordain for us."

It is against this internal mechanism of avoidance and transference of the truth about ourselves that the religions of the world contend.

The Bhagavad Gita [sacred text of the Hindu religion] is on the surface a tale of battle, its justification and its necessity. [Indian leader Mohandas K.] Gandhi was one of many to point out that it is wiser and more correct to read this story as a spiritual battle which takes place in the soul of Arjuna, the warrior. Gandhi said that he drew great lessons about satyagraha, truth force, and ahimsa, nonviolence, partly from reading the Gita.

If we win the war with ourselves, we will know peace and be at peace with the rest of the world.

The Islamic concept of jihad is similar. Jihad is a personal striving for goodness, purity, spiritual depth and understanding, and compassion that characterize the truest meaning of this holy war of the Muslim believer. It is a holy war against the believer's worst impulses.

The Tao Te Ching [ancient Chinese scripture] teaches that "peace throughout the world . . . begins with you and me." Taoism teaches us to look inward and esteem ourselves. Learn simplicity. Be open to what others can teach us. Be in harmony with nature. Face our fears. Learn to relieve the tensions of our bodies. Detach ourselves from complicated things. Laugh!

As we take control of our inner lives, as we practice wu-wei, non-effort, non-striving, receptivity, we create in ourselves and in those around us a calmness, a beauty, an order that enables us to further the cause of peace because we are living it.

The General and the Abbot

There is a story in the Korean Zen tradition that tells of a time when a rebel army swept into a town and conquered it. All the monks at the local temple fled, except for the abbot. The general in charge of the armed forces came into the temple and became annoyed when the abbot did not show him enough respect.

"Don't you know," the general shouted at the abbot, "that you are looking at a man who can run you through without blinking?"

"And you," the abbot replied calmly, "are looking at a man who can be run through without blinking."

The general stared at the abbot, bowed in respect, and left, not to return.

Inner Peace

If our heart is truly at peace, violence cannot conquer it and violence will not erupt from it.

This was the message of the prophet Jeremiah when he spoke of the religion of the heart.

It was the message of Jesus when he talked of cleansing the heart before one prays at services.

It was the message of Martin Luther King, Jr. when he said that he had been to the mountaintop and he was not afraid of dying.

Coming to terms with ourselves, learning to love and accept who we are without deception or excess, being unafraid to die if living would violate our integrity, we are then able to love others and avoid the scars of violence and war.

> *"If we win the war with ourselves, we will know peace and be at peace with the rest of the world."*

Among the Unitarian Universalists this is a central teaching. Do not look for saviours to rescue us. Look inside to find strength, intelligence, sensitivity, courage, and peacefulness. The work of peace begins in our own individual souls.

Peace begins inside us. This is a major teaching of the religions of the world. A major purpose of all religious communities is to help us practice this inner peace.

It must not stop there. The religions of the world teach that we must act for justice. There is an ineradicable link between peace and justice.

War and justice do not go together. In war our lives are at stake. Our highest value is survival. Justice takes second place, if it has any place at all.

In war we forget that those whom we fight against are our fellow travelers on this earth, our brothers and sisters in humanity. How can we strive for justice if the face we see is not that of our neighbor but of an enemy?

That is why the Tao Te Ching teaches that with those with whom we contend we should strive not to be opponents but partners in transcending conflict and discovering equitable solutions.

It is why Jesus taught that we should love our enemies and do good to those who despise us.

In Judaism the faithful are enjoined to care for the widow and the orphan and to treat the stranger as one of their own. Righteousness should flow down like waters and justice like a mighty stream.

Homelessness and hunger, economic inequalities, discrimination on the basis of gender or sexual orientation or religion or birth or any of the other categories of people who are oppressed only ultimately lead to disorder, disturbance, violence, and not infrequently war.

> *"[Peace is possible] if we can rid ourselves of the curse of holy war."*

If there is to be peace, there must be justice. Where justice is found, there will be peace.

All religions teach the lesson of consequences, that we reap what we sow. If we want peace and justice, we must sow the seeds that will raise up the flowers of kindness and cooperation, caring and sharing, restraint and equitability.

The Example of the Arapesh

A long time ago someone did just that among the Arapesh in New Guinea. Aggressive behaviour is not approved of by this gentle people. Kindness is the norm. Blood feuds do not exist and those who commit violence are looked on with pity, not admired or made into objects of vengeance.

The aim of all people in this society is to grow things: plants, pigs, children. Conflict resolution at its most extreme involves the parties isolating themselves from one another. Religious ritual is centered on the theme of the worthiness of all to do the work of living together without anger or hatred.

In the Arapesh society, because there is peace there is also justice. Because justice matters to these people and they have found a way of building it into their society, there is also peace. The whole of the community is organized for the welfare of all its people. The means of achieving that welfare are themselves part of the ends being sought.

This is a central truth in our heritage as liberal religious people—that we reap what we sow, that working for justice is a mandate of our religious faith, that working for justice is part of the way we can work for peace. From King John Sigismund's Decree of Toleration in 1568 that brought peace among warring religious parties in Transylvania because all were treated the same under this De-cree to the efforts of Unitarian Universalists today to provide gender equity, full rights of citizenship regardless of sexual orientation, fairer standards of racial justice, equitable economic practices, and hosts of other areas where UU's are involved, peace and justice have been linked in our thoughts and actions.

Peace and justice are inseparable. This is a universal teaching of the religions of the world.

Is peace possible?

The Curse of Holy War

It is if we can rid ourselves of the curse of holy war, the curse of divine sanc-tion for our slaughter of the other guy, the curse of thinking we are chosen as God's emissaries and so can do as we like.

Let us rid ourselves of those curses.

Is peace possible?

It is if we are willing to take seriously the need to begin peace-making with our own personal lives.

Let each of us begin that task today.

Is peace possible?

It is if we commit ourselves to work for a world that is just and equitable for every single human being.

Let us make that commitment.

Could there possibly be a worthier cause to which we could commit ourselves than to prove to the world the possibility of peace.

Capitalism Causes War

by John Molyneux

About the author: *John Molyneux is a frequent contributor to the* Socialist Worker.

The invasion of Iraq is only the latest in a line of "interventions" by the United States. Before Iraq were the wars in Afghanistan and the Balkans. And before those many can remember Somalia and the 1991 Gulf War.

While America was waging these wars, there were also numerous other bloody conflicts raging around the world—in Algeria, Angola, Congo, Somalia, Rwanda, Chechnya, Azerbaijan and many other places. Indeed, when one looks back over the 20th century the world appears to have been more or less continuously at war.

Wars of the Twentieth Century

The picture is dominated by the First and Second World Wars, which claimed approximately 16 million and 50 million lives respectively. But, prior to 1914, there were also the Boer War, the Russian-Japanese War, the Balkan Wars, the US-Spanish War over Cuba and numerous colonial wars. Between the world wars, there was the Russian Civil War (War of Allied Intervention), the Japanese War on China, the Italian invasion of Abyssinia, the Irish War of Independence and Civil War, and the Spanish Civil War.

After 1945 there was the overarching Cold War, and innumerable sub-conflicts in Korea, Malaysia, Aden, Greece, Cuba, Guatemala, Vietnam, Cambodia, Zimbabwe, Mozambique, India, Pakistan, Bangladesh, Biafra, Ireland, El Salvador. The list is almost endless. At the start of every war, the leaders speak of fighting for peace, security, freedom, democracy. At the end the peace proves only an interval before the next war. And so it is today. Now [that President George W.] Bush has occupied Iraq, he is turning his attentions to North Korea and Iran. What explains the prevalence of war, which destroys so many lives and involves such a vast waste of human resources?

Why, after thousands of years of history, centuries of so-called Western civilisation and enlightenment, is war still with us and, if anything, more common and terrible than ever? One can, of course, shrug one's shoulders and put it down to human nature. But this leads nowhere except to resignation or even justification for war. It is also false.

It cannot account for the fact that for tens of thousands of years human beings as hunters and gatherers lived virtually without war.

Nor can it explain why some parts of the world live for long periods in peace (for example Scandinavia) while other parts like the Middle East are hotbeds of conflict.

With the exception of popular uprisings, wars are not waged by "people", but by governments and states. Despite propaganda to the contrary, states act not on the basis of instincts, feelings or ideals, but overwhelmingly on the basis of vested interests. And not the interests of their populations, but the interests of the ruling classes who control the state.

The Capitalist System

To explain the unending sequence of wars in the modern world, we have first to grasp the fact that the economic system we live under, capitalism, has within it a built-in tendency to war. Capitalism is a system of competitive exploitation. Exploitation—the daily extraction of wealth by a minority from the labour of the majority—in itself generates bitter and permanent conflict.

To contain and repress this conflict the exploiters, the rich, create state machines—special bodies of armed men, prisons, police and so on—which stand above society. In addition to controlling their own people, these states have the capacity to wage war on other states and peoples for terri-

"The economic system we live under, capitalism, has within it a built-in tendency to war."

tory, trade, resources and so on. This is why there have been wars as long as there has been exploitation—about 5,000 years.

The emergence of capitalism, roughly 500 years ago, intensified this. Under capitalism every business is locked in permanent competition with other businesses. This competition runs through the whole system—the corner shop competes with the corner shop, the department store with other stores, the textile company with other textile companies.

Competiton and Accumulation

Ultimately, the competition is about accumulation of capital. But it includes struggle over land, raw materials, labour, markets and everything which contributes to profit. This competitive drive made capitalism more dynamic than any previous economic system, such as feudalism, but also more destructive and dangerous.

Within capitalist nations the state serves not only to hold down the workers but also, by and large, to keep the competition between capitalist firms within legal, non-violent limits. But the competition does not go away, it is channelled through the state and reproduced internationally, leading repeatedly to war.

In the 18th and early 19th centuries the British state fought a series of wars against France for the control of India, Canada, the West Indies and, ultimately, Europe. Britain's victory in these wars, together with the industrial revolution, ensured that in the 19th century it became the world's dominant state with the largest empire ever seen.

Imperialist Capitalism

However, the horrific wars of the 20th century were a product not just of capitalism in general, but of the particular phase of capitalism, known as imperialism, which set in at the end of the 19th century. By this time capitalist industry had spread to all Europe's major powers and had changed from competition between relatively small firms to competition between giant monopolies operating internationally. The result was the conquest and colonisation of almost all the rest of the world by the main imperialist powers.

"The potential for future conflicts is horrific, and will remain so while capitalism survives."

In itself this process involved a host of colonial wars in which poorly armed "natives" were slaughtered by immensely superior forces. But it also prepared the ground for war on a hitherto unimagined scale.

The fact that the world was already divided up meant that any change in the balance of economic and military power between the European states led to a struggle to redivide the world. In particular, Germany emerged as Europe's major economic power at the turn of the century.

Because it had only become a unified country in 1870, Germany had missed out on the 19th century drive for colonies. But it was determined to get its "fair" share, either in Africa and Asia, or on central and eastern Europe. Britain, France and Russia were equally determined to stop it. This was the real cause of the horrendous bloodbath of the First World War. The ruling classes of Europe sent their workers and young men to kill each other in their millions for the sake of colonies and profit. The Second World War was fundamentally a continuation of the First. The British government did not fight because they were opposed to fascism, but rather to defend the British Empire.

Profit and Conquest

The US came into the war not to liberate the French people, but to defend its interests in the Pacific against the threat from Japan and because it feared an eventual challenge from Germany. The wars of the present period derive from the same fundamental imperialist drives for profit and conquest, now operating in the new situation created by the collapse of the Soviet Union and its empire in 1989–91.

The US ruling class sees this as an opportunity to establish a "New World Order" dominated by American big business.

Central to this project is control of the word's major oil supplies. For the US state 11 September 2001 was a further "window of opportunity". It convinced people like vice president Dick Cheney, defence secretary Donald Rumsfeld and his deputy Paul Wolfowitz, and those around them that they had a chance to pursue this strategy through aggression.

Their aims are to gain control of Iraqi oil, to consolidate their hold on the Middle East and central Asia, and to send a message to the world that no state can defy American power or challenge it in the future.

Capitalism Breeds War

This is what makes the present situation so dangerous. Australia and Britain, as usual, have positioned themselves as allies of the US on the world stage. But neither France nor Germany, who aspire to lead Europe, Russia, or China (which is rapidly growing as an economic power), let alone the people of the Middle East and the rest of the world, are content to simply bow down before US capital.

The potential for future conflicts is horrific, and will remain so while capitalism survives. This is why, if we want a peaceful world, a world free of B-52s, cluster bombs, and the threat of nuclear holocaust, we have to both resist this war to the maximum and build a movement to end the capitalist system which breeds war by its very nature.

Socialism Causes War

by Anthony Gregory

About the author: *Anthony Gregory is a writer and musician who has written for* Libertarian Enterprise *and* Rational Review.

Socialists who still embrace the discredited ideas of Marx believe that the ultimate value of a service or product is the labor put into it. As they see it, profits exploit workers by providing them with compensation worth less than the labor they put into their work. Even socialists who dismiss many of Marx's doctrines have a soft spot for the idea that profits are exploitation, and employees should receive wages according to the sheer effort they put into something. It is this sympathy to the labor theory of value that leads socialists to call for a "living wage," even though many jobs don't produce enough wealth to pay for such a wage.

War Is Labor Intensive

I peruse the news accounts about [the 2003 Iraq war] and think about the billions of dollars spent on the war. I think about the Americans and Iraqis killing each other, and the expensive bombs and weapons employed in that senseless violence. I think to myself: Wow, this war sure requires a lot of labor to keep it going. I wonder if socialists would value it more than something that would require much *less* labor, like a peace agreement.

There are a lot of things that most people value that require much less labor to produce and maintain than a war. Ten billion dollars worth of food does a lot more good than a hundred billion dollars worth of bombing campaigns. Some things that leftists especially claim to value—such as an untouched rainforest—they value specifically because so *little* human labor has been invested.

Should we champion an economic system that would value things based solely on how much work they require, when there are so many historical examples of incredibly laborious enterprises that didn't seem to benefit very many people at all? Aside from a small ruling class, who benefited from the incredibly labor-intensive destruction involved in World War I?

Central Planners

Almost everyone would be better off if the United States packed up and left Iraq. Unfortunately, the central planners have used the power of the state to wage a war that the free market would have never produced, and the planners want to maintain that war.

Sure, [defense contractor] Halliburton and some other companies benefited from the war. Leftists cried that the war was about oil and corporate profits. Even if that's true, it's hard to imagine those companies so attracted to war in a free market, in which they would have to fork over hundreds of billions of dollars to hire soldiers and make bombs just to go and steal oil. It wouldn't be profitable, and people would look on in horror.

> *"The central planners have used the power of the state to wage a war that the free market would have never produced."*

In a free market, I doubt that a company would have been able to convince the American people to spend hundreds of billions of dollars—about a thousand dollars per person—to pay for the Iraq War. Americans would have done their homework and researched the credibility of WMD [weapons of mass destruction] allegations [the claim that Iraq possessed weapons of mass destruction] before they were convinced the war was worth it to them. Even if they were won over by the humanitarian reasons for ousting [Iraqi leader Saddam Hussein], they would have wanted assurances that their money would be used in a way that would not hurt the very people it was meant to help.

Since the government supplies the funding for war, taxpayers kid themselves into believing the war makes sense. I would guess that some people figure they have to pay for war no matter what, and so convince themselves, just to stay sane, that their money is going to a good cause. Americans would feel ripped off beyond belief to think so much of their income, forcefully taken from them, was spent on hurting people far more than helping people.

Many on the Left complain that the money the government spends on war should go to jobs. Of course they are right, but if they want the government to create jobs by spending that money, rather than giving it back to the people who earned it, they should recognize that wars are the quintessential way that governments "create" jobs.

War as a Government Program

War is the archetypal government program and the perfect example of trying to use the coercive state to create value out of violence and destruction.

Of course, domestic government programs, from public schools to drug prohibition, also require far more labor to maintain than they are worth, and hurt far more people than they help, but wars are worse in these regards than anything else the state inflicts on people.

Only in a free market will true value determine which projects, large and small, people undertake. Politicians base their decisions on what's politically viable, and when they make a miscalculation that kills and maims countless people all for nothing, the worst that happens to them is that they get voted out of office, and must live the rest of their lives in luxury and with cushy tax-funded pensions. After a politician is voted out of office the system remains in place, and someone new is elected and given more power than anyone should ever have. The government continues creating disasters and hurting innocents, and the new ruler is held no more accountable for bad decisions than the replaced ruler. The Iraq War fits well within democratic principles, though it doesn't make economic sense.

It never really makes economic sense for people to spend billions on killing thousands, when they have to foot the bill and take responsibility for their actions, such as they would in a free market. One day that might be the order of the day, and we won't have so many wars.

But as long as there are so many socialists who don't see how central planning of the economy leads to war, and as long as there are so many conservatives who don't see that war is the apex of socialism, both socialism and war will continue to plague America.

Pacifism Causes War

by Thomas Sowell

About the author: *Columnist Thomas Sowell is the author of* Basic Economics: A Citizen's Guide to the Economy.

Although most Americans seem to understand the gravity of the situation that terrorism has put us in—and the need for some serious military response, even if that means dangers to the lives of us all—there are still those who insist on posturing, while on the edge of a volcano. In the forefront are college students who demand a "peaceful" response to an act of war. But there are others who are old enough to know better, who are still repeating the pacifist platitudes of the 1930s that contributed so much to bringing on World War II.

Root Causes

A former ambassador from the weak-kneed Carter administration says that we should look at the "root causes" behind the [September 11, 2001] attacks on the World Trade Center and the Pentagon. We should understand the "alienation" and "sense of grievance" against us by various people in the Middle East.

It is astonishing to see the 1960s phrase "root causes" resurrected at this late date and in this context. It was precisely this kind of thinking, which sought the "root causes of crime" during that decade, creating soft policies toward criminals, which led to skyrocketing crime rates. Moreover, these soaring crime rates came right after a period when crime rates were lower than they had been in decades.

On the international scene, trying to assuage aggressors' feelings and look at the world from their point of view has had an even more catastrophic track record. A typical sample of this kind of thinking can be found in a speech to the British Parliament by Prime Minister Neville Chamberlain in 1938: "It has always seemed to me that in dealing with foreign countries we do not give ourselves a chance of success unless we try to understand their mentality, which is not always the same as our own, and it really is astonishing to contemplate how the identically same facts are regarded from two different angles."

Like our former ambassador from the Carter era, Chamberlain sought to "remove the causes of strife or war." He wanted "a general settlement of the grievances of the world without war." In other words, the British prime minister approached Hitler with the attitude of someone negotiating a labor contract, where each side gives a little and everything gets worked out in the end. What Chamberlain did not understand was that all his concessions simply led to new demands from Hitler—and contempt for him by Hitler.

What Winston Churchill [British prime minister after Chamberlain] understood at the time, and Chamberlain did not, was that Hitler was driven by what Churchill called "currents of hatred so intense as to sear the souls of those who swim upon them." That was also what drove the men who drove the planes into the World Trade Center.

Blood on Their Hands

Pacifists of the 20th century had a lot of blood on their hands for weakening the Western democracies in the face of rising belligerence and military might in aggressor nations like Nazi Germany and imperial Japan. In Britain during the 1930s, Labor Party members of Parliament voted repeatedly against military spending, while Hitler built up the most powerful military machine in Europe.

> *"Pacifists of the 20th century had a lot of blood on their hands."*

Students at leading British universities signed pledges to refuse to fight in the event of war.

All of this encouraged the Nazis and the Japanese toward war against countries that they knew had greater military potential than their own. Military potential only counts when there is the will to develop it and use it, and the fortitude to continue with a bloody war when it comes. This is what they did not believe the West had. And it was Western pacifists who led them to that belief.

Actual Consequences

Then as now, pacifism was a "statement" about one's ideals that paid little attention to actual consequences. At a Labor Party rally where Britain was being urged to disarm "as an example to others," economist Roy Harrod asked one of the pacifists: "You think our example will cause Hitler and Mussolini to disarm?"

The reply was: "Oh, Roy, have you lost all your idealism?" In other words, the issue was about making a "statement"—that is, posturing on the edge of a volcano, with World War II threatening to erupt at any time. When disarmament advocate George Bernard Shaw was asked what Britons should do if the Nazis crossed the channel into Britain, the playwright replied, "Welcome them as tourists."

What a shame our schools and colleges neglect history, which could save us from continuing to repeat the idiocies of the past, which are even more dangerous now in a nuclear age.

The Military-Industrial Complex Causes War

by Manuel Valenzuela

About the author: *Manuel Valenzuela is an attorney, consultant, freelance writer, and the author of* Echoes in the Wind.

> "In the councils of government, we must guard against the acquisition of unwarranted influence, whether sought or unsought, by the military industrial complex. The potential for the disastrous rise of misplaced power exists and will persist.

> "We must never let the weight of this combination endanger our liberties or democratic processes. We should take nothing for granted. Only an alert and knowledgeable citizenry can compel the proper meshing of the huge industrial and military machinery of defense with our peaceful methods and goals, so that security and liberty may prosper together."

> —Dwight D. Eisenhower, 1961

In the United States last year [2003] there were over 11,000 deaths by firearms. No other nation comes even close to matching this appetite for death. That is 8,000 more than died [during the September 11, 2001, terrorist attacks], but about the same number as those innocent Iraqi civilians that perished by our actions in Gulf War II. And the costs to American society from injuries and death due to firearms is more than $60 billion (USA). Those who produce instruments of death are not ignorant, however; they know the statistics, they simply brush them aside. Profit, after all, is much more important than stopping Americans from arming themselves to the teeth and killing each other. What else explains the gun lobby's attempts to go against common sense? The Second Amendment (right to keep and bear arms) must be honored and preserved, they say, even if the Founding Fathers never imagined the killing power of today's firearms. It is no coincidence, then, that the same nation that allows so many of its citizens to die at the hands of loaded weapons would naturally export its appetite for human death abroad.

Manuel Valenzuela, "Perpetual War, Perpetual Terror," *Briarpatch,* vol. 33, October 2004, p. 39.

Supplying the World with Weapons

Today, the USA is responsible for 40 percent of all worldwide weapons' sales. Tanks, fighter jets, artillery, helicopters, missiles, landmines, machine guns, mortars, bullets, grenades, guns, you name it, Guns'R'U.S. has it. Our nation supplies the world in instruments of death.

The United States' Military Industrial Complex (MIC) makes a killing from death, suffering and destruction. It exists only if people die. Its signature is everywhere; in the millions of landmines buried worldwide and the millions of amputee victims, many of them children. It can be seen in civil wars that ravage the world, from Africa to Asia to Latin America. From sea to shining sea, our weapons we can see, from the exponentially growing threat of weapons of mass destruction (WMDs)—many of which were distributed at one time by our own government—to the military hardware of tyrants, dictators, war criminals and warlords.

The MIC's front for assuring continual human violence is the USA government, the Pentagon in particular. President [George W.] Bush has granted the Pentagon a military budget of $400 billion for the next fiscal year. That's $400,000,000,000.00 (USA). This, of course, does not include our little warmongering expedition to the Fertile Crescent [the 2003 Iraq war], which by last estimates had already cost an additional $160 billion more. With so much of our money going to the "Department of War," one has to wonder where our priorities are. Certainly not in education, healthcare or in the creation of jobs.

The Pentagon's Revolving Door

The Pentagon and the Military Industrial Complex are one and the same, having morphed over time to form the most lethal killing institution the world has ever seen. Through a sliding and revolving door that turns citizen soldiers into armament industry executives and company officers into military policy makers, the MIC has embedded itself into the military branch of the USA government, thereby assuring itself of unlimited contracts, access, information and profit. Military industry executives and lobbyists have also slithered deep into top administration positions, occupying vitally important posts that decide national and foreign policy. Top government officials now sit on boards of today's biggest suppliers of military might. One need only look to the Carlyle Group to find the marriage between government and the MIC. George Bush the First had until recently sat on the board of this powerful yet clandestine group. This intertwined dancing tango of cronyism is exactly what Dwight D. Eisenhower warned about in 1961. Like a virus, the MIC has spread itself throughout the hallways of the Pentagon, penetrating from top to bottom through the disease called greed.

> *"The United States' Military Industrial Complex . . . makes a killing from death, suffering and destruction."*

Now one and the same, the Pentagon and the MIC have a common interest, motive and ability to shape how funds are used and wars are waged.

The Pentagon is the Department of War, not Defense. It is in business to kill, kill and kill some more. Without war, violence and weapons there is no Pentagon. And so to survive, to remain a player, wars must be created, weapons must be allocated, profits must be made and the Military Industrial Complex must continue exporting and manufacturing violence and conflict throughout the globe. And, as always, in the great tradition of the United States, enemies must exist. Indians, English, Mexicans, Spanish, Nazis, Koreans, Communists and now the ever-ambiguous Terrorists.

The End of the Cold War

When the Cold War came to an end, so too did the great profits of the MIC. Reductions in the Pentagon budget threatened the lifeblood of the industry; a new enemy had to be unearthed. There is no war, and hence no profit, without evildoers—without terrorists lurking at every corner, waiting patiently for the moment to strike, instilling fear into our lives, absorbing our attention.

We are told our nation is in imminent danger, that we are a mushroom cloud waiting to happen. And so we fear; transforming our mass uneasiness into nationalistic and patriotic fervor, wrapping ourselves up in the flag and the Military Industrial Complex. We have fallen into the trap and have become the subservient slaves of an engine run by greed, interested not in peace but constant war, constant killing and constant sacrifice to the almighty dollar. Brainwashed to believe that War is Peace we sound the drums of war, marching our sons and daughters to a battle that cannot be won by sword or gun.

> *"The Pentagon is the Department of War, not Defense."*

Us and Them

We are programmed to see the world as a conflict between Us and Them, or Good versus Evil, and we must inflict death on those who are not with us and on those against us. The MIC preys on our human emotions and psychology, exploiting our still fragile memories of the horrors of 9/11, manipulating us to believe that what they say and do is right for us all. We unite against the enemy, fearing for our lives, complacent and obedient, blindly descending like a plague of locusts onto foreign land, devastating, usurping, conquering and devouring those who have been deemed enemies of the state, those who harbor and live among them, "evil ones" and "evildoers" and "haters of freedom," all for the sake of profit and pillage, ideology and empire.

The so-called "War on Terror" is but a charade; a fear-engendering escapade, designed to last into perpetuity, helping guarantee that the Military Industrial Complex will grow exponentially in power. It is a replacement for a Cold War long ago retired, unable to deliver a massive increase in defense spending. Terrorists and the countries that harbor them have replaced the Soviet Union and Communists as enemy number one. With a war that may go on indefinitely, pursuing an enemy that lives in shadows and in the haze of ambiguity, the MIC will grow ever more powerful, conscripting hundreds of thousands of our youth, sending them to guide, operate and unleash their products of death.

> *"We are programmed to see the world as a conflict between Us and Them, or Good versus Evil."*

Rumblings of bringing back the draft are growing louder, and if you think your children and grandchildren will escape it, think again. In a war without end, in battles that do not cease, the MIC will need fresh human flesh to replace those who perish and fall wounded. Empire building needs bodies and drones to go with military might; instruments of death need trigger fingers and human brains. In this so-called "war on terror" the MIC will continue its reprogramming of expendable young men and women from peaceful civilians to warmongering killing machines. After all, "War is Peace."

Perpetual War

A perpetual war is what the MIC has sought all along. A lifetime of combat, a lifetime of profit, a lifetime of power. Assembly lines of missiles, bombs, tanks and aircraft operate without pause, helping expand a sluggish economy and the interests of the Pax Americana. Profit over people, violence before peace, the American killing machine continues on its path to human extinction, and it is the hands and minds of our best and brightest building and creating these products of decimation.

While we look over our shoulders for terrorists and evildoers, the world ominously looks directly at us, not knowing on which nation the storm of satellite-guided missiles will rain down on next. Every action has an equal and opposite reaction. In becoming preemptive warmongers, we are also becoming victims of our own making, helping assure a swelling wrath of revenge, resentment and retaliation against us. If we kill we will be killed, if we destroy we will be destroyed. The MIC is leading us down a steep canyon of fury, making us a pariah, a rogue country in the eyes of the world. We are becoming that which we fear most, a terrorist state.

As political scientist and ex-marine C. Douglas Lummis has said, "Air bombardment is state terrorism, the terrorism of the rich. It has burned up and blasted apart more innocents in the past six decades than have all the anti-state terrorists who have ever lived. Something has benumbed our consciousness against this reality." Today we are seen, along with Israel, as the greatest threats to world peace. When hundreds of thousands throughout the planet call Bush "the world's number one terrorist," that less than admirable distinction is automatically imputed onto the nation as a whole and the citizens in particular. This can be seen in the world's perception and treatment of us today.

When the day comes, not too far in the future, when one of our cities goes up in a mushroom cloud or in a vapor of suffocation, or when tens of thousands of citizens die of biological or chemical demons, we must dive deep into our national psyche and question why we allowed those in power to guide us down the road of cause and effect, action and reaction. And, in the end, we must realize that those same WMDs we once so gleefully created and exported have come back to our shores, haunting us and our children for the suffering we have helped spread throughout the world through our idleness; impotence to act and automaton-like acquiescence.

Can you imagine spending $400 billion to alleviate poverty in the Middle East? Can you imagine spending $400 billion to improve the lives of millions who today have nothing to live for, except martyrdom? Wouldn't $400 billion go further than perpetual bloodshed in the insidious war on terror if we alleviated the suffering and poverty of the world's poor by helping to provide jobs, education and medicines which would in turn spawn a sense of goodwill towards the USA?

Quest for Empire

Could it be remotely possible that our foreign policy, our support for puppet dictators and monarchs, our quest for empire and resources and our unyielding military, financial and political support of the dehumanization of the Palestinian people by Israel all leads to the subjugation, injustice, humiliation and misery of hundreds of millions of people? Could this be why we are so hated throughout a world where billions have nothing while we bathe in abundance—the spoils of war? As long as the MIC acts in our name while plundering humanity, we will be hated. Gandhi once said that "an eye for an eye only leads to more blindness." If that is so, then our nation is on a collision course with an ominous black hole whose darkness we shall not escape and whose exit we will never again see. Unless . . .

Wars Are Fought Because They Are Profitable

by Evan Augustine Peterson III

About the author: *Evan Augustine Peterson III is an attorney and executive director of the American Center for International Law.*

"The sinews of war are endless profits."
—Cicero, Orationes Philippicæ, v, c (c. 60 B.C.)

"Blessed are the peacemakers, for they shall be called children of God."
—Jesus the Christ, "The Beatitudes," Matthew 5:9 (NRSV)

Every nation that authentically seeks to become a peacemaking society must make an introspective pit-stop, somewhere along its pilgrimage to nonviolence, to wrestle self-critically with this thorny question: "What is this strange killer instinct doing inside of human nature—both mine and yours?" As the above quotations would indicate, two mutually-exclusive paths exist—the national path to war's filthy lucre or the national path to God's just peace—and yet there are no easy answers to this difficult question.

However, as if to provide an answer, a group of social scientists from the Nationalism and Ethnic Conflict Research Group devoted their entire conference in June of 2004—entitled "Why Neighbors Kill: Explaining The Breakdown Of Ethnic Relations"—to understanding human nature's genocidal warmaking instinct [1]. To deepen their inquiry into the bellicose side of human nature, these scholars posed the following 3 questions:

1. Anthropological—"Individual animals fight but do not collectively engage in war; what, then, causes human beings to wage war against each another?"

2. Psychological—"What causes people to polarize into: (a) 'Us'—one's sense of psychological identification with a group, based on kinship, contract, ethnicity, religion, tribe, or nationality, which forms 'The Self'; versus (b) 'Them'—those who fall outside the boundaries of one's group, the unpeople we designated as 'The Other'?"

3. Sociological—"Social scientists know that manifestations of trouble or propagandistic brainwashing will create a shared sense of threat, which in turn causes people both to retreat into the security of the group and to polarize their identities into 'Us' and 'Them'—but what actually causes people to go to war?"

In answering their third question, these scholars concluded that a hierarchical network of social planning is required to mobilize people for war. It must include:

A. A top level, to create the vision (e.g., the Plan for the New American Century's ["PNAC"] neoconservatives had already planned the invasion of Iraq by 1997–8) [2].

B. A middle level, to administer the top tier's plan, to give the orders, to arouse peoples' fighting instinct by waving the bloody shirt and reciting a history of injustice (e.g., "After [the September 11, 2001, terrorist attacks], everything must be different!"), and to transfer aggression (e.g., "We must attack Iraq, or our cities will be destroyed by [Iraqi leader Saddam Hussein's] deadly WMD [weapons of mass destruction] arsenal—in the form of a mushroom cloud!").

C. And a bottom level, to be manipulated into doing the fighting, the killing [3], and the dying through propagandistic fearmongering, demonization of the foe until he is reduced to a subhuman beast [4], peer-pressure (e.g., "It's your patriotic duty to kill those freaking 'hajis'!") [5], and narcotizing drugs [6].

Therefore, when viewed from the illuminating standpoint of the social sciences, it appears inevitable that there is a first step in the multicausative genesis of MILITARISM—which is an essential component of any nation's decline into FASCISM [7]—and that is deliberate top-down social organization to produce the infrastructural capacity with which to conquer other peoples and nations through force of arms.

> *"Militarism's belligerently self-righteous jingoistic mindset tends to originate with the economic interests of upper class."*

To achieve the societal transition to militarism, the upper classes must indoctrinate themselves with a morally-blind imperialist war-profiteering mentality before they will organize the lower classes into a hierarchical society that can harvest the poisonous fruits of war. Hence, militarism's belligerently self-righteous jingoistic mindset tends to originate with the economic interests of upper class, and then to disseminate downward.

Furthermore, so as not to unduly place blame for the phenomenon of militaristic fascism onto any one socioeconomic class, it should be reiterated that human nature itself contains the seeds that have repeatedly sprouted, throughout history, into the lethal tree of war. Or, as the renowned ethologist Konrad Lorenz once trenchantly observed, "The need today is for a gentler humankind, for the hand that wielded the axe against the ice and the saber-toothed tiger now cradles the machine gun equally as lovingly."

Additionally, as [ancient Roman statesman] Cicero wryly observed some 2,064 years ago, war can be extraordinarily profitable for those who invest in, or are members of, the military-industrial complex. And, as political economist Joseph Schumpeter correctly pointed out in his magnum opus, *Capitalism, Socialism and Democracy* (Perennial, 1962), global capitalism inherently contains within itself the very real danger that even a democratic nation could become economically addicted to war—and hence to militarism—for several reasons, but primarily to lessen the recessionary impact of "creative destruction" during its volatile business cycles.

Indeed, the twenty-first century began with a global recession that was a major factor in proximately causing at least one illegal war of aggression, from which one might infer that multinational corporate capitalism's postmodern version of "creative destruction" is going to be significantly more destructive than creative!

This is NOT to contend that capitalism is itself the sole cause of wars! Rather, it is to state that global capitalism, when objectively viewed in its sociopolitical context, can truthfully be said to exacerbate the bellicose propensities in human nature by cyclically supplying nations—especially the industrialized nations—with an economic motive to engage in militaristic warmongering.

The Bottom Line: America's national consciousness is undergoing an incremental regression toward fascism because hubristic nations are always locked into a blinkered mindset of self-righteous denial, which cannot recognize its own darker nature, and which seeks to exalt itself among the nations as if it was "the shining city upon a hill," but which instead sets itself up to experience a long hard fall into militaristic fascism; and that's why any nation's pilgrimage beyond militarism to a mature state of nonviolent peacemaking requires that its citizens must genuinely recognize the darker impulses within human nature, and then become self-critical enough to stop feeding the feral beast that lurks within us all—individually and collectively [8–10].

Notes

1. Olivia Ward's 6-5-04 CD essay, "Battling to Understand Our Genocidal Instinct," at: http://www.commondreams.org/headlines04/0605-01.htm

2. PNAC's neocon agenda for "Iraq/Middle East [1997–2000]," at: http://newamerican century.org/iraqmiddleeast2000-1997.htm

3. Esther Schrader's 2-4-05 CD/LAT article, "General Draws Fire For Saying 'It's Fun To Shoot' The Enemy," reports that USMC Lt. General James Mattis, while speaking before 200 people at the San Diego Convention Center on 2-1-05, publicly stated that: "Actually, it's fun to fight. It's a hell of a hoot. It's fun to shoot some people." And then again, referring to the US invasion of Afghanistan, he said: "So it's a hell of a lot of fun to shoot them!" A local TV reporter said the audience—a military contractors' convention—erupted into loud laughter and applause upon hearing these comments: http://www.commondreams.org/headlines05/0204-22.htm

4. Luc Santes' 5-11-04 NYT essay, "Tourists And Torturers," at: http://www.nytimes.com/ 2004/05/11/opinion/11SANT.html?ex=1107752400&en=2b12aaf8d4113c24&ei=5070 &oref=login&th

5. Bob Herbert's CD/NYT essay, "'Gooks' To 'Hajis'," at: http://www.commondreams.org/ views04/0521-08.htm

6. A. Beyond narcotizing drugs, the US military is using stimulant drugs in Iraq, as reported in Tom Spears' 10-11-03 TOW article, "New Drug May Help Soldiers Stay Awake: Doctors Unsure Of Long-Term Effects," at: http://www.modafinil.com/article/ soldiers.html

   B. Moreover, the Pentagon has been researching the use of drugs as biochemical weapons, as reported in The Sunshine Project's 2-11-03 SP article, "Pentagon Perverts Pharma: Liability & Public Image In The Pentagon's Drug Weapons Research," at: http://www.sunshineproject.org/publications/pr/pr110203.html

7. A. Ritt Goldstein's 7-8-04 CD/AT article, "US: Patriotic Pride And Fear," reports that writings by Canadian psychologist Daniel Burston and American political scientist Michael Parenti have come to the same disturbing conclusion—albeit from the different perspectives of their own disciplines—that the Bushite USA seems to be undergoing the process of a societal regression into fascism: http://www.commondreams.org/views04/ 0709-09.htm

   B. Lew Rockwell's 12-31-04 LR essay, "The Reality Of Red-State Fascism," explains why he thinks fascism has appeared among the USA's red-state bourgeoisie: http:// www.lewrockwell.com/rockwell/red-state-fascism.html

   C. In TU History Professor Gary Leupp's excellent 1-13-05 CP essay, "Everybody's Talkin' About Christian Fascism: Fightin' For The Lord," he breaks down the overbroad charge about "Christian Fascism" into two groups—Christian fundamentalists and Jewish neocons—and then concludes that generalized "American Fascism" doesn't exist yet. However, Professor Leupp never defines "fascism," so it remains unclear whether his conclusion is correct: http://counterpunch.org/leupp01132005.html

8. Joan Chittister's 1-28-05 CD/NCR essay, "What The Rest Of The World Watched On Inauguration Day," analyzes the mindset that blithely ignores the personal and global consequences of the US military's recent unjust shooting of an unarmed family of seven civilian noncombatants at a checkpoint in Tal Afar, Iraq: http://www.commondreams. org/views05/0128-35.htm

9. Agence France Presse's 2-2-05 CD/AFP article, "Rumsfeld Asks for Restoration of Nuclear 'Bunker Buster' Program," reports that DoD Secretary Rumsfeld is currently seeking to restore $27 million in Congressional funding for the Robust Nuclear Earth Penetrator ("RNEP") program, colloquially known as the "bunker buster mini-nuke": http:// www.commondreams.org/headlines05/0202-10.htm

10. Evan Augustine Peterson III's 9-29-04 ICH essay, "Does Mr. Bush's Foreign Policy Mirror The American Peoples' Soul?," correlates Mr. Bush's militarization of US foreign policy with the increasing bellicosity of this nation's collective consciousness: http: //www.informationclearinghouse.info/article6977.htm

Competition for Resources Causes War

by John Gray

About the author: John Gray is a professor of European thought at the London School of Economics and the author of False Dawn *and* Two Faces of Liberalism.

The economic theory that underpins the global free market ultimately rejects the very idea of resource scarcity.

An Infinite Supply

If demand exceeds supply, resources will become expensive. As a result, new supplies will be found—or technological alternatives developed.

In this view, so long as market pricing is in place and technological innovation continues, economic growth cannot be derailed by scarcity. For all practical purposes, natural resources are infinite.

The idea that human invention can overcome natural scarcity is not new. The Positivists [adherents of a philosophy concerned with the logical analysis of scientific knowledge] believed that industrialization would enable humanity to conquer scarcity.

Industrialism Breeds Abundance?

Following them in this faith, Karl Marx—the philosopher who originated the notion of communism—imagined that industrialism would make possible a condition of abundance in which, in turn, both markets and the state would become obsolete.

And before Marx, the belief that human ingenuity could overcome scarcity had long been a mainstay of utopian thought.

For example, Charles Fourier—the early 19th century French utopian thinker—is reputed to have believed that a time would come when the oceans would be made of lemonade.

John Gray, *Al Qaeda and What It Means to Be Modern*. New York: The New Press, 2003. Copyright © 2003 by John Gray. Reproduced by permission of The New Press, (800) 233-4830.

His prognostications were no more far-fetched than those of late 20th century free-market economists.

Like Marxists, neoliberals imagine that with the triumph of industrialization, there will be no more wars of scarcity.

In that sense, America's neoliberal missionaries ironically embraced the weakest aspects of Marx's thought. They emulated his historical determinism— but lacked his Homeric vision of historical conflict.

Overestimated Capitalism

Karl Marx, after all, knew that capitalism is endemically unstable. In contrast, his American followers imagined it had reached an equilibrium that would last forever.

Marx perceived that capitalism was destroying bourgeois life. His American "disciples" were confident that bourgeois life would soon be universal.

Abandoning the Global Free Market

Either way, the sub-Marxian, neoliberal worldview that shaped U.S. policies in the 1990s could not last. Well before the terrorist attacks of [September 11, 2001], the United States was losing interest in globalization.

Later, when President [George W.] Bush imposed tariffs on steel and farm products, it became clear that maintaining the global free market was no longer a priority. It is probably only a matter of time before the United States thumbs its nose at the World Trade Organization.

> *"By the 1990s, resource scarcity had become a source of war."*

In that event, trade will return to being a matter of bilateral negotiations among governments and blocs. The international system will revert to being a society of sovereign states.

The Myth of Infinite Resources

Back in the 1970s, it was the Club of Rome that argued that finite natural resources could not support exponentially rising population and production. Despite all its impressive findings, its report failed to dent the faith that industrial societies had discovered the secret of perpetual growth.

History outran the prescience of economists. By the 1990s, resource scarcity had become a source of war. The Gulf War was waged to prevent Kuwaiti and Saudi oil supplies falling out of western control. A decade later, control of energy supplies dominates strategic thinking.

A Familiar Problem

The limits to growth have not disappeared. They have returned as geopolitics. 21st century wars will be resource wars, made more dangerous and intractable by being intertwined with ethnic and religious enmities.

Lest we forget, rivalry for scarce natural resources played a central role in the 20th century's largest wars. Competition for oil supplies was a formative influence on the Second World War.

A U.S. embargo on oil exports to Japan was the deciding factor in tipping the balance of opinion in the Japanese military in favor of war. The prospect of seizing Soviet oil production facilities was a major factor in Hitler's decision to invade Russia in 1941.

The Era of Oil Wars

If history is any guide, the coming century will be punctuated by oil wars.

Behind intensifying rivalries for natural resources are increasing human numbers. Continued population growth worldwide increases the human impact on the planet as a whole. The result is increasing geopolitical conflict.

Necessity Trumps Government

When the necessities of life are at stake, humans will not wait for technical innovation or the market to operate. They will demand—and obtain—political action.

We do well to remember that the price mechanism is a creature of state power. It operates only so long as the state is intact. When scarcity amounts to a threat to subsistence, market pricing breaks down. The state becomes an instrument of rationing or conquest.

Increasing resource scarcity would be dangerous even if the global environment were stable. As a matter of fact, though, it is increasingly unstable. The geopolitical risks of resource scarcity are being aggravated by climate change.

Natural Consequences

Over the coming century, global warming may well overtake scarcity in energy supplies as a source of geopolitical conflict.

In some areas, it means desertification—in others flood. Food production is likely to be disrupted.

Feeding Wars of Scarcity

Ultimately, globalization begets de-globalization.

By intensifying competition for natural resources and hastening the spread of weapons of mass destruction, the dissemination of new technology throughout the world magnifies some of the most dangerous human conflicts.

Neoliberal utopians expected that globalization would fill the world with liberal republics, linked together in peace and trade. As it appears, history is responding with a flowering of war, tyranny—and empire.

War Is Central to the Human Condition

by David Limbaugh

About the author: *David Limbaugh is an attorney and the author of* Absolute Power.

"Is war our biological destiny?" That is the question posed in a recent *New York Times* article by Natalie Angier.

"In these days of hidebound militarism and round-robin carnage . . . it's fair to ask: Is humanity doomed? Are we born for the battlefield—congenitally, hormonally incapable of putting war behind us? Is there no alternative to the bullet-riddled trapdoor, short of mass sedation or a Marshall Plan [the American effort to rebuild Europe after World War II] for our DNA?"

After all, says Angier, our biological ancestors were also prone to war. I know—it probably shocks you that this person implies we evolved from apes and were not brought into being by a Divine Creator.

She wrote, "Nor are humans the only great apes to indulge in the elixir. . . . Common chimpanzees," she says, "engage in war and share 98 percent of their genes with humans. The other 2 percent they share with liberals. Just kidding. . . .

Psychobabble

Not to worry! There are researchers studying "warfare, aggression and the evolutionary roots of conflict" who believe our inclination toward war is "by no means innate." These researchers believe that you don't need to be a Pollyanna to conceive of a future "in which war is rare and universally condemned."

And upon what do these enlightened researchers base their conclusions? Well, they have the results of "game theory experiments." It appears that human subjects, "in laboratories around the world," respond by compromising when faced with a risk of everyone losing. Instead of adopting a "cheating strategy" where there is a risk of everyone losing, they cooperate and earn a "smaller but more reliable reward." These "cooperative networks" rapidly reach a point of "fixation."

For those of us unschooled in psychobabble, I think this means that once the participants experience the benefits of cooperation, the process becomes "fixed" or relatively permanent. But that's just a guess.

> **"Wars are not the result of genetics, but of our spiritual condition."**

What can we extrapolate from these findings? That "it's easy to get cooperation to evolve to fixation, for it to be the successful strategy." And what's more, according to these geniuses, "There is no such quantifiable evidence or theoretical underpinning in favor of Man the Warrior."

Actual Human Experience

Oh? How about thousands of years of recorded history for starters? Or does our actual human experience not compare to these controlled laboratory experiments? In other words, if the neighborhood bully has harassed your kid every day for the last year, you should disregard that as an illusion if some erudite group of professors conducts an experiment showing that bullies are prone to cooperation that eventually evolves to fixation. Yes, and I'm sure the professors will tell us that terrorists are interested in negotiation and cooperation as well— as opposed to a fixation on WMD [weapons of mass destruction].

What a relief to discover, as postmodernists have understood for years, that reality is a social construct! If the bully is fixating on depositing speed bumps on your son's face, you can console yourself with the laboratory results.

Humanism

The scary thing about this humanistic thought process is that these people actually believe humans can be remolded like laboratory animals into completely peaceful behavior. This delusional idealism is nothing new. Massachusetts legislator Horace Mann, prominent in the 1830s, was instrumental in an education reform movement that eventually led to centralized control of education in this country. He believed that through social transformation in the public schools, "nine-tenths of the crimes in the penal code would become obsolete."

Those peddling the notion that war can be made obsolete have a political agenda as well. That shoe drops in the last paragraph of the *Times* article, in which Angier quotes Dr. Frans de Waal, a primatologist and professor of psychology (a horrifying combination in my view) at Emory University. De Waal and others, says Angier, believe "the way to foment peace is to encourage interdependency among nations."

I'm far from an isolationist or protectionist, considering myself a free trader. But there is a dangerous trend in this country to forfeit our sovereignty, from the Supreme Court relying on foreign law, to pressure to join the International

Criminal Court, to the drive to cede our authority over environmental decisions to international bodies hostile to America, capitalism and Western civilization.

Sin Is Human Nature

These humanistic types just don't seem to understand that sin is part of human nature and wars are not the result of genetics, but of our spiritual condition. If the way to war is through international cooperation to the point of "fixation" on one-world government, count me out. This government would probably resort to "mass sedation or a Marshall Plan for our DNA." There are certain things worse than war.

Chapter 2

Is the War on Terror Justified?

Chapter Preface

In his September 20, 2001, address to a joint session of Congress, President George W. Bush declared that in response to the terrorist attacks on New York and Washington that had occurred nine days earlier, the United States was now engaged in a global war on terrorism. What he described as "a new kind of war" led to large-scale military operations first in Afghanistan and then in Iraq. Despite the fact that these actions represented the largest commitment of American military resources since the 1991 Gulf War, some argued that the force levels in both Iraq and Afghanistan were too low and questioned whether committing a nation to war with insufficient troop levels is justifiable. They believe that these conflicts have stretched the military too thin, resulting in calls for a reinstitution of the draft, which has not been used since 1973.

Proponents of a draft argue that despite its 2.6 million personnel, the U.S. military desperately needs more troops. In 2004 Congressman Charles Rangel of New York proposed legislation to reinstate the draft (the legislation failed by a large margin). "I am saying that war is hell and if indeed our country's security is in jeopardy, then we must as a country be prepared to make sacrifices," Rangel said.

Some argue that if the entire nation is to be committed to war, the risk and loss of combat should be shared by all parts of society—rich and poor, urban and rural, black and white. They claim that if the war on terror truly is a fight for national survival, fighting it using only volunteers is unjustifiable, and that for fairness, the draft should be reinstituted. Senator Chuck Hegel asks, "Why shouldn't all Americans have to pay some price, make some sacrifice? Why is it that the middle class, lower-middle class [who tend to volunteer for military service] are the ones doing the fighting and dying?"

However, opponents of the draft argue that the all-volunteer military is made up of "willing warriors" who have chosen the path of military service and are better suited to completing missions. Military recruiters contend that conscripts are less enthusiastic and less devoted to the service. President Bush and Secretary of Defense Donald Rumsfeld agree that a draft is not necessary, and have suggested that proponents of a draft and increased troop levels are looking at the war on terror through the prism of World War II. They believe that the changing nature of modern conflicts makes a large military force unnecessary. They desire to transform the U.S. military from a large, lumbering force more suited to the infantry and tank battles of World War II into a sleeker, more technologically savvy force capable of fighting terrorists anywhere around the globe. In one of the 2004 presidential debates, Bush said, "We don't need mass armies anymore." Rumsfeld suggests that the large population of the United

States ensures that the pool of available volunteers is big enough. "We've got 295 million people in this country," he said. "We don't need a draft."

Regardless of whether a new draft is instituted, the United States is likely to be conducting the war on terror well into the foreseeable future. The authors of the viewpoints in the following chapter debate whether or not the war on terror is justified.

The War Against Iraq Was Necessary to Combat Terrorism

by Stephen F. Hayes

About the author: *Stephen F. Hayes is a staff writer for the* Weekly Standard.

[Terrorist leader] Osama bin Laden and [former Iraqi president] Saddam Hussein had an operational relationship from the early 1990s to 2003 that involved training in explosives and weapons of mass destruction, logistical support for terrorist attacks, [terrorist group] al Qaeda training camps and safe haven in Iraq, and Iraqi financial support for al Qaeda—perhaps even for Mohamed Atta [one of the terrorists responsible for the terrorist attacks of September 11, 2001]—according to a top secret U.S. government memorandum obtained by *The Weekly Standard.*

The memo, dated October 27, 2003, was sent from Undersecretary of Defense for Policy Douglas J. Feith to Senators Pat Roberts and Jay Rockefeller, the chairman and vice chairman of the Senate Intelligence Committee. It was written in response to a request from the committee as part of its investigation into prewar intelligence claims made by the administration. Intelligence reporting included in the 16-page memo comes from a variety of domestic and foreign agencies, including the FBI, the Defense Intelligence Agency, the Central Intelligence Agency, and the National Security Agency. Much of the evidence is detailed, conclusive, and corroborated by multiple sources. Some of it is new information obtained in custodial interviews with high-level al Qaeda terrorists and Iraqi officials, and some of it is more than a decade old. The picture that emerges is one of a history of collaboration between two of America's most determined and dangerous enemies.

According to the memo—which lays out the intelligence in 50 numbered points—Iraq–al Qaeda contacts began in 1990 and continued through mid-

March 2003, days before the Iraq War began. Most of the numbered passages contain straight, fact-based intelligence reporting, which in some cases includes an evaluation of the credibility of the source. This reporting is often followed by commentary and analysis. . . .

Reporting from the early 1990s remains somewhat sketchy, though multiple sources place Hassan al-Turabi and Ayman al Zawahiri, bin Laden's current No. 2, at the center of the relationship. The reporting gets much more specific in the mid-1990s:

> 8. Reporting from a well placed source disclosed that bin Laden was receiving training on bomb making from the IIS's [Iraqi Intelligence Service] principal technical expert on making sophisticated explosives, Brigadier Salim al-Ahmed. Brigadier Salim was observed at bin Laden's farm in Khartoum in Sept.–Oct. 1995 and again in July 1996, in the company of the Director of Iraqi Intelligence, Mani abd-al-Rashid al-Tikriti.

> 9 . . . Bin Laden visited Doha, Qatar (17–19 Jan. 1996), staying at the residence of a member of the Qatari ruling family. He discussed the successful movement of explosives into Saudi Arabia, and operations targeted against U.S. and U.K. interests in Dammam, Dharan, and Khobar, using clandestine al Qaeda cells in Saudi Arabia. Upon his return, bin Laden met with Hijazi and Turabi, among others.

And later more reporting, from the same "well placed" source:

> 10. The Director of Iraqi Intelligence, Mani abd-al-Rashid al-Tikriti, met privately with bin Laden at his farm in Sudan in July 1996. Tikriti used an Iraqi delegation traveling to Khartoum to discuss bilateral cooperation as his "cover" for his own entry into Sudan to meet with bin Laden and Hassan al-Turabi. The Iraqi intelligence chief and two other IIS officers met at bin Laden's farm and discussed bin Laden's request for IIS technical assistance in: a) making letter and parcel bombs; b) making bombs which could be placed on aircraft and detonated by changes in barometric pressure; and c) making false passport [sic]. Bin Laden specifically requested that [Brigadier Salim al-Ahmed], Iraqi intelligence's premier explosives maker—especially skilled in making car bombs—remain with him in Sudan. The Iraqi intelligence chief instructed Salim to remain in Sudan with bin Laden as long as required.

The analysis of those events follows:

> The time of the visit from the IIS director was a few weeks after the Khobar Towers bombing. The bombing came on the third anniversary of a U.S. [Tomahawk missile] strike on IIS HQ (retaliation for the attempted assassination of former President [George H.W.] Bush in Kuwait) for which Iraqi officials explicitly threatened retaliation.

Contacts in the Late 1990s

In addition to the contacts clustered in the mid-1990s, intelligence reports detail a flurry of activities in early 1998 and again in December 1998. A "former senior Iraqi intelligence officer" reported that "the Iraqi intelligence service station in Pakistan was Baghdad's point of contact with al Qaeda. He also said bin Laden visited Baghdad in Jan. 1998 and met with Tariq Aziz."

> 11. According to sensitive reporting, Saddam personally sent Faruq Hijazi, IIS deputy director and later Iraqi ambassador to Turkey, to meet with bin Laden at least twice, first in Sudan and later in Afghanistan in 1999. . . .

> 14. According to a sensitive reporting [from] a "regular and reliable source," [Ayman al] Zawahiri, a senior al Qaeda operative, visited Baghdad and met with the Iraqi Vice President on 3 February 1998. The goal of the visit was to arrange for coordination between Iraq and bin Laden and establish camps in an-Nasiriyah and Iraqi Kurdistan under the leadership of Abdul Aziz.

That visit came as the Iraqis intensified their defiance of the U.N. inspection regime, known as UNSCOM, created by the cease-fire agreement following the Gulf War. UNSCOM demanded access to Saddam's presidential palaces that he refused to provide. As the tensions mounted, President Bill Clinton went to the Pentagon on February 18, 1998, and prepared the nation for war. He warned of "an unholy axis of terrorists, drug traffickers, and organized international criminals" and said "there is no more clear example of this threat than Saddam Hussein."

> *"The picture that emerges is one of a history of collaboration between two of America's most determined and dangerous enemies."*

The day after this speech, according to documents unearthed in April 2003 in the Iraqi Intelligence headquarters by journalists Mitch Potter and Inigo Gilmore, Hussein's intelligence service wrote a memo detailing coming meetings with a bin Laden representative traveling to Baghdad. Each reference to bin Laden had been covered by liquid paper that, when revealed, exposed a plan to increase cooperation between Iraq and al Qaeda. According to that memo, the IIS agreed to pay for "all the travel and hotel costs inside Iraq to gain the knowledge of the message from bin Laden and to convey to his envoy an oral message from us to bin Laden." The document set as the goal for the meeting a discussion of "the future of our relationship with him, bin Laden, and to achieve a direct meeting with him." The al Qaeda representative, the document went on to suggest, might provide "a way to maintain contacts with bin Laden."

Four days later, on February 23, 1998, bin Laden issued his now-famous *fatwa* on the plight of Iraq, published in the Arabic-language daily, *al Quds al-Arabi:* "For over seven years the United States has been occupying the lands of Islam in the holiest of places, the Arabian Peninsula, plundering its riches, dictating to its rulers, humiliating its people, terrorizing its neighbors, and turning its bases in the Peninsula into a spearhead through which to fight the neighboring Muslim peoples." Bin Laden urged his followers to act: "The ruling to kill all Americans and their allies—civilians and military—is an individual duty for every Muslim who can do it in any country in which it is possible to do it."

Although war was temporarily averted by a last-minute deal brokered by U.N. Secretary General Kofi Annan, tensions soon rose again. The standoff with Iraq came to a head in December 1998, when President Clinton launched Operation Desert Fox, a 70-hour bombing campaign that began on December 16 and ended three days later, on December 19, 1998.

Bin Laden Offered Safe Haven

According to press reports at the time, Faruq Hijazi, deputy director of Iraqi Intelligence, met with bin Laden in Afghanistan on December 21, 1998, to offer bin Laden safe haven in Iraq. CIA reporting in the memo to the Senate Intelligence Committee seems to confirm this meeting and relates two others.

> 15. A foreign government service reported that an Iraqi delegation, including at least two Iraqi intelligence officers formerly assigned to the Iraqi Embassy in Pakistan, met in late 1998 with bin Laden in Afghanistan.

> 16. According to CIA reporting, bin Laden and Zawahiri met with two Iraqi intelligence officers in Afghanistan in Dec. 1998.

> 17. . . . Iraq sent an intelligence officer to Afghanistan to seek closer ties to bin Laden and the Taliban in late 1998. The source reported that the Iraqi regime was trying to broaden its cooperation with al Qaeda. Iraq was looking to recruit Muslim "elements" to sabotage U.S. and U.K. interests. After a senior Iraqi intelligence officer met with Taliban leader [Mullah] Omar, arrangements were made for a series of meetings between the Iraqi intelligence officer and bin Laden in Pakistan. The source noted Faruq Hijazi was in Afghanistan in late 1998.

> 18. . . . Faruq Hijazi went to Afghanistan in 1999 along with several other Iraqi officials to meet with bin Laden. The source claimed that Hijazi would have met bin Laden only at Saddam's explicit direction.

An analysis that follows No. 18 provides additional context and an explanation of these reports:

> Reporting entries #4, #11, #15, #16, #17, and #18, from different sources, corroborate each other and provide confirmation of meetings between al Qaeda operatives and Iraqi intelligence in Afghanistan and Pakistan. None of the reports have information on operational details or the purpose of such meetings. The covert nature of the relationship would indicate strict compartmentation [sic] of operations.

Saddam's Strategy

Information about connections between al Qaeda and Iraq was so widespread by early 1999 that it made its way into the mainstream press. A January 11, 1999, *Newsweek* story ran under this headline: "Saddam + Bin Laden?" The story cited an "Arab intelligence source" with knowledge of contacts between Iraq and al Qaeda. "According to this source, Saddam expected last month's American and British bombing campaign to go on much longer than it did. The dictator believed that as the attacks continued, indignation would grow in the Muslim world, making his terrorism offensive both harder to trace and more effective. With acts of terror contributing to chaos in the region, Turkey, Jordan, Saudi Arabia, and Kuwait might feel less inclined to support Washington. Saddam's long-term strategy, according to several sources, is to bully or cajole Muslim countries into breaking the embargo against Iraq, without waiting for the United Nations to lift it formally."

Intelligence reports about the nature of the relationship between Iraq and al Qaeda from mid-1999 through 2003 are conflicting. One senior Iraqi intelligence officer in U.S. custody, Khalil Ibrahim Abdallah, "said that the last contact between the IIS and al Qaeda was in July 1999. Bin Laden wanted to meet with Saddam, he said. The guidance sent back from Saddam's office reportedly ordered Iraqi intelligence to refrain from any further contact with bin Laden and al Qaeda.

> *"Saddam's long-term strategy . . . is to bully or cajole Muslim countries into breaking the embargo against Iraq, without waiting for the United Nations to lift it formally."*

The source opined that Saddam wanted to distance himself from al Qaeda."

The bulk of reporting on the relationship contradicts this claim. One report states that "in late 1999" al Qaeda set up a training camp in northern Iraq that "was operational as of 1999." Other reports suggest that the Iraqi regime contemplated several offers of safe haven to bin Laden throughout 1999.

> 23. . . . . Iraqi officials were carefully considering offering safe haven to bin Laden and his closest collaborators in Nov. 1999. The source indicated the idea was put forward by the presumed head of Iraqi intelligence in Islamabad (Khalid Janaby) who in turn was in frequent contact and had good relations with bin Laden.

Some of the most intriguing intelligence concerns an Iraqi named Ahmed Hikmat Shakir:

> 24. According to sensitive reporting, a Malaysia-based Iraqi national (Shakir) facilitated the arrival of one of the Sept 11 hijackers for an operational meeting in Kuala Lumpur (Jan 2000). Sensitive reporting indicates Shakir's travel and contacts link him to a worldwide network of terrorists, including al Qaeda. Shakir worked at the Kuala Lumpur airport—a job he claimed to have obtained through an Iraqi embassy employee.

One of the men at that al Qaeda operational meeting in the Kuala Lumpur Hotel was Tawfiz al Atash, a top bin Laden lieutenant later identified as the mastermind of the October 12, 2000, attack on the USS *Cole.*

> 25. Investigation into the bombing of the USS *Cole* in October 2000 by al Qaeda revealed no specific Iraqi connections but according to the CIA, "fragmentary evidence points to possible Iraqi involvement."

> 26. During a custodial interview, Ibn al-Shaykh al-Libi [a senior al Qaeda op-

erative] said he was told by an al Qaeda associate that he was tasked to travel to Iraq (1998) to establish a relationship with Iraqi intelligence to obtain poisons and gases training. After the USS *Cole* bombing in 2000, two al Qaeda operatives were sent to Iraq for CBW-related [chemical and biological weapons] training beginning in Dec 2000. Iraqi intelligence was "encouraged" after the embassy and USS *Cole* bombings to provide this training.

The analysis of this report follows.

CIA maintains that Ibn al-Shaykh's timeline is consistent with other sensitive reporting indicating that bin Laden asked Iraq in 1998 for advanced weapons, including CBW and "poisons."

Additional reporting also calls into question the claim that relations between Iraq and al Qaeda cooled after mid-1999:

27. According to sensitive CIA reporting, . . . the Saudi National Guard went on a kingdom-wide state of alert in late Dec 2000 after learning Saddam agreed to assist al Qaeda in attacking U.S./U.K. interests in Saudi Arabia.

A 9/11 Connection

And then there is the alleged contact between lead 9/11 hijacker Mohamed Atta and an Iraqi intelligence officer in Prague. The reporting on those links suggests not one meeting, but as many as four. What's more, the memo reveals potential financing of Atta's activities by Iraqi intelligence.

The Czech counterintelligence service reported that the Sept. 11 hijacker [Mohamed] Atta met with the former Iraqi intelligence chief in Prague, [Ahmed Khalil Ibrahim Samir] al Ani, on several occasions. During one of these meetings, al Ani ordered the IIS finance officer to issue Atta funds from IIS financial holdings in the Prague office.

And the commentary:

CIA can confirm two Atta visits to Prague—in Dec. 1994 and in June 2000; data surrounding the other two—on 26 Oct 1999 and 9 April 2001—is complicated and sometimes contradictory and CIA and FBI cannot confirm Atta met with the IIS. Czech Interior Minister Stanislav Gross continues to stand by his information.

It's not just Gross who stands by the information. Five high-ranking members of the Czech government have publicly confirmed meetings between Atta and al Ani. The meeting that has gotten the most press attention—April 9, 2001—is also the most widely disputed. Even some of the most hawkish Bush administration officials are privately skeptical that Atta met al Ani on that occasion. They believe that reports of the alleged meeting, said to have taken place in public, outside the headquarters of the U.S.-financed Radio Free Europe/Radio Liberty, suggest a level of sloppiness that doesn't fit the pattern of previous high-level Iraq–al Qaeda contacts.

Whether or not that specific meeting occurred, the report by Czech counterintelligence that al Ani ordered the Iraqi Intelligence Service officer to provide

IIS funds to Atta might help explain the lead hijacker's determination to reach Prague, despite significant obstacles, in the spring of 2000. (Note that the report stops short of confirming that the funds were transferred. It claims only that the IIS officer requested the transfer.) Recall that Atta flew to Prague from Germany on May 30, 2000, but was denied entry because he did not have a valid visa. Rather than simply return to Germany and fly directly to the United States, his ultimate destination, Atta took pains to get to Prague. After he was refused entry the first time, he traveled back to Germany, obtained the proper paperwork, and caught a bus back to Prague. He left for the United States the day after arriving in Prague for the second time.

> *"Other reports suggest that the Iraqi regime contemplated several offers of safe haven to bin Laden throughout 1999."*

Contacts After September 11

Several reports indicate that the relationship between Saddam and bin Laden continued, even after the September 11 attacks:

> 31. An Oct. 2002 . . . report said al Qaeda and Iraq reached a secret agreement whereby Iraq would provide safe haven to al Qaeda members and provide them with money and weapons. The agreement reportedly prompted a large number of al Qaeda members to head to Iraq. The report also said that al Qaeda members involved in a fraudulent passport network for al Qaeda had been directed to procure 90 Iraqi and Syrian passports for al Qaeda personnel.

The analysis that accompanies that report indicates that the report fits the pattern of Iraq–al Qaeda collaboration:

> References to procurement of false passports from Iraq and offers of safe haven previously have surfaced in CIA source reporting considered reliable. Intelligence reports to date have maintained that Iraqi support for al Qaeda usually involved providing training, obtaining passports, and offers of refuge. This report adds to that list by including weapons and money. This assistance would make sense in the aftermath of 9-11.

The Terrorist Insurgency

Colin Powell, in his February 5, 2003, presentation to the U.N. Security Council, revealed the activities of Abu Musab al Zarqawi. Reporting in the memo expands on Powell's case and might help explain some of the resistance the U.S. military is currently facing in Iraq.

> 37. Sensitive reporting indicates senior terrorist planner and close al Qaeda associate al Zarqawi has had an operational alliance with Iraqi officials. As of Oct. 2002, al Zarqawi maintained contacts with the IIS to procure weapons and explosives, including surface-to-air missiles from an IIS officer in Baghdad. According to sensitive reporting, al Zarqawi was setting up sleeper cells

in Baghdad to be activated in case of a U.S. occupation of the city, suggesting his operational cooperation with the Iraqis may have deepened in recent months. Such cooperation could include IIS provision of a secure operating bases [*sic*] and steady access to arms and explosives in preparation for a possible U.S. invasion. Al Zarqawi's procurements from the Iraqis also could support al Qaeda operations against the U.S. or its allies elsewhere.

38. According to sensitive reporting, a contact with good access who does not have an established reporting record: An Iraqi intelligence service officer said that as of mid-March the IIS was providing weapons to al Qaeda members located in northern Iraq, including rocket propelled grenade (RPG)-18 launchers. According to IIS information, northern Iraq-based al Qaeda members believed that the U.S. intended to strike al Qaeda targets during an anticipated assault against Ansar al-Islam positions.

The memo further reported pre-war intelligence which "claimed that an Iraqi intelligence official, praising Ansar al-Islam, provided it with $100,000 and agreed to continue to give assistance."

Critics of the Bush administration have complained that Iraq-al Qaeda connections are a fantasy, trumped up by the warmongers at the White House to fit their preconceived notions about international terror; that links between Saddam Hussein and Osama bin Laden have been routinely "exaggerated" for political purposes; that hawks "cherry-picked" bits of intelligence and tendentiously presented these to the American public. . . .

> *"Several reports indicate that the relationship between Saddam and bin Laden continued, even after the September 11 attacks."*

One of the most interesting things to note about the 16-page memo is that it covers only a fraction of the evidence that will eventually be available to document the relationship between Iraq and al Qaeda. For one thing, both Saddam and bin Laden were desperate to keep their cooperation secret. (Remember, Iraqi intelligence used liquid paper on an internal intelligence document to conceal bin Laden's name.) For another, few people in the U.S. government are expressly looking for such links. There is no Iraq–al Qaeda equivalent of the CIA's 1,400-person Iraq Survey Group currently searching Iraq for weapons of mass destruction.

Instead, CIA and FBI officials are methodically reviewing Iraqi intelligence files that survived the three-week war last spring [2003]. These documents would cover several miles if laid end-to-end. And they are in Arabic. They include not only connections between bin Laden and Saddam, but also revolting details of the regime's long history of brutality. It will be a slow process.

So Feith's memo to the Senate Intelligence Committee is best viewed as sort of a "Cliff's Notes" version of the relationship. It contains the highlights, but it is far from exhaustive.

Another 9/11 Connection

One example. The memo contains only one paragraph on Ahmed Hikmat Shakir, the Iraqi facilitator who escorted two September 11 hijackers through customs in Kuala Lumpur. U.S. intelligence agencies have extensive reporting on his activities before and after the September 11 hijacking. That they would include only this brief overview suggests the 16-page memo, extensive as it is, just skims the surface of the reporting on Iraq-al Qaeda connections.

Other intelligence reports indicate that Shakir whisked not one but two September 11 hijackers—Khalid al Midhar and Nawaq al Hamzi—through the passport and customs process upon their arrival in Kuala Lumpur on January 5, 2000. Shakir then traveled with the hijackers to the Kuala Lumpur Hotel where they met with Ramzi bin al Shibh, one of the masterminds of the September 11 plot. The meeting lasted three days. Shakir returned to work on January 9 and January 10, and never again.

Shakir got his airport job through a contact at the Iraqi embassy. (Iraq routinely used its embassies as staging grounds for its intelligence operations; in some cases, more than half of the alleged "diplomats" were intelligence operatives.) The Iraqi embassy, not his employer, controlled Shakir's schedule. He was detained in Qatar on September 17, 2001. Authorities found in his possession contact information for terrorists involved in the 1993 World Trade Center bombing, the 1998 embassy bombings, the 2000 attack on the USS *Cole*, and the September 11 hijackings. The CIA had previous reporting that Shakir had received a phone call from the safe house where the 1993 World Trade Center attacks had been plotted.

The Qataris released Shakir shortly after his arrest. On October 21, 2001, he flew to Amman, Jordan, where he was to change planes to a flight to Baghdad. He didn't make that flight. Shakir was detained in Jordan for three months, where the CIA interrogated him. His interrogators concluded that Shakir had received extensive training in counter-interrogation techniques. Not long after he was detained, according to an official familiar with the intelligence, the Iraqi regime began to "pressure" Jordanian intelligence to release him. At the same time, Amnesty International complained that Shakir was being held without charge. The Jordanians released him on January 28, 2002, at which point he is believed to have fled back to Iraq.

Was Shakir an Iraqi agent? Does he provide a connection between Saddam Hussein and September 11? We don't know. We may someday find out.

But there can no longer be any serious argument about whether Saddam Hussein's Iraq worked with Osama bin Laden and al Qaeda to plot against Americans.

The War on Terror Is Necessary to Combat Radical Islam

by Jonathan Rosenblum

About the author: *Jonathan Rosenblum is director of Jewish Media Resources, a leading media organization dedicated to furthering an understanding of Torah Judaism.*

The second anniversary of [the terrorist attacks of] September 11 has now passed, and Americans are increasingly divided over the nature of its legacy. In the ensuing two years, some Americans (and most Europeans) have managed to convince themselves that they are living in a world pretty much the same as the one they saw themselves inhabiting on September 10, 2001.

For most Americans, however, September 11 constituted a wake-up call, alerting us to the fact that all our previous paradigms for interpreting reality have to be reexamined in light of a new enemy: Islamic terrorism.

World War IV

The consequences of this debate are enormous. If one believes that America today is essentially a nation at peace, then the rate of casualties and money invested in [the Iraq war and its aftermath] is intolerable. If, on the other hand, we are in the middle of what Elliot Cohen has termed World War IV against Islamic terrorism, then the number of American casualties has to be weighed against some remarkable achievements, including the removal of the Taliban [terrorist-supporting regime] in Afghanistan, [former Iraqi president] Saddam Hussein in Iraq, and the capture or killing of two-thirds of [the terrorist group] Al Qaeda's top leadership.

From the moment the hijacked commercial airliners crashed into the Twin

Towers and the Pentagon, President [George W.] Bush has lined up with those who view the world as dramatically altered for the foreseeable future by September 11. Bush reiterated that belief in his September 7, 2003 speech to the nation in which he described the progress in the ongoing "war on terror."

Radical Islam

Despite the progress in that war described by the president, the dystopia pictured the Hudson Institute's Max Singer, in which September 11 turns out to be only the prologue to a series of such attacks throughout the West cannot be dismissed out of hand. The spread of radical Islam around the globe has not abated. Saudi-exported Wahhabism fuels Islamic terrorism against Western targets in Southeast Asia. Sharia, Islamic law in all its cruelty, is the law of the land in Nigeria, one of America's most important oil suppliers. And the threat posed by terrorist-sponsoring states will be multiplied many times if Iran succeeds in acquiring nuclear weapons.

The source of the seething hatred of the West that gave rise to Islamic terrorism in the first place has not lessened over the past two years. That hatred has its source in the failure of Moslem, and in particular Arab societies, vis-á-vis the West. As the London-based Arab columnist Zuheir Abdallah wrote recently: "What have we offered civilization, in terms of human sciences or inventions or anything else of value, from the beginning of the industrial revolution to the present? Unfortunately, the answer is: almost nothing."

Arab Failure

A U.N.-sponsored study by Arab intellectuals last year [2002] detailed the collective failure of the Arab world in every field of human endeavor. Over the last twenty years, Arab nations have experienced the second lowest growth in per capita income in the world, and between 1960 and 2000, productivity in the Arab world actually declined.

The bitterness of Arab failure is heightened by its contrast to the prosperity all around. Harvard historian Michael Ignatieff describes the "remorseless growth [in Arab lands] of lawless shanty towns that collect populations of unemployed or underemployed males who can see the promise of globalized prosperity in the TVs in every café, but cannot enjoy it themselves."

President Bush quite rightly noted, in his September 7 speech, that this Arab failure and the hatred it generates is an immediate threat to the United States: "The Middle East will either become a place of progress and peace, or it will become an exporter of violence and terror that takes more lives in America and in other free nations."

Appeasement vs. Confrontation

In the battle against Islamic terrorism, the usual choice between military confrontation and some form of appeasement/accommodation does not exist for two reasons. The first is that appeasement is impossible with enemies who view one's very existence as an affront. The United States and the West are hated by Moslem terrorists not for what they have done but for what they are.

The second is that nothing encourages Islamic terrorism more than the perception of Western lack of resolve. "In the writings and speeches of [terrorist] Osama bin Laden and of his allies and disciples," writes Bernard Lewis, "hatred of America is less significant than contempt—the perception that America is a paper tiger,' that its people have become soft and pampered—'hit them and they will run.'" In that sense, the *Boston Globe*'s Jeff Jacoby is surely right that 9/11 had its roots 22 years earlier when the U.S. embassy in Teheran was seized and America found no response and in the subsequent two decades of terror attacks on U.S. targets around the globe that went unavenged.

> *"The spread of radical Islam around the globe has not abated."*

President Bush is correct that the massive American military response in Iraq and Afghanistan [in 2003 and 2002, respectively] has gone far to remove the impression that free nations are "decadent and weak." But that impression of Western cowardice has not been completely removed, and it can be quickly revived by any sign of a lack of American determination in Iraq.

The Importance of Iraq

Iraq is thus crucial for two reasons. First, it provides the best opportunity to create a model for an Arab society that is more than a tribal autocracy. Again President Bush put the matter clearly: "The terrorists thrive on the support of tyrants and the resentments of oppressed peoples. When tyrants fall, and resentment gives way to hope, men and women in every culture reject the ideologies of terror . . . Everywhere that freedom takes hold, terror will retreat."

Second, Iraq is the ultimate test of American resolve. That is why even those Americans who opposed the war should pray that America is not perceived as retreating from Iraq, as it once retreated from Beirut. Not for the sake of the Iraqis—though that would be reason enough for such prayers—but for our own sake. A lack of American determination will embolden terrorists around the world and thereby render the West more vulnerable to future 9/11s.

Our enemies clearly understand this. Islamic terrorists of various stripes have poured into Iraq from Iran, Syria, and Saudi Arabia because they recognize how much of a threat a free, fairly governed, and economically dynamic state would be to their vision. Their targets, points out Michael Gove in the *Times of London*, from the sabotage of Iraq's crumbling infrastructure to the assassination of future leaders in a pluralist Iraq, such as Ayatollah Mohammed Said al-Hakim, have all been carefully chosen to prevent "the transformation of Iraq into a different sort of Arab country." The collection of killers "desperately trying to undermine Iraq's progress and throw the country into chaos," mentioned by the

President in his speech, is a sign not of American failure but of the magnitude of the threat to them of American success.

Success Is Not Guaranteed

That success is far from guaranteed and certainly will not be achieved on the cheap or without a long-term American commitment. In today's world, Ignatieff sharply observes, American imperialism is the precondition for democracy. But an inept or indecisive American imperialism would be the worst possible scenario. The process of developing democratic institutions in Iraq must be guided by Iraqis themselves, writes Bernard Lewis, the foremost modern student of the Arab world. But that development must be underwritten by American money and power.

"Premature democratization—holding elections and transferring power, in a country which has had no experience of such things for decades, can only lead to disaster, as in Algeria. Democracy is the best and therefore the most difficult of all forms of government," concludes Lewis.[1]

President Bush showed in his September 7 speech that he understands clearly what is at stake in Iraq. The war on terror, he said, "would be a lengthy war, a different type of war, fought on many fronts and places. Iraq is now the central front. Enemies of freedom are making a desperate stand there—and there they must be defeated."

America is engaged in promoting freedom in Iraq, the President explained, in no small part to make itself more secure. Both are worthy goals, and if the President succeeded in explaining the connection in a way that Americans can understand, they will be a lot closer to being achieved.

1. Iraq held free elections for the first time in the winter of 2005.

The War on Terror Is Making America Safer

by J. Michael Waller

About the author: *J. Michael Waller is a staff writer for* Insight *magazine.*

The United States and its allies are chewing their way through terror networks on every populated continent. On any given day, international terrorists and their leaders are surrendering, being captured or killed. Terrorist commanders from Iraq to Indonesia face life sentences in prison or await execution. Those who remain find their networks in tatters, their funding sources starting to dry up and fewer places to hide.

Things have changed in the two years since [the September 11, 2001, terrorist attacks]. The terrorists now are the prey, though still a dangerous one.

Some say the United States is being too aggressive in fighting terrorism, citing insensitivity to other cultures abroad and alleged abuses of civil liberties at home. Others, such as Defense Secretary Donald Rumsfeld, insist that the United States isn't fighting hard enough or creatively enough and has yet to take a strategic approach to a war expected to take years or even decades.

No Instant Gratification

The civilized world faces more ugly and painful realities ahead, and the elites aren't getting their customary instant gratification of a quick, tidy victory. Yet despite deep and emotional divisions over the ouster of Saddam Hussein, the Arab-Israeli hostilities, the sheer aggressiveness of the U.S.-led offensive against the world's terrorists and their friends and Washington's inept communication with the rest of the world, the United States still has the support of most of the countries that matter. That's important, Bush-administration officials say, because the toughest part may be yet to come.

President George W. Bush has racked up an impressive string of victories in a little more than two years. He led an unheard-of Marine invasion and Naval bombardment of landlocked Afghanistan [in 2002], destroying the terrorist, Wahhabi-backed Taliban regime, tearing up the sanctuaries of al-Qaeda [terrorists] and freeing a grateful people from a Dark Ages nightmare. He commanded an audacious and spectacularly successful invasion of Iraq [in 2003], breaking records of military history in a campaign that ousted [former Iraqi president] Saddam Hussein and ripped up the totalitarian Ba'athist Party.

While human casualties have been low, the political and diplomatic casualties for the administration have been costly. Sold to the public and the world on legalistic grounds as enforcement of U.N. resolutions, the Iraq war was and is, according to the new White House line, a central front against terrorism.

Diplomatic Successes

Still, Iraq has produced major diplomatic successes for the United States. In mid-October [2003], within hours of Sen. Edward Kennedy (D-Mass.) assailing the Iraq war as a "fraud" built on "lies," the United Nations—including Russia, Syria and even France—voted unanimously, in effect, to ratify U.S. control of Iraq and to recognize the provisional Iraqi governing council in Baghdad.

The United States is far from alone. More than 40 countries are supporting the Iraq operation. Depending on the count, as many as 70 countries are helping the United States either overtly or covertly to wage war on the terrorists, administration officials tell *Insight.* No major terrorist attack has succeeded on U.S. soil since Sept. 11, 2001, and the terrorists have far less freedom to operate as the war goes on around the world. The State Department's annual report on terrorism, released earlier this year [2003], shows a 44 percent drop in attacks by "international terrorists" in 2002 from the previous year and down to its lowest level since 1969—more than three decades ago.

Foreign Cooperation

Even some of the regimes the State Department has designated as state sponsors of terrorism, including Syria and Sudan, have found it necessary to extend varying degrees of cooperation. "Friendly" governments such as Saudi Arabia and the Persian Gulf state of Qatar have stopped, as far as can be seen, funding Taliban-like movements that sheltered al-Qaeda. European allies, some supportive of U.S. policy and others openly critical, actively have been working together and with Washington to defund and neutralize terrorist entities. Asian allies, particularly the Philippines, Indonesia, Singapore and Thailand, have put their combat forces to work as well as their police. Quick actions by the United States and other countries have foiled plans for scores—some say hundreds—of terrorist attacks and have disrupted or destroyed terror networks from Manila to Miami. Even Saudi Arabia and Iran are cracking

> *"The terrorists now are the prey, though still a dangerous one."*

down at home on al-Qaeda and other terrorist groups.

"Since Sept. 11, 2001, more than 3,000 al-Qaeda leaders and foot soldiers have been taken into custody around the globe, nearly 200 suspected terrorist associates have been charged with crimes in the U.S. and as many as 100 terrorist attacks or plots have been broken up worldwide," the FBI says in an assessment statement. Some administration officials estimate privately that the United States and its partners have killed thousands of terrorists and trainees. More than half of the senior leadership of al-Qaeda has been captured or killed, according to an official Justice Department estimate.

The Patriot Act

New laws and legal procedures, especially the 2001 USA PATRIOT Act, have provided the FBI and others with the authority to go after terrorist cells at home much more aggressively—so much so that civil libertarians have joined with terrorist-linked groups to complain. The Treasury Department's March 2002 raids of suspected terrorist financing fronts in Northern Virginia were possible in part because the USA PATRIOT Act had provided additional authority for federal judges to issue search warrants, according to a sealed federal affidavit in support of the raids. *Insight* had obtained a copy of the affidavit, since unsealed.

"President George W. Bush has racked up an impressive string of victories."

In February, the FBI arrested the alleged leader of the North American cell of the Palestinian Islamic Jihad terrorist group, also thanks to the USA PATRIOT Act. Sources close to the arrest tell this magazine that the FBI for years had been watching Sami al-Arian, a professor at the University of South Florida and an occasional Washington lobbyist against antiterrorist legislation, but because of quirks in the law could not arrest him until the USA PATRIOT Act provided certain legal authority.

Those new powers include allowing counterterrorist investigators to use decades-old, court-approved legal tools and procedures designed to fight narcotics trafficking and organized crime, increasing information-sharing among agencies, updating statutes to be current with new technologies and levying stiffer penalties not only for the terrorists but for those who aid and abet them. To date more than 150 terrorist suspects in the United States have pleaded guilty or been convicted in federal court. According to the Justice Department, some of them, including six members of a terror cell that was based in Lackawanna, N.Y., are helping authorities.

Painful Reforms

The post-9/11 war footing has forced the federal government to undertake painful reforms to meet the new terrorist threat. Different security and intelligence services, which at times had been loath to cooperate with one another, have improved their coordination and information-sharing, with tangible results. The feds arrested suspected terrorist Abdullah al-Muhajir, a convict once known as José Padilla, as he plotted to detonate a radiological device or "dirty bomb" designed to spew radioactive fallout in a U.S. city. Attorney General John Ashcroft said at the time of Padilla's arrest in 2002, "Because of the close cooperation among the FBI, the CIA, Defense Department and other federal agencies, we were able to thwart this terrorist."

> *"More than half of the senior leadership of al-Qaeda has been captured or killed, according to an official Justice Department estimate."*

Less visible to the public is the most massive national-security transformation of the U.S. government since the aftermath of World War II. The new Department of Homeland Security (DHS), a merger of 22 government agencies under a single coordinating umbrella, is still a work in progress but is symptomatic of a much larger transformation.

One of the antiterrorism roles of DHS is to keep the public informed, demystifying the terrorist threat and helping people understand in simple language, via its ready.gov Website and other educational means, what the average citizen can do to protect himself from terrorism. For Rumsfeld and others, however, the transformation of government is too modest and too slow. "My impression is that we have not yet made truly bold moves, although we have made many sensible, logical moves in the right direction," he wrote in a private Oct. 16 memo to aides, "but are they enough?" Even in the Pentagon, where he spearheaded a long-term defense transformation effort before 9/11, progress is slow: "It is not possible to change DoD [Department of Defense] fast enough to successfully fight the global war on terror; an alternative might be to try to fashion a new institution, either within DoD or elsewhere—one that seamlessly focuses the capabilities of several departments and agencies on this key problem."

The FBI, the Treasury Department, DHS and other agencies claim to be making headway against terrorist networks already in place inside the country. They disrupted or uprooted al-Qaeda cells from Oregon to Michigan to New York, arresting nearly two-dozen suspects, and already are landing guilty pleas or convictions. They are making headway against other U.S.-based terrorist networks as well. Larry Mefford, outgoing FBI assistant director for counterterrorism, told a Senate subcommittee in June, "Islamic Sunni extremism spearheaded by al-Qaeda, but which also includes Hamas and other groups, continues to inflict casualties on innocent people worldwide. Hezbollah and Hamas in particular maintain a sizable presence in the U.S."

According to a Justice Department memorandum: "Hundreds of suspected terrorists have been identified and tracked throughout the United States."

Mefford said, "Since Sept. 11, 2001, the FBI has investigated more than 4,000 terrorist threats to the U.S., and the number of active FBI investigations into potential terrorist activity has quadrupled since 9/11. Working with our partners in local and state law enforcement and with the U.S. intelligence community, we have also disrupted terrorist activities in over 35 instances inside the United States since Sept. 11, 2001. These include both domestic and international terrorism matters and consist of a variety of preventive actions, including arrests, seizure of funds and disruption of terrorist recruiting and training efforts."

More Work to Be Done

With all that activity, the FBI has yet to make the transformation to a strategic terrorism-fighting organization. FBI Director Robert Mueller told a House panel in June that the bureau had to transform its "intelligence effort from tactical to strategic if [it] is to be successful in preventing terrorism and more proactive in countering foreign intelligence adversaries and disrupting and dismantling significant criminal activity." Rumsfeld, in a memo to senior military and Pentagon leaders, appears to agree that the United States as a whole has not taken a strategic approach to fighting terrorism: "The U.S. is putting relatively little effort into a long-range plan, but we are putting a great deal of effort into trying to stop terrorists."

Top terrorist-hunters acknowledge that the war will be long and difficult, and there is a lot that the United States simply does not know. "Since our understanding of terrorist groups and the underlying philosophy behind these movements continue to develop," said Mefford, "the FBI's assessment of the overall threat continues to evolve."

As Rumsfeld put it in his Oct. 16 memorandum: "Today, we lack metrics to know if we are winning or losing the global war on terror," noting that extremists throughout the world are training new generations of terrorists in madrassas (Islamic religious schools). "Are we capturing, killing or deterring and dissuading more terrorists every day than the madrassas and the radical clerics are recruiting, training and deploying against us?" And terrorist authorities concur, confirming that Rumsfeld and his people are responding to precisely the right question.

Claims That Iraq Was a Terrorist Threat Are Unfounded

by Peter Bergen

About the author: *Peter Bergen is the author of* Holy War, Inc.: Inside the Secret World of Osama bin Laden.

Americans supported the war in Iraq not because Saddam Hussein was an evil dictator—we had known that for many years—but because President [George W.] Bush had made the case that Saddam might hand off weapons of mass destruction to his terrorist allies to wreak havoc on the United States. As of this writing, there appears to be no evidence that Saddam had either weapons of mass destruction or significant ties to terrorist groups like al Qaeda. Yet the belief that Saddam posed an imminent threat to the United States mounted to a theological conviction within the administration, a conviction successfully sold to the American public. So it's fair to ask: Where did this faith come from?

Influence of the Neoconservatives

In the past year, there has been a flood of stories about the thinking of neoconservative hawks such as Richard Perle, until March [2003] the chairman of the influential Defense Policy Board and a key architect of the president's get-tough-on-Iraq policy. Perle has had a long association with the American Enterprise Institute (AEI), a conservative think tank that was also home to other out-of-power hawks during the Clinton years such as John Bolton, now under secretary of state for arms control and international security affairs. It was at AEI that the idea took shape that overthrowing Saddam should be a fundamental goal of U.S. foreign policy. Still, none of the thinker/operatives at AEI, or indeed any of the other neocon hawks such as Paul Wolfowitz, were in any real way experts on Iraq or had served in the region. Moreover, the majority of those in and out of government who were Middle East experts had grave concerns about the wisdom of invading Iraq and serious doubts about claims that Saddam's regime posed an urgent threat to American security. What, then, gave neoconservatives like Wolfowitz and Perle such abiding faith in their own positions?

Historians will be debating that question for years, but an important part of the reason has to do with someone you may well have never heard of: Laurie Mylroie. Mylroie has an impressive array of credentials that certify her as an expert on the Middle East, national security, and, above all, Iraq. She has held faculty positions at Harvard and the U.S. Naval War College and worked at the Washington Institute for Near East Policy, as well as serving as an advisor on Iraq to the 1992 Clinton presidential campaign. During the 1980s, Mylroie was an apologist for Saddam's regime, but reversed her position upon his invasion of Kuwait in 1990, and, with the zeal of the academic spurned, became rabidly anti-Saddam. In the run up to the first Gulf War, Mylroie with *New York Times* reporter Judith Miller wrote *Saddam Hussein and the Crisis in the Gulf*, a well-reviewed bestseller translated into more than a dozen languages.

Until this point, there was nothing controversial about Mylroie's career. This would change with the bombing of the World Trade Center in 1993, the first act of international terrorism within the United States, which would launch Mylroie on a quixotic quest to prove that Saddam's regime was the most important source of terrorism directed against this country. She laid out her case in *Study of Revenge: Saddam Hussein's Unfinished War Against America*, a book published by AEI in 2000 which makes it clear that Mylroie and the neocon hawks worked hand in glove to push her theory that Iraq was behind the '93 Trade Center bombing. Its acknowledgements fulsomely thanked John Bolton and the staff of AEI for their assistance, while Richard Perle glowingly blurbed the book as "splendid and wholly convincing." Lewis "Scooter" Libby, now Vice President [Dick] Cheney's chief of staff, is thanked for his "generous and timely assistance." And it appears that Paul Wolfowitz himself was instrumental in the genesis of *Study of Revenge:* His then-wife is credited with having "fundamentally shaped the book," while of Wolfowitz, she says: "At critical times, he provided crucial support for a project that is inherently difficult."

None of which was out of the ordinary, except for this: Mylroie became enamored of her theory that Saddam was the mastermind of a vast anti-U.S. terrorist conspiracy in the face of virtually all evidence and expert

> *"There appears to be no evidence that Saddam had either weapons of mass destruction or significant ties to terrorist groups like al Qaeda."*

opinion to the contrary. In what amounts to the discovery of a unified field theory of terrorism, Mylroie believes that Saddam was not only behind the '93 Trade Center attack, but also every anti-American terrorist incident of the past decade, from the bombings of U.S. embassies in Kenya and Tanzania to the leveling of the federal building in Oklahoma City to [the September 11, 2001, terrorist attacks]. She is, in short, a crackpot, which would not be significant if she were merely advising say, Lyndon LaRouche. But her neocon friends who went on to run the war in Iraq believed her theories, bringing her on as a consultant at the Pentagon, and they seem to continue to entertain her eccentric belief that Saddam is the fount of the entire shadow war against America.

Hussein on the Brain

According to Bob Woodward's book *Bush at War*, immediately after 9/11 Wolfowitz told the cabinet: "There was a 10 to 50 per cent chance Saddam was involved." A few days later, President Bush told his top aides: "I believe that Iraq was involved, but I'm not going to strike them now." However, the most comprehensive criminal investigation in history—involving chasing down 500,000 leads and interviewing 175,000 people—has turned up no evidence of Iraq's involvement, while the occupation of Iraq by a substantial American army has also uncovered no such link. Moreover, the U.S. State Department's counterterrorism office, which every year releases an authoritative survey of global terrorism, stated in its 2000 report: "[Iraq] has not attempted an anti-western attack since its failed attempt to assassinate former President Bush in 1993 in Kuwait." In other words, by 9/11, Saddam's regime had not engaged in anti-American terrorism for almost a decade.

The First Trade Center Attack

Ideas do not appear out of nowhere, so how is it that key members of the Bush administration believed that Iraq had been so deeply involved in terrorism directed at U.S. targets for many years? For that we must turn to Mylroie's *Study of Revenge*, which posits that Iraq was behind the first Trade Center attack, a theory that is risible as hundreds of national security and law enforcement professionals combed through the evidence of the '93 bombing, certainly looking, amongst other things, for such a connection, and found no evidence. But Mylroie claims to have discovered something that everyone else missed: the mastermind of the plot, a man generally known by one of his many aliases, "Ramzi Yousef," was an Iraqi intelligence agent who some time after Iraq's invasion of Kuwait in 1990 assumed the identity of a Pakistani named Abdul Basit whose family lived there. This was a deduction which she reached following an examination of Basit's passport records and her discovery that Yousef and Basit were four inches different in height. On this wafer-thin foundation she builds her case that Yousef must have therefore been an Iraqi agent given access to Basit's passport following the Iraq occupation. However, U.S. investigators say that "Yousef" and Basit are in fact one and the same person, and that the man Mylroie describes as an Iraqi agent is in fact a Pakistani with ties to al Qaeda.

Mylroie appears never to have absorbed the implications of Occam's Razor, the basic philosophical and scientific principle generally understood to be: "Of two competing theories or explanations, all other things being equal, the simpler one is to be preferred." In this case the simpler—and more accurate—explanation of Yousef/Basit's identity is that he was part of the al Qaeda network, not working for Baghdad. Indeed, an avalanche of evidence demonstrates that Yousef was part of the loosely knit al Qaeda organization, evidence that Mylroie does not consider as it would undermine all her suppositions.

When Yousef flew to New York from Pakistan in 1992 before the bombing of the Trade Center, he was accompanied by Ahmad Ajaj, who was arrested at Kennedy Airport on immigration charges, and was later found to have an al Qaeda bomb-making manual in his luggage. Al Qaeda member Jamal al-Fadl told a New York jury in 2000 that he saw Yousef at the group's Sadda training camp on

> *"Mylroie became enamored of her theory that Saddam was the mastermind of a vast anti-U.S. terrorist conspiracy in the face of virtually all evidence and expert opinion to the contrary."*

the Pakistan-Afghanistan border some time between 1989 and 1991. When Yousef lived in the Philippines in the early 1990s, his partner in terrorism was Wali Khan Amin Shah, who had trained in Afghanistan under bin Laden. A number of Yousef's co-conspirators had ties to a Brooklyn organization known as the Afghan Refugee Center. This was the American arm of an organization bin Laden founded in Pakistan during the mid-1980s that would later evolve into al Qaeda. Yousef's uncle, Khalid Sheikh Mohammed, sent him money for the Trade Center attack, and would later go on to become al Qaeda's military commander and the chief planner of 9/11. I could go on. The point is that the 1993 attack was plotted not by Iraqi intelligence, but by men who were linked to al Qaeda.

In addition to ignoring Yousef's many connections to al Qaeda, Mylroie is clearly aware that in 1995, he gave what would be his only interview to the Arabic newspaper *al Hayat* since she alludes to it in her book *Study of Revenge*. "I have no connection with Iraq," said Yousef to his interviewer, adding for good measure that "the Iraqi people must not pay for the mistakes made by Saddam." "Yousef," who traveled under a variety of false identities, confirmed that his real name was indeed Abdul Basit and that he was a Pakistani born in Kuwait, and also admitted that he knew and admired Sheikh Omar Abdel Rahman, one of al Qaeda's spiritual gurus, whom the U.S. government would later convict of plotting terror attacks in New York. Yousef went on to say that he wanted to "aid members" of Egypt's Jihad group, a terrorist organization then led by Ayman al-Zawahiri, who is now bin Laden's deputy. Yousef's interview has the ring of truth as he freely volunteered that he knew Sheikh Rahman, the cleric whom the U.S. government had by then already identified as the inspiration for several terrorist conspiracies in New York during the early '90s and also explained that he was part of an Islamic movement which planned to carry out attacks in Saudi Arabia to avenge the arrests of Sheikh Salman al-Audah and Sheikh Safar al-Hawali, radical clerics who have profoundly influenced both bin Laden and al Qaeda. Yousef knew that he was likely facing a lifetime in prison at the time of this interview, and so had little reason to dissemble. In *Study of Revenge*, Mylroie is careful not to mention the substance of what Yousef said here as it demolishes her theory that he was an Iraqi agent.

Moreover, Mylroie's broader contention that the first Trade Center attack was an Iraqi plot is, to put it mildly, not shared by the intelligence and law-enforcement officials familiar with the subsequent investigation. Vince Cannistraro, who headed the C.I.A.'s Counterterrorist Center in the early 1990s, told me, "My view is that Laurie has an obsession with Iraq and trying to link Saddam to global terrorism. Years of strenuous effort to prove the case have been unavailing." Ken Pollack, a former C.I.A. analyst, scarcely to be described as "soft" on Saddam—his book *The Threatening Storm: The Case for Invading Iraq* made the most authoritative argument for toppling the dictator—dismissed Mylroie's theories to me: "The NSC [National Security Council] had the intelligence community look very hard at the allegations that the Iraqis were behind the 1993 Trade Center attack. Finding those links would have been very beneficial to the U.S. government at the time, but the intelligence community said that there were no such links."

No Evidence

Mary Jo White, the no-nonsense U.S. attorney who successfully prosecuted both the Trade Center case and the al Qaeda bombers behind the 1998 attacks on U.S. embassies in Africa, told me that there was no evidence to support Mylroie's claims: "We investigated the Trade Center attack thoroughly, and other than the evidence that Ramzi Yousef traveled on a phony Iraqi passport, that was the only connection to Iraq." Neil Herman, the F.B.I. official who headed the Trade Center probe, explained that following the attacks, one of the lower-level conspirators, Abdul Rahman Yasin, did flee New York to live with a family member in Baghdad: "The one glaring connection that can't be overlooked is Yasin. We pursued that on every level, traced him to a relative and a location, and we made overtures to get him back." However, Herman says that Yasin's presence in Baghdad does not mean Iraq sponsored the attack: "We looked at that rather extensively. There were no ties to the Iraqi government." In sum, by the mid-'90s, the Joint Terrorism Task Force in New York, the F.B.I., the U.S. Attorney's office in the Southern District of New York, the C.I.A., the N.S.C., and the State Department had all found no evidence implicating the Iraqi government in the first Trade Center attack.

Perles of Wisdom

As Mylroie was fighting against the tide of expert opinion to prove her case that Saddam was behind the '93 bombing, her neocon colleagues at AEI and elsewhere were formulating an alternative vision of U.S. foreign policy to challenge what they saw as the feckless and weak policies of the Clinton administration. Mylroie's research and expertise on Iraq complemented the big-think strategizing of the neocons, and a symbiotic relationship developed between them, as evidenced by the garlands that the neocons bestowed upon her for her work. Wolfowitz gushingly blurbed *Study of Revenge*: "[Her] provocative and disturbing book argues that . . . Ramzi Yousef, was in fact an agent of Iraqi intelligence. If so, what would that tell us about the extent of Saddam Hussein's ambitions? How would it change our view of Iraq's continuing efforts to retain weapons of mass destruction and to acquire new ones? How would it affect our judgments about the collapse of U.S. policy toward Iraq and the need for a fundamentally new policy?" (How, indeed . . .) James Woolsey, another prominent Iraq hawk who headed the C.I.A. between 1993 and 1995, also weighed in: "Anyone who wishes to continue to deal with Saddam by ignoring his role in international terrorism . . . and by giving only office furniture to the Iraqi resistance now has the staggering task of trying to refute this superb work." *Study of Revenge* was reissued after 9/11 as *The War Against America*, Woolsey contributing a new foreword that described Mylroie's work as "brilliant and brave."

> *"By 9/11, Saddam's regime had not engaged in anti-American terrorism for almost a decade."*

It is possible, of course, that the neocons did not find Mylroie's research to be genuinely persuasive, but rather that her findings simply fit conveniently into their own desire to overthrow Saddam. Having blurbed her first book as "wholly convincing," Richard Perle now says that "not everything she says is convincing" and that Mylroie's thinking was "not very important" to the development of his own views on Iraq. At the same time, Perle continues to praise Mylroie's investigative skills, even saying she should be put in charge of "quality control" at the C.I.A. So there are reasons to think that people like Perle actually were persuaded by her research. As the one member of the neocon team with serious credentials on Iraq, Mylroie offered opinions which would naturally have carried special weight. That she was a genuine authority, whose "research" confirmed their worst fears about Saddam, could only have strengthened their convictions.

The evidence that the hawks really believed her theories can be seen in their statements and actions following September 11. Shortly thereafter, Woolsey was dispatched to the United Kingdom on an extraordinary trip, apparently sanctioned by Wolfowitz, to check out a key aspect of Mylroie's argument about Yousef. During the early '90s, Abdul Basit, the Pakistani whose identity Yousef had supposedly assumed, attended a Welsh college to study electrical engineering. Mylroie writes that Basit was quite different in appearance from Yousef, thus further proving her contention that Yousef was a substitute, a fact that could be proved by visiting Basit's former college in Wales. As Woolsey has made no comment on his trip to the United Kingdom, it's fair to assume that his efforts to replicate these findings did not meet with success. However, around the second anniversary of 9/11, Vice President Dick Cheney continued to echo Mylroie's utterances when he told NBC's Tim Russert that Iraq was "the geographic base of the terrorists who have had us under assault for many years, but most especially on 9/11," a demonstrably false theory that Mylroie has been vigorously touting since this past summer [2003].

Conspiracy Theory

In July, Mylroie published a new book *Bush vs. the Beltway*, which reprised many of the themes of *Study of Revenge*. The subtitle of her new tome tells you where the book is headed: *How the CIA and the State Department Tried to Stop the War on Terror.* The book charges that the U.S. government actually suppressed information about Iraq's role in anti-American terrorism, including in the investigation of 9/11. Luckily, *Bush vs. the Beltway*, which reads in part like Bush 2004 campaign literature, does have at least one heroic figure: "There is an actual hero, in the person of the president who could not be rolled, spun or otherwise diverted from his most solemn obligation."

Bush vs. the Beltway, the subject of additional hosannas from both Woolsey and Perle, claims that Khalid Sheik Mohammed, the now-captured mastermind of 9/11, is an Iraqi intelligence agent, like Ramzi Yousef, who adopted the identity of a Pakistani living in Kuwait. Funnily enough, the U.S. government doesn't seem to have explored this intriguing theory. Why not? According to Mylroie, a plot is afoot to prevent Mohammed's unmasking. Shortly after *Bush vs. the Beltway* was published, she appeared as an expert witness before the blue-ribbon commission investigating 9/11, testifying that "there is substantial reason to believe that these masterminds [of both the '93 and 9/11 Trade Center attacks] are Iraqi intelligence agents." Mylroie explained that this had not been discovered by the U.S. government because "a senior administration official told me in specific that the question of the identities of the terrorist masterminds could not be pursued because of bureaucratic obstructionism." So we are expected to believe that the senior Bush administration officials whom Mylroie knows so well could not find anyone in intelligence or law enforcement to investigate the supposed Iraqi intelligence background of the mastermind of 9/11, at the same time that 150,000 American soldiers had been sent to fight a war in Iraq under the rubric of the war on terrorism. Please.

> *"There is no evidence linking [Saddam Hussein] to any act of anti-American terrorism for the past decade, while there is a mountain of evidence that implicates al Qaeda."*

Further undermining Mylroie's theory about Khalid Sheik Mohammed is the fact that since his apprehension in Pakistan, KSM, as he's known to law enforcement, has specifically denied any connection to Iraq, at the same time that he has offered up actionable intelligence about terror plots in the United States. A senior U.S. counter-terrorism official told me that KSM, like several other high-ranking al Qaeda operatives, has disgorged much useful information following the use of coercive methods that include making him "uncomfortable and withholding water and sleep." As a result of KSM's interrogations, Iyman Faris, a trucker living in Ohio, was arrested for plotting to cut through the cable supporting the Brooklyn Bridge and was sentenced in October to 20 years in prison.

Zeitgeist Heist

Mylroie declined to be interviewed for this article "with regret," so the only chance I have had to talk with her came this past February, when we both appeared on Canadian television to discuss the impending war in Iraq and Saddam's putative connections to terrorism. As soon as the interview started, Mylroie began lecturing in a hectoring tone: "Listen, we're going to war because President Bush believes Saddam Hussein was involved in 9/11. Al Qaeda is a front for Iraqi intelligence . . . [the U.S.] bureaucracy made a tremendous blunder that refused to acknowledge these links . . . the

> *"Her specious theories of Iraq's involvement in anti-American terrorism have now become part of the American zeitgeist."*

people responsible for gathering this information, say in the C.I.A., are also the same people who contributed to the blunder on 9/11 and the deaths of 3,000 Americans, and so whenever this information emerges they move to discredit it." I tried to make the point that Mylroie's theories defied common sense, as they implied a conspiracy by literally thousands of American officials to suppress the truth of the links between Iraq and 9/11, to little avail.

Hysterical Hyperbole

At the end of the interview, Mylroie, who exudes a slightly frazzled, batty air, started getting visibly agitated, her finger jabbing at the camera and her voice rising to a yell as she outlined the following apocalyptic scenario: "Now I'm going to tell you something, OK, and I want all Canada to understand, I want you to understand the consequences of the cynicism of people like Peter. There is a very acute chance as we go to war that Saddam will use biological agents as revenge against Americans, that there will be anthrax in the United States and there will be smallpox in the United States. Are you in Canada prepared for Americans who have smallpox and do not know it crossing the border and bringing that into Canada?"

This kind of hysterical hyperbole is emblematic of Mylroie's method, which is to never let the facts get in the way of her monomaniacal certainties. In the case

91

of the 1995 Oklahoma City bombing, she has said that Terry Nichols, one of the plotters, was in league with Ramzi Yousef. Richard Matsch, the veteran federal judge who presided over the Oklahoma City bombing case, ruled any version of this theory to be inadmissible at trial. Mylroie implicates Iraq in the 1996 bombing of a U.S. military facility in Saudi Arabia which killed 19 U.S. servicemen. In 2001, a grand jury returned indictments in that case against members of Saudi Hezbollah, a group with ties not to Iraq, but Iran. Mylroie suggests that the attacks on two U.S. embassies in Africa in 1998 might have been "the work of both bin Laden and Iraq." An overseas investigation unprecedented in scope did not uncover any such connection. Mylroie has written that the crash of TWA flight 800 into Long Island Sound in 1996 likely was an Iraqi plot. A two-year investigation by the National Transportation Safety Board ruled it was an accident. According to Mylroie, Iraq supplied the bomb-making expertise for the attack which killed 17 U.S. sailors on the USS *Cole* in Yemen in 2000. No American law enforcement official has made that claim. Mylroie blames Iraq for the post-9/11 anthrax attacks around the United States. Marilyn Thompson, *The Washington Post*'s investigations editor, who has written an authoritative book on those attacks, says, "The F.B.I. has essentially dismissed this theory and says there is no evidence to support it." A U.S. counter-terrorism official remarked: "Mylroie probably thinks the Washington sniper was an Iraqi."

In her book *Bush vs. the Beltway*, Mylroie approvingly quotes the maxim "we should not love our opinions like our children." It's long overdue that she heed this excellent piece of advice. Saddam is guilty of many crimes, not least the genocidal policies he unleashed on the Marsh Arabs and the Iraqi Kurds, but there is no evidence linking him to any act of anti-American terrorism for the past decade, while there is a mountain of evidence that implicates al Qaeda.

Unfortunately, Mylroie's researches have proven to be more than merely academic, as her theories have bolstered the argument that led us into a costly war in Iraq and swayed key opinion-makers in the Bush administration, who then managed to persuade seven out of 10 Americans that the Iraqi dictator had a role in the attacks on Washington and New York. So, her specious theories of Iraq's involvement in anti-American terrorism have now become part of the American zeitgeist. Meanwhile, in a recent, telling quote to *Newsweek*, Mylroie observed: "I take satisfaction that we went to war with Iraq and got rid of Saddam Hussein. The rest is details." Now she tells us.

The War on Terror Is Being Fought to Benefit American Corporations

by Norman Council

About the author: Norman Council is a behavioral health care administration professional and an assistant professor. He is also a freelance writer of fiction, poetry, and political commentary and the managing editor of Newtopia Magazine.

Since it was clear that we were headed in that direction, plaintive comments from the "peace" movement have asserted that the second Iraq war [in 2003] is, like the first one, a power grab aimed at assuring continued American access to Middle Eastern oil. This position continues to be articulated today and, to many, is simply acknowledged fact.

Many dispute these assertions, espousing instead the idea that the war is about freedom, democracy or national security. However, the most meaningful critique of the assertion that Middle Eastern wars are about oil is not that they go too far in asserting connection to the West's addiction to oil, but that they do not go far enough. In the end, all war is about economics, but it is overly simplistic to attribute the US strategy in the Middle East to a single cause, or more to the point, a single commodity.

The Real Reason for the War in Iraq

In these times of shifting justification for the war, it is difficult to ascertain the true rationale for it. This difficulty is compounded by the fact that we have not actually heard, in all of the various justifications, anything that could actually be accepted as a "real" rationale. This is because the real reasons are at the same time more complex and nuanced and more mundane than the general public is willing to attend to.

This war is not about security, democracy, or the ending of tyranny or even terrorism; the war in Iraq is the first salvo of a trade war. It is the first in what will eventually be a series of wars whose purpose is to establish the security necessary for the United States to dominate the agenda and process of globalization. It is the first step toward bringing all nations into what Thomas P.M. Barnett, in the March 2003 issue of *Esquire* magazine described as "the globalizing world . . . its rule sets, its norms, and all the ties that bind countries together in mutually assured dependence."

Barnett (author of *The Pentagon's New Map: War and Peace in the Twenty-first Century*, he served in the Office of Secretary of Defense from November 2001 until June 2003) is disarmingly candid in his advocacy of a military strategy aimed at reconciling what he refers to as the "Non-Integrating Gap" nations, which he characterizes as "regions plagued by politically repressive regimes, widespread poverty and disease, routine mass murder, and—most important—the chronic conflicts that incubate the next generation of global terrorists," with the "Functioning Core" or regions where "network connectivity, financial transactions, liberal media flows, and collective security" engender "stable governments, rising standards of living, and more deaths by suicide than murder." (This last providing an interesting, perhaps unconscious, commentary on the effect of globalization on personal life quality.)

> *"All war is about economics."*

Barnett divides the countries of the world into three distinct categories:

1. The Core—those nations who get it: North America, much of South America, the European Union, Putin's Russia, Japan and Asia's emerging economies (most notably China and India), Australia, New Zealand, and South Africa.
2. The Gap—the guys who don't get it—among them, Sudan, Afghanistan, northwestern Pakistan, Somalia, Yemen.
3. And last, but not least, the Seam; those nations that function—sometimes unwittingly and involuntarily—as borders or buffers between the Core and the Gap—such as Mexico, Brazil, Morocco, Algeria, Greece, Turkey, Thailand, Malaysia, the Philippines, and Indonesia.

Constitutional Liberalism

Ostensibly the United States favors the emergence of "democracy," in the world—that is governments put into place by a universally enfranchised people. In fact, this is not at all what we seek, or at least what we seek as a primary outcome. Despite President [George W.] Bush's [October 18, 2004] acknowledgement that an Islamic theocracy may be the choice of the Iraqi people, what we seek in Iraq—in the end all that we will accept in that or any other "Gap" country such as Afghanistan, Myanmar, Indonesia and numerous other Asian and Middle Eastern countries—is the exportation of a variant of what Fareed Zakaria, in his book *The Future of Freedom* refers to as "constitutional liberalism," a form of government consistent with Barnett's vision: "free and fair elections, but also . . . the rule of law, a separation of powers and the protection of basic liberties of speech, assembly, religion and property." Our efforts express a prejudice so ingrained in our thinking that Ira Chernus—Professor of Religious Studies University of Colorado at Boulder—concluded that: ". . . every word of this mainstream debate reinforces the basic view both sides share: the Iraqis must choose between order, American-style, and the endless misery of chaotic savagery."

Democracy American-Style

Thus, even from the most generous of perspectives, it is not "democracy" that we seek to export to these countries, but American democracy, which Zakaria makes clear, is—by design—quite undemocratic. Our constitution limits specifically and generally the actions that can be taken by any branch of government, including "the people." In Zakaria's interesting analysis of the evolution of Western liberal (using here the older, original connotation of the word) democracy, it is not voting that has been of importance, but the emergence of a nongovernmental elite whose interests gave it a vested interest in how the government was run. The rule of law for instance is only coincidentally directed at the "common man." For the most part the rule of law is in place to protect the interests—and property—of the elite. This elite was originally a landed aristocracy, but since the late 17th century it has increasingly been a capitalist elite—those who own the means of production. Today it is the corporati—the CEO's, board members and major equity partners of US multinational corporations.

Zakaria makes clear that the capitalist democracy that is unique to America took several hundred years to develop and did so in a crucible that is not likely to be reproduced in the

> *"What we seek is to make the world safer for capitalism."*

Middle East, Asia or Africa, or at least not be reproduced in the period of time necessary to secure those regions for the incursion of global capitalism. But that is okay, because the agenda is not really to make these countries democratic; to hell with making the world safer for democracy—what we seek is to make the world safer for capitalism.

Capitalism First

Zakaria traces a specific and well defined path to freedom and liberty for the people of any country: capitalism and the rule of law first, then democracy. His view is that capitalism, with its inherent capacity to facilitate the accumulation of wealth and power independent of some ruling body, facilitates the development of an independent judiciary and the rule of law. It does this, according to Zakaria, because governments need money to run—to press their policies—and to get this money from an independent bourgeoisie, it must bargain for it. In the bargain come the protections for the interests of the capitalists, who in turn facilitate the growth of the economy.

In the course of his treatise, Zakaria actually delineates order as a third precursor for democracy. That is, capitalism, though somewhat dependent on the chaos of open markets, cannot thrive in anarchy, and order does not arise from anarchy; it must be imposed. This point is made in numerous examples by Zakaria but the most illuminating is this rather convoluted quote from political scientist Myron Weiner who stated that "every single country in the Third World that emerged from colonial rule since the Second World War with a population of at least one million (and almost all the smaller colonies as well) with a continuous democratic experience is a former British colony." The meaning here is clear. Order, whether imposed by imperial or dictatorial means, is a necessary precursor to liberty. Zakaria, illustrates the counterpoint to this assertion by using numerous examples of countries who attempted democracy in the first blush of liberation and failed miserably—in fact are still failing.

> *"Order, whether imposed by imperial or dictatorial means, is a necessary precursor to liberty."*

Lest one think that the agenda ascribed here is based only the philosophical musings of Zakaria or Barnett consider these words from the Bush administration's National Security Strategy (NSS). "In the twenty-first century, only nations that share a commitment to protecting basic human rights and guaranteeing political and economic freedom will be able to unleash the potential of their people and assure their future prosperity." Freedom equals economic prosperity, and who is to assure that freedom? Consider further, ". . . the United States will use this moment of opportunity to extend the benefits of freedom across the globe. We will actively work to bring the hope of democracy, development, free markets, and free trade to every corner of the world."

The Reason for the War on Terror

Thus we arrive at the raison d'etre of the war on terror. It is the dream to impose democracy—the imposition of which, in this twisted way of thinking, constitutes not a violation of freedom, but the advocacy of it—on the world, but in order to do that, the ground must be prepared, so to speak. We make the world safe for democracy by first making it exploitable by capitalists, and to make it exploitable by capitalists we must first impose order.

And it is here that American arrogance moves from merely frightening to terrifying. In a national security policy memorandum, developed by current Deputy Defense Secretary Paul Wolfowitz under the supervision of then Secretary of Defense Dick Cheney, one finds the following: "Our first objective is to prevent the re-emergence of a new rival. This is a dominant consideration underlying the new regional defense strategy and requires that we endeavor to prevent any hostile power from dominating a region whose resources would, under consolidated control, be sufficient to generate global power. These regions include Western Europe, East Asia, the territory of the former Soviet Union, and Southwest Asia."

While Cheney was later forced to retract this document after it was leaked, its basic tenets live on in the NSS, viz "The U.S. national security strategy will be based on a distinctly American internationalism that reflects the union of our values and our national interests."

US Domination

"In essence," explained Jay Bookman of *The Atlanta Journal-Constitution*, "(the National Security Strategy) lays out a plan for permanent U.S. military and economic domination of every region on the globe, unfettered by international treaty or concern. And to make that plan a reality, it envisions a stark expansion of our global military presence."

The "war on terror" is, of course, not the first time that a nation or government has used its military to impose its policies on a diverse set of once sovereign states. And, like the Pax Britannica or Pax Romana before it, this effort at establishing a Pax Americana arises from a realization that American prosperity, like that of ancient Rome or 19th century Britain is dependent on our capacity to control events outside of our borders. The trouble is, in this effort the "value" of democracy is for sale, as it is US prosperity that is sought, not the prosperity of the world at large. In fact, what is sought is prosperity for the US multinational corporations, who, according to this perspective, are the engine of economic prosperity.

Barnett points out that "Iraq is but the first step in this process. The real reason I support a war like this is that the resulting long-term military commitment will finally force America to deal with the entire Gap as a strategic threat environment." Terrorism has become heir apparent as the new engine for the Pax Americana. In this it has replaced communism as the best excuse to use the American military as a tool for forwarding its foreign and economic policy.

Unilateral Intervention

Using the war on terror as a device, the US now has reason to intervene, unilaterally if it sees fit, into any society it deems as a haven for terrorists. The situation in Sudan makes it clear, however, that intervention is based on something other than the needs and interests of the citizens of the country. Whereas the suffering of the people in Sudan is readily comparable to that of the people of Iraq under Saddam [Hussein], the US has no plan for military intervention into Sudan. The reason is straightforward: Sudan has no information and financial infrastructure, no products of interest to the US and has no strategic position in the global marketplace.

We seek to establish in the "Gap" in months, years or even decades, what has taken centuries to evolve in the West. And, despite the rhetoric about the establishment of democracy, the history of US foreign policy demonstrates a rather clear bias toward dictatorship as it has viewed that as the fastest path to "stability" which can be functionally defined as access to the economic assets of the country.

Examples abound of US tacit acceptance or outright support of dictatorships in the Middle East—examples include Egypt, Jordan and Saudi Arabia—while maintaining significant level of hostility to a government in Iran, which supports a basic concept of the rule of law (though not English Common Law). In fact an argument could be made that Iran is a far more stable government than that of Russia, which is in the process of deterioration to the domain of a KGB strongman.[1] The difference between Russia and Iran of course is that the US has access to Russian assets and does not have access to those of Iran.

It's the Stupid Economy

It is not only the means of the Pax Americana that presents problems for the world, it is the goal itself: the outcome of globalization.

There are more than 60,000 multinational corporations worldwide. Prior to the late 70's and early 80's most of the direct investment in foreign countries took place through lending institutions. Following the 1983 Mexican default and the domino effect throughout Latin America, foreign investment shifted from a focus on debt to a new structure, Foreign Direct Investment (FDI), a process directed mainly by multinational corporations. FDI is technically defined as a 10% holding or greater by foreign interests in assets located within a nation's borders, although today FDI usually means 100% ownership by a multinational corporation.

Foreign Direct Investment, has many advantageous features, particularly as compared to debt. As FDI amounts to direct control of assets by the multinational, default by a borrower, which in the past was most likely a government, is far less of a likelihood. At the same time there are opportunities for real growth in the county, with improved infrastructure, improved

> *"We make the world safe for democracy by first making it exploitable by capitalists."*

wages and technology and skills transfers that contribute to the overall well being of the local economy, as well as the quality of life in the community. Although historical experience makes it clear that these improvements are by no means guaranteed.

In fact, despite the potential for trickle down of these benefits, the down sides associated with FDI are as problematic as the upsides are potentially beneficial.

---

1. Vladimir Putin, the president of Russia, previously served as an officer in the KGB, the security service of the former Soviet Union.

When issues such as "repatriation" of earnings (i.e. the return of profits of FDI to the home country of the multinational) resulting in decapitalization of the local economy, damage to competition for local companies and resulting market dominance by the multinational, and environmental damage resulting from the off-loading of highly polluting processes to countries where environmental laws are not strong, and one is left with a lukewarm feeling about FDI, at best. At worst, in countries like Bolivia and Venezuela, FDI has been seen as a tool for robbing the people of those countries of their national assets.

> *"Terrorism has become heir apparent as the new engine for Pax Americana."*

After an exhaustive review of the literature Andrew Charlton and Joseph E. Stiglitz made this conclusion in a preliminary draft for *Initiative for Policy Dialogue Capital Market Task Force:* "In general, this literature establishes a compelling case for caution: capital market liberalization is not robustly associated with economic growth in developing countries, but it does appear to exacerbate macroeconomic volatility and increase the incidence of financial crises." In short, despite assertions to the contrary, a rational view of cross-border capitalization is that it is generally better for the multinational than it is for countries and their populations in the "Gap."

Global Marketplace

As Western financial markets are liberalized (i.e. deregulated) the resulting competition sends financial institutions into the global market-place. Concomitant deregulation of local economies has supported that development. But this inflow of foreign capital, generally sucked up by multinationals to expand production, is far from a boon. If a country becomes dependent on foreign capital, sudden shifts in foreign capital flows can create financing difficulties and economic downturns.

These financial crises are very costly. In 1973–1997, researchers studied 44 crises in developed countries and 95 in emerging markets and found that average output losses were 6.25 and 9.21 percent of GDP [gross domestic product] respectively. These crises have a disproportionate impact on people, particularly hurting the poor through loss of wages and employment shocks, but also through high inflation, relative price changes, and cutbacks in public spending. . . .

One of the main consequences of globalization is that, when the domestic financial system integrates with the rest of the world, it becomes harder for countries to oversee the transactions outside its borders. While it may be possible for the local authorities to regulate the activities of the local subsidiary of an international bank, it is more difficult to regulate the international operations that are linked to the local bank.

Sergio L. Schmukler, Senior Economist for the Development Research Group of the World Bank notes that "As economies become more integrated, governments have less policy instruments and have to rely more on international financial policies. For example, governments tend to have fewer options about their monetary policy and exchange rate policy . . . bank regulation and supervision by one government is more difficult when liabilities and prices are denominated in foreign currency . . . in the midst of contagious crises, governments tend to lack sufficient resources to stop a currency attack and an individual government can do little to stop crises being originated in foreign countries."

In fact, what the research on financial liberalization (code for cross border financial services) and globalization indicates is that economic growth is associated with improvements in indicators of well-being; that is when the people are better off, the economy improves. There is no research that supports the idea that an economy can be forcefully "grown" from outside and that it will then run on its own and provide improvements to the local people of that economy.

Indeed, when Alex Cobham, Supernumerary Fellow in Economics at St. Anne's College, University of Oxford, and Director of the Political Economy section of the Oxford Council for Good Governance, surveyed the linkages between capital account liberalization and poverty and he found "a number of potential mechanisms by which liberalization can contribute to monetary inequality and undermine government attempts to address other elements of poverty including the provision of health and education." Leading him to conclude that "Given the now-broad acceptance that growth benefits have thus far been inconsequential, the implied net poverty impact of liberalization is negative."

> *"The 'war on terror' is the perfect storm."*

Confused by the Facts

What has all of this to do with the "war on terror"? As both Zakaria and Barnett note, in order for capitalism (usually in the form of FDI by multinationals) to succeed certain things must be in place. One is "the rule of law." Another is that local markets need to be effectively secured. In part, this is accomplished through the "liberalization" of the finance sector across borders, but more importantly, securing local markets requires the elimination of forces resistant to American influence.

In effect, what we have in American foreign policy is a rationale for moving forward with a process that has limited demonstrable benefit for the local economy and in fact has a marked tendency to destabilize it, deprive the local government of the regulatory capacity to protect itself, and leave the local people subject to forces originating in other countries or, more to the point, within the operations of US multinational corporations.

Undaunted, the neocons move inexorably forward. Never one to be confused by the facts, once its mind is made up, the Bush administration presses forward its military agenda of globalization and will brook no resistance. The United

States' plays on the international stage are characterized by the startling arrogance of Barnett's assumptions: "The International system today lacks any sort of recognized institutional rule set for processing a politically bankrupt state . . . The UN [United Nations] is at best a legislative branch for the global community, whereas the U.S. is clearly the closest thing we have to an executive Leviathan able to prosecute criminal actors across the system."

His rational for the war on terror is clear "[terrorist leader Osama] Bin Laden and Al Qaeda [terrorists] are pure products of the Gap—in effect, its most violent feedback to the Core. They tell us how we are doing in exporting security to these lawless areas (not very well) and which states they would like to take 'offline' from globalization and return to some seventh-century definition of the good life."

The Perfect Storm

The "war on terror" is the perfect storm. Having established an international policy based on corporate imperialism, the United States has instituted a military response to the resulting pan-nationalistic guerilla war that is guaranteed to engender more terror, enhancing both the status and market share of the "military-industrial complex", the US multinational corporations and legions of "contractors" who feed off of the continuous need for administration of and reconstruction following military intervention. The United States is the only body extant that can provide the security necessary for economic expansion, but in so doing, it creates the conditions from which the rebellious strike out, thus justifying the arguments for greater security and more "preemptive" intervention.

This new war is a warmer version of the Cold War; or better—Cold War: the Sequel. As Bush states in the preface to the NSS "The great struggles of the twentieth century between liberty and totalitarianism ended with a decisive victory for the forces of freedom—and a single sustainable model for national success: freedom, democracy, and free enterprise." In essence the NSS outlines the strategy for extending US hegemony and imposing its model of prosperity on the world.

> *"This new war is a warmer version of the Cold War; or better—Cold War: the Sequel."*

This war will be fought in fits and starts and result ultimately in an overextension of United States' resources, leading to the same kinds of mistakes that the Cold War did— such as the classic one of outfitting Osama bin Laden[2] during Afghanistan's occupation by the Soviet Union, or supporting Saddam (and his use of WMD's [weapons of mass destruction]) in a proxy war against Iran (at the time, believed to be in the Soviet sphere). The engine driving this new war is the same

---

2. The United States covertly aided terrorist leader Osama bin Laden in his efforts to oust the Soviet Union from Afghanistan in the 1980s.

as the old—pressing the message of capitalism and "prosperity" forward in the name of democracy. However, as pointed out by Charles V. Peña, director of defense policy studies at the Cato Institute, the NSS ". . . prescribes a global security strategy based on the false belief that the best and only way to achieve U.S. security is by forcibly creating a better and safer world in America's image."

Wolfowitz, Cheney, et al envision themselves as this generation's George Marshall [U.S. Army general in World War II and later secretary of state] and Dean Acheson [influential U.S. secretary of state]. Sadly, in the end, the only real beneficiaries of their work will be the people who can offload their assets to offshore accounts.

The War on Terror Is Creating More Terrorists

by the *Progressive*

About the author: *The* Progressive *is a journal focused on peace, social and economic justice, and civil rights.*

The Bush Administration claims that the Iraq campaign, far from being an illegal war and a botched occupation, is actually a defense of the United States.

Even though Bush has overthrown Saddam [Hussein], the alleged threat incarnate, Administration officials are still repeating the same mantra. Only now it's not Saddam who threatens the United States from Iraq; it's the terrorists who have flowed into Iraq. But whose fault is that?

"Every American needs to believe this: that if we fail here in this environment, the next battlefield will be the streets of America," said General Ricardo Sanchez, the U.S. commander in Iraq. Paul Bremer, de facto king of Iraq, has said virtually the same thing. As has Bush, who told the American Legion, "Our military is confronting terrorists in Iraq . . . so our people will not have to confront terrorist violence in New York, or St. Louis, or Los Angeles."

A Terrorist Magnet

Again on September 7 [2003], in his speech to the nation, [George W.] Bush said U.S. troops were fighting the enemy in Iraq today "so that we do not meet him again on our own streets, in our own cities." Yet it is Bush's Iraq War that has made such encounters more likely.

Bush's Iraq folly has made the United States less safe in at least three ways: It has bred the very terrorism it ostensibly set out to vanquish, it has diverted resources from the fight against Al Qaeda [terrorists], and it has alienated people and countries that were providing crucial help in that fight.

Back in July, General Sanchez described Iraq as a "terrorist magnet." While such a designation may be partially a propaganda ploy, there is evidence that terrorists from outside Iraq have been swarming in to take on the U.S. occupiers.

The *Financial Times* warned that "increasing numbers of Saudi Arabian Islamists are crossing the border into Iraq, in preparation for jihad, or holy war, against U.S. and U.K. forces." And the *New York Times* reported that Iraq is becoming the place to go if you want to take on the United States. "In much the same way as the Russian invasion of Afghanistan stirred an earlier generation of young Muslim militants to fight the infidel, the American presence in Iraq is prompting a rising tide of Muslim militants to slip into the country to fight the foreign occupier," wrote Neil MacFarquhar of the *New York Times*. He interviewed Mullah Mustapha Kreikar, the spiritual leader of Ansar al-Islam, who said, "There is no difference between this occupation and the Soviet occupation of Afghanistan in 1979. . . . The resistance is not only a reaction to the American invasion, it is part of the continuous Islamic struggle since the collapse of the caliphate."

> *"Bush's Iraq folly has made the United States less safe."*

For radical Muslims, "the imperative to free Iraq is profound," Daniel Benjamin and Steven Simon, authors of *The Age of Sacred Terror*, wrote in *Time* magazine. "The country is in the heartland of Dar al-Islam, the true realm of the faith, not some backwater like Afghanistan. For 500 years, Baghdad was home to the Caliph, the leader of all Muslims, the equivalent of both Pope and King. For them, the U.S. occupation of this land is an existential affront. . . . That requires the radicals to bloody the Americans—the more savagely the better."

Breeding Terrorists

But even if not a single foreign terrorist had entered Iraq, the U.S. occupation would be breeding terrorists there. With Iraqi citizens suffering more in material ways now than they did before the war, with the U.S. military's often heavy-handed treatment of Iraqi civilians, and with the failure of the U.S. military to provide adequate safety in places like Baghdad and Najaf, it can hardly be a surprise that some in Iraq view the United States as an illegitimate occupying force. A fraction of those people will be susceptible to calls for a nationalist uprising or a jihad against the United States.

In his September 7 speech, Bush said U.S. troops were facing resistance from only two groups: "former members of the old Saddam regime" and "foreign terrorists." By omitting reference to anyone else who may be resisting, Bush was dodging his own responsibility for creating terrorists.

A Disastrous War

"We're making terrorists faster than we're killing them," says Stephen Zunes, chair of the Peace and Justice Studies Program at the University of San Francisco and author of *Tinderbox: U.S. Middle East Policy and the Roots of Terrorism*. "The Iraq War is a disaster in terms of our security needs."

More than the war in Afghanistan, more even than the ongoing U.S. support for Israel's occupation of Palestine, it is the U.S. war in Iraq that has sparked the new flames of terror, says Zunes.

"U.S.-Israeli policy has been there a while, and Afghanistan is remote and non-Arab, while Iraq is right in the Arab heartland and there are actual American troops on the ground," he says. Bush's Iraq War and occupation have "reinforced the worst images and stereotypes of America in that part of the world."

The Iraq War also has diverted resources away from rooting out Al Qaeda, which represents the real and announced and proven threat to U.S. lives.

It's undeniable that by pouring so much military and intelligence effort into conquering and occupying Iraq (as well as into the manhunt for Saddam), the Bush Administration has handicapped its efforts to go after Al Qaeda.

"Strategic analysts, military commanders, and intelligence officers have been distracted by the Iraq War," Zunes says. "Iraq has been the single biggest setback as far as the resources we need to fight terrorism."

Consequently, Al Qaeda has been able to regroup around the world, and even the Taliban have come out of their caves with ferocity in Afghanistan.

Unwilling to Cooperate

The U.S. ability to round up Al Qaeda forces depended, in no small part, on the willingness of people in the Muslim world to cooperate with Washington. Today, much of the Muslim world is in no mood to cooperate.

"In the immediate aftermath of [the September 11, 2001, terrorist attacks], the United States enjoyed unprecedented sympathy and support in the Muslim world," Zunes says. "Now Bush has turned that into unprecedented hostility." As a result, says Zunes, "people are less willing to be supportive of efforts to track down and root out these terrorist cells."

> *"Even if not a single foreign terrorist had entered Iraq, the U.S. occupation would be breeding terrorists there."*

And it's not just people. It's countries, too. Take the case of Syria. "After September 11, the Syrian leader, Bashar Assad, initiated the delivery of Syrian intelligence to the United States," Seymour Hersh wrote in *The New Yorker* back on July 28. "The Syrians had compiled hundreds of files on Al Qaeda, including dossiers on the men who participated—and others who wanted to participate—in the September 11 attacks. Syria also penetrated Al Qaeda cells throughout the Middle East and in Arab exile communities throughout Europe. That data began flowing to CIA and FBI operatives."

With such cooperation, Syria was hoping to ingratiate itself with Washington. But Assad would not back Bush's Iraq War effort, and this infuriated hardliners like Defense Secretary Donald Rumsfeld, who in late March went after Damascus, accusing it of supplying Iraq with military items like night vision goggles and of possibly harboring Iraqi weapons of mass destruction. "Members of the intelligence community I spoke to characterized the evidence against Syria as highly questionable," Hersh reported.

But the damage had been done, and the flow of helpful information from Damascus to Washington dried up. Some officials were angry that the Administration decided to "choose confrontation with Syria over day-to-day help against Al Qaeda," Hersh notes. "In a sense, the issue was not so much Syria itself as a competition between ideology and practicality—and between the drive to go to war in Iraq and the need to fight terrorism."

An Obsession with Iraq

That Bush subordinated the need to fight terrorism to his own Iraq obsession should appall American citizens across the spectrum.

As his wont, Bush, in his speech to the nation, wrapped his Iraq campaign in the shroud of September 11. Three times, he explicitly mentioned that date, and he alluded to it several other times, including right at the top. Cynically, Bush has fueled a mass misconception. While there is no credible evidence connecting Saddam Hussein to September 11, 69 percent of Americans still believe he was involved in the attacks, according to a recent *Washington Post* poll.

In his speech, Bush plumbed new depths when he called his war against Iraq one of the "most humane" military campaigns in history. According to Iraqbodycount.net, between 6,118 and 7,836 Iraqi civilians have died so far. What's so "humane" about that?

The only proper thing for Bush to do now is to cede control of Iraq to the United Nations or directly to the Iraqi people.[1] He had no right to invade. He has no right to occupy.

It's a sin to spend most of his requested $87 billion for this low cause. And it's a sin to keep 130,000 U.S. soldiers there, daily in harm's way. No one should die for Halliburton and ExxonMobil and Bechtel—or for George W. Bush, Donald Rumsfeld, and Paul Wolfowitz.

---

1. Iraq held its first free elections in 2005, thereby establishing its own democratic government.

Chapter 3

How Should Wars Be Conducted?

Chapter Preface

In 1949 the four Geneva Conventions for the protection of war victims were ratified by 125 nations. This led directly to the most famous tribunals for war crimes, the Nuremberg trials, in which officials of the defeated Nazi regime faced international justice. Adolf Hitler's assistant, Martin Bormann, who was directly linked to orders for enslaving and annihilating people in the occupied territories, was convicted of war crimes and crimes against humanity, and was sentenced to death by hanging. Hermann Goering, second in command to Hitler, was convicted of crimes against peace, war crimes, and crimes against humanity, and was also sentenced to death by hanging. In all, twenty-one major Nazi figures were tried; eighteen were convicted, and eleven were sentenced to death. Despite widespread support, however, the legality of the Nuremberg trials was questioned, even by some on the Allied side. A leading U.S. senator, Robert Taft, suggested that the trial was in fact ex post facto law—criminalizing an action after it had been committed. Some asked why only Germans were on trial, since atrocities almost certainly had been committed by all sides.

Under international law, a war crime is a punishable offense for violations of the laws of war. Examples of war crimes include attacking a surrendering combatant and mistreating prisoners of war. However, since war consists primarily of killing people and destroying property, some wonder how certain acts of violence or destruction can be classified as criminal acts while others are not.

Although internationally accepted legal definitions of war crimes were only written in the twentieth century, the idea is actually ancient. In fact, rules of war originated centuries ago. Legal and religious texts, including the Bible and Roman law, specified which actions in war were permissible and which were not. A more selfish, fundamental principle probably hastened the eventual codification of the rules of war—self-interest. Many engaging in warfare came to understand that any extreme acts of violence or destruction they took could be visited on them as revenge at a later date.

The laws of war are composed of two concepts: the *jus ad bellum* (rules related to the legality of a war, such as the legitimacy of self-defense) and the *jus in bello* (rules related to the conduct of war, such as prohibitions against deliberately targeting civilians). *Jus in bello* is usually more difficult to enforce. War, after all, is by its nature brutal. But in the modern era, especially in wars conducted in Europe, three measurements evolved to gauge criminal conduct in war: whether the force applied is in proportion or excessive, whether noncombatants are intentionally attacked, and whether explicitly banned techniques or weapons (such as chemical weapons) are used.

The chief criticism of war crimes trials is that they are unfair—war crimes are usually charged against the vanquished and defined by the victor, critics point out. According to Princeton University professor Gary Bass, "No international tribunal will ever hold Russia to account for Chechnya, or China for . . . Tibet, let alone the U.S. This is an international implement that's going to be used by stronger powers against weaker powers."

Despite these complaints, most people agree that certain actions, even within the context of war, are so repellent that they must be punished as crimes of war. The authors in the following chapter debate what tactics or policies violate the rules of war.

Preemptive War Is a Legitimate Option for Fighting Terrorism

by David Horowitz

About the author: *David Horowitz is editor of* Front Page Magazine *and the author of several books, including* Unholy Alliance: Radical Islam and the American Left.

Even as American forces complete their liberation of Iraq [in 2003] and the world celebrates their victory, domestic opponents of the Bush administration have stepped up their attacks on the national security policy that led to the result.

In particular, they have challenged the doctrine of military "pre-emption," which is the policy of readiness to initiate action in order to quell an imminent threat. In short, to take the battle to the enemy camp.

Opponents argue that pre-emption is a radical departure from previous American foreign policies; that it is an immoral doctrine; and that it sets a dangerous example for other nations.

These objections are held to be so grave as to justify fracturing the traditional bipartisan consensus on national defense and dividing the home front—even in the face of enemies who are supporters of terror, armed with weapons of mass destruction, and motivated by religious fanaticisms that appear impervious to rational dissuasion and traditional military deterrence.

At the very outset, there is a problem in taking these arguments as seriously as their proponents intend them. The same voices raised no similar complaint during the eight foreign policy years of the Clinton administration.

Yet every use of military force by the Clinton administration can be reasonably said to have been an act of pre-emption according to the standards invoked in the present liberal attack. These actions include the missile strikes on the Sudan, Afghanistan and Iraq, and the air attacks of the Kosovo War whose goal was a regime change in Belgrade.

Clinton's Preventive Wars

The 1998 missile strike on the Sudan was an unannounced, unprovoked attack that destroyed that Third World nation's only medicine factory. Yet it provoked no opposition outcry on the left.

The Clinton air strike violated every principle of the current liberal critique of Bush foreign policy. The target of the attack was an alleged chemical weapons factory (which the administration subsequently was forced to concede contained no chemical weapons facility).

Yet there were no inspections, U.N. [United Nations] or otherwise, preceding the attack to determine whether the factory was actually producing chemical weapons, as the Clinton White House claimed. There was not even a presidential phone call to the head of a state with whom the United States had diplomatic relations to request such an inspection.

The strike in the Sudan was ordered without a U.N. resolution, without a congressional authorization and without approval from the Joint Chiefs of Staff (who actually opposed it). Yet no critic of the current Bush foreign policy on Iraq expressed concern over the aggression.

This is in dramatic contrast to the present critique of a war policy that is based on 12 years of disregarded U.N. resolutions and thwarted U.N. inspections, and two congressional resolutions (under two presidents) supporting a regime change by force.

The 1998 decisions by the Clinton administration to fire 450 cruise missiles into Iraq (and 72 into Afghanistan) were also justified by no attack on the United States on the part of Afghanistan or Iraq, and were not authorized by either Congress or the United Nations.

The Clinton air war against Iraq was initiated in response to the expulsion of U.N. inspectors by [Iraqi president] Saddam Hussein. But no act of Congress nor U.N. Security Council resolution legitimized this military assault.

Clinton's attack on Afghanistan was justified by administration officials as a response to the blowing up of two U.S. embassies in Kenya and Tanzania by unknown terrorists. But the Clinton administration provided no more evidence of a connection between Afghanistan and those attacks than was provided by the Bush administration of the connection between the World Trade Center bombing and Iraq.

> *"Opponents argue that pre-emption is a radical departure from previous American foreign policies."*

In both cases, the judgment to launch a military response was made by those charged with responsibility for America's national security. But in only one case did the absence of a proven connection become the basis for a critique of the action.

The Clinton-led attack on Yugoslavia was a pre-emptive war that was not even justified as "national defense." [Serbian president] Slobodan Milosevic and the government of Yugoslavia did not threaten, let alone attack the United States. There were no Serbian terrorist organizations linked to attacks on the United States or American citizens, nor was Yugoslavia accused of harboring such organizations.

Slobodan Milosevic and the government of Yugoslavia were never regarded by anyone as constituting a national security threat to the United States or the NATO alliance. Yet, without provocation, the Clinton administration organized a coalition attack on Yugoslavia from the air and proceeded to bomb targets in that country until a regime change was achieved.

> *"The First World War, in fact, was a pre-emptive war from the American point of view."*

The targets included the capital city of Belgrade, with as large a civilian population as Baghdad. Yet there was no U.N. resolution authorizing this attack, nor did liberal critics of the present Bush policy complain about the lack of one.

Nor was there a congressional declaration of war or authorization (as there was in Iraq) for the use of force. The attack on Yugoslavia was a pre-emptive war to save the lives of Albanian Muslims. There was no other rationale for conducting it, nor did anyone in the United States or Europe ask for one.

Past Wars of Pre-Emption

Nor is there anything new in the doctrine of pre-emption itself. The First World War, in fact, was a pre-emptive war from the American point of view. America did not enter the war because it was attacked (it wasn't), nor did Germany declare war on the United States.

For three years Americans had watched the war from the sidelines. It was a European conflict in which America had no national stake. Then, in 1917, the United States decided to go to war to prevent a German victory, claiming that its goal was "to make the world safe for democracy."

The second war with Germany was different, but only slightly. The very same people who now claim to oppose pre-emption have long faulted the United States for remaining neutral during the Spanish Civil War of the 1930s. If fascism had been defeated in Spain, they argue, there might not have been a Second World War at all.

It's an interesting point. But it is also an argument for a pre-emptive policy. Lives could have been saved (in fact, tens of millions of lives) if the United States and the Western powers had taken the initiative and used force to stop Hitler early—in the Rhineland, in Austria and in Czechoslovakia, before he was able to amass the military strength that made the Second World War inevitable.

The war against Hitler was itself pre-emptive. It is true that Hitler declared war on the United States after the attack on Pearl Harbor. But Hitler did not attack the United States. The United States went to war with Hitler to pre-empt the possibility of a German attack on the United States.

Pre-Emptive War Makes Sense

Thus, pre-emptive war has made sense in the past. Why should not the same prudent defense policy make sense now? In fact, it has. The pre-emptive war against Iraq actually began a dozen years ago at the end of the Gulf War when the United States and Britain instituted the "no-fly zones" to protect the Kurds from potential poison gas attacks.

This was an invasion of Iraqi air space. But no one besides Iraq and its allies objected, and the Kurds thrived under the protection. The present victory over Saddam Hussein has removed the threat of his weapons of mass destruction as well as the terrorism he has for so long sponsored.

The threat of pre-emptive war is a form of protection. It tells Iran and Syria— the sponsors of Hezbollah and Hamas and al-Qaeda terrorists who have killed American citizens—that the consequences of their covert aggressions can be deadly to them.

Syria and Iran have already done no less than the Taliban regime in Afghanistan when we attacked it. Should the United States tie its hands and force its citizens to wait for another World Trade Center scale attack before allowing them a response?

Critics of the war in Iraq claimed that the administration should have allowed Saddam Hussein more time to continue his evasion of the U.N. resolutions and focused on the nuclear threat from North Korea instead.

What credibility would American demands to North Korea have had, however, if we had continued to appease Saddam and ignore his defiance of U.N. resolutions? Far from being a distraction, the pre-emptive war against Saddam Hussein has enhanced the ability of the United States to deter North Korea from its sinister plans.

In sum, the arguments against the doctrine of pre-emption are historically baseless and logically incoherent. On the other hand, they present obstacles to a national consensus that can prove dangerous. Division at home on matters of national security is the surest way to undermine the credibility of an American deterrent and create the possibility of an enemy assault.

Critics should think twice before encouraging such outcomes.

Preemptive War Is Not a Legitimate Option for Fighting Terrorism

by Noam Chomsky

About the author: *Noam Chomsky is an educator and linguist who has taught at the Massachusetts Institute of Technology since 1955. He is the author of* Hegemony or Survival: America's Quest for Global Dominance.

September 2002 was marked by three events of considerable importance, closely related. The most powerful state in history announced a new National Security Strategy asserting that it will maintain global hegemony permanently. Any challenge will be blocked by force, the dimension in which the US reigns supreme. At the same time, the war drums began to beat to mobilize the population for an invasion of Iraq [in 2003]. And the campaign opened for the mid-term congressional elections, which would determine whether the administration would be able to carry forward its radical international and domestic agenda.

The new "imperial grand strategy," as it was termed at once in the leading establishment journal, presents the US as "a revisionist state seeking to parlay its momentary advantages into a world order in which it runs the show," a "unipolar world" in which "no state or coalition could ever challenge" it as "global leader, protector, and enforcer." These policies are fraught with danger even for the US itself, the author warned, joining many others in the foreign policy elite.

Imperial America

What is to be "protected" is US power and the interests it represents, not the world, which vigorously opposed the conception. Within a few months, studies revealed that fear of the United States had reached remarkable heights, along with distrust of the political leadership. An international Gallup poll in December [2002], barely noted in the US, found virtually no support for Washington's announced plans for a war in Iraq carried out "unilaterally by America and its allies": in effect, the US-UK "coalition."

Washington informed the UN [United Nations] that it can be "relevant" by endorsing Washington's plans, or it can be a debating society. The US has the "sovereign right to take military action," the administration moderate [former secretary of state] Colin Powell informed the World Economic Forum, which also strenuously opposed Washington's war plans: "When we feel strongly about something we will lead," he informed them, even if no one is following us. [President George W.] Bush and [British prime minister Tony] Blair underscored their contempt for international law and institutions at their Azores Summit on the eve of the invasion. They issued an ultimatum—not to Iraq, but to the [UN] Security Council: capitulate, or we will invade without your meaningless seal of approval. And we will do so whether or not [former Iraqi president] Saddam Hussein and his family leave the country. The crucial principle is that the US must effectively rule Iraq.

> *"The most powerful state in history announced a new National Security Strategy asserting that it will maintain global hegemony permanently."*

President Bush declared that the US "has the sovereign authority to use force in assuring its own national security," threatened by Iraq with or without [Iraqi leader Saddam Hussein], according to the Bush doctrine. Washington will be happy to establish an "Arab façade," to borrow the term of the British during their day in the sun, while US power is firmly implanted at the heart of the world's major energy-producing region. Formal democracy will be fine, but only if it is of the submissive kind accepted in Washington's "backyard," at least if history and current practice are any guide.

Preventive War

The grand strategy authorizes Washington to carry out "preventive war": *Preventive*, not pre-emptive. Whatever the justifications for pre-emptive war might be, they do not hold for preventive war, particularly as that concept is interpreted by its current enthusiasts: the use of military force to eliminate an invented or imagined threat, so that even the term "preventive" is too charitable. Preventive war is, very simply, the "supreme crime" condemned at Nuremberg.[1]

That was understood by those with some concern for their country. As the US invaded Iraq, historian Arthur Schlesinger wrote that Bush's grand strategy is "alarmingly similar to the policy that imperial Japan employed at Pearl Harbor, on a date which, as an earlier American president said it would, lives in infamy." FDR [President Franklin Delano Roosevelt] was right, he added, "but today it is we Americans who live in infamy." It is no surprise that "the global

---

1. War crimes trials were held in Nuremberg, Germany, after World War II.

wave of sympathy that engulfed the United States after [the September 11, 2001, terrorist attacks] has given way to a global wave of hatred of American arrogance and militarism," and the belief that Bush is "a greater threat to peace than Saddam Hussein."

For the political leadership, mostly recycled from more reactionary sectors of the Reagan–Bush I administrations [the administrations of Ronald Reagan and George H.W. Bush], "the global wave of hatred" is not a particular problem. They want to be feared, not loved. It is natural for [U.S. secretary of defense] Donald Rumsfeld to quote the words of Chicago gangster Al Capone: "You will get more with a kind word and a gun than with a kind word alone." They understand as well as their establishment critics that their actions increase the risk of proliferation of weapons of mass destruction (WMD) and terror. But that too is not a major problem. Far higher in the scale of priorities are the goals of establishing global hegemony and implementing their domestic agenda: dismantling the progressive achievements that have been won by popular struggle over the past century, and institutionalizing these radical changes so that recovering them will be no easy task.

It is not enough for a hegemonic power to declare an official policy. It must establish it as a "new norm of international law" by exemplary action. Distinguished commentators may then explain that law is a flexible living instrument, so that the new norm is now available as a guide to action. It is understood that only those with the guns can establish "norms" and modify international law.

Defenseless Foes

The selected target must meet several conditions. It must be defenseless, important enough to be worth the trouble, and an imminent threat to our survival and ultimate evil. Iraq qualified on all counts. The first two conditions are obvious. For the third, it suffices to repeat the orations of Bush, Blair, and their colleagues: the dictator "is assembling the world's most dangerous weapons [in order to] dominate, intimidate or attack"; and he "has already used them on whole villages leaving thousands of his own citizens dead, blind or transfigured. . . . If this is not evil then evil has no meaning."

President Bush's eloquent denunciation surely rings true. And those who contributed to enhancing evil should certainly not enjoy impunity: among them, the speaker of these lofty words and his current associates, and those who joined them in the years when they were supporting the man of ultimate evil long after he had committed

> *"Washington informed the UN that it can be 'relevant' by endorsing Washington's plans, or it can be a debating society."*

these terrible crimes and after the war with Iraq—because of our duty to help US exporters, the Bush I administration explained. It is impressive to see how easy it is for political leaders, while recounting the monster's worst crimes, to suppress

116

the crucial words: "with our help, because we don't care about such matters." Support shifted to denunciation as soon as their friend committed his first authentic crime: disobeying (or perhaps misunderstanding) orders by invading Kuwait.[2] Punishment was severe—for his subjects. The tyrant escaped unscathed, and was further strengthened by the sanctions [on his] regime then imposed by his former allies.

> *"Preventive war is, very simply, the 'supreme crime' condemned at Nuremberg."*

Also easy to suppress are the reasons why Washington returned to support for Saddam immediately after the Gulf war, as he crushed rebellions that might have overthrown him. The chief diplomatic correspondent of the *New York Times* explained that "the best of all worlds" for Washington would be "an iron-fisted Iraqi junta without Saddam Hussein," but since that goal seemed unattainable, we would have to be satisfied with second best. The rebels failed because Washington and its allies held the "strikingly unanimous view [that] whatever the sins of the Iraqi leader, he offered the West and the region a better hope for his country's stability than did those who have suffered his repression." All of this is suppressed in the commentary on the mass graves of the victims of Saddam's US-authorized paroxysm of terror, now offered as justification for the war on "moral grounds." It was all known in 1991, but ignored for reasons of state.

War Fever

A reluctant domestic population had to be whipped to a proper mood of war fever. From early September [2002], grim warnings were issued about the dire threat Saddam posed to the United States and his links to al-Qaeda, with broad hints that he was involved in the 9/11 attacks. Many of the charges "dangled in front of [the media] failed the laugh test," the editor of the *Bulletin of Atomic Scientists* commented, "but the more ridiculous [they were,] the more the media strove to make whole-hearted swallowing of them a test of patriotism."

The propaganda assault had its effects. Within weeks, a majority of Americans came to regard Saddam Hussein as an imminent threat to the US. Soon almost half believed that Iraq was behind the 9/11 terror. Support for the war correlated with these beliefs. The propaganda campaign proved just enough to give the administration a bare majority in the mid-term elections, as voters put aside their immediate concerns and huddled under the umbrella of power in fear of the demonic enemy.

The brilliant success of "public diplomacy" was revealed when the President "provided a powerful Reaganesque finale to a six-week war" on the deck of the aircraft carrier *Abraham Lincoln* on May 1. The reference, presumably, is to Reagan's proud declaration that America was "standing tall" after conquering

---

2. Iraq invaded Kuwait in 1990 but was ejected by a US-led coalition in 1991.

the nutmeg capital of the world [Grenada] in 1983, preventing the Russians from using it to bomb the US. Reagan's mimic was free to declare—without concern for skeptical comment at home—that he had won a "victory in a war on terror [by having] removed an ally of al Qaeda." It is immaterial that no credible evidence was provided for the alleged link between Saddam Hussein and his bitter enemy [al-Qaeda leader] Osama bin Laden and that the charge was dismissed by competent observers. Also immaterial is the only known connection between the victory and terror: the invasion appears to have been a "huge setback in the 'war on terror'," by sharply increasing al-Qaeda recruitment, as US official concede.

The *Wall Street Journal* recognized that Bush's carefully-staged *Abraham Lincoln* extravaganza "marks the beginning of his 2004 re-election campaign," which the White House hopes "will be built as much as possible around national-security themes." The electoral campaign will focus on "the *battle* of Iraq, not the war," chief Republican political strategist Karl Rove explained: the war must continue, if only to control the population at home. Before the 2002 elections, he had instructed Party activists to stress security issues, diverting attention from unpopular Republican domestic policies. All of this is second-nature to the recycled Reaganites now in office. That is how they held on to political power during their first tenure in office, regularly pushing the panic button to evade public opposition to the policies that left Reagan the most disliked living President by 1992, ranking alongside Nixon.

Despite its narrow successes, the intensive propaganda campaign left the public unswayed in more fundamental respects. Most continue to prefer UN rather than US leadership in international crises, and by 2-1, prefer that the UN, rather than the United States, should direct reconstruction in Iraq.

> *"It is understood that only those with the guns can establish 'norms' and modify international law."*

When the occupying army failed to discover WMD, the administration's stance shifted from "absolute certainty" that Iraq possessed WMD to the position that the accusations were "justified by the discovery of equipment that potentially could be used to produce weapons." Senior officials suggested a "refinement" in the concept of preventive war that entitles the US to attack "a country that has deadly weapons in mass quantities." The revision "suggests instead that the administration will act against a hostile regime that has nothing more than the intent and ability to develop [WMD]." Lowering of the bars for the resort to force is the most significant consequence of the collapse of the proclaimed argument for the invasion.

Old Europe

Perhaps the most spectacular propaganda achievement was the lauding of the president's "vision" to bring democracy to the Middle East in the midst of an extraordinary display of hatred and contempt for democracy. One illustration was the distinction between Old and New Europe, the former reviled, the latter hailed for its courage. The criterion was sharp: Old Europe consists of governments that took the same position as the vast majority of their populations; the heroes of New Europe followed orders from Crawford, Texas [President George W. Bush's private residence], disregarding an even larger majority, in most cases. Political commentators ranted about disobedient Old Europe and its psychic maladies, while Congress descended to low comedy.

At the liberal end of the spectrum, Richard Holbrooke stressed "the very important point" that the population of the eight original members of New Europe is larger than that of Old Europe, which proves that France and Germany are "isolated." So it does, unless we succumb to the radical left heresy that the public might have some role in a democracy. [Writer] Thomas Friedman urged that France be removed from the permanent members of the Security Council, because it is "in kindergarten," and "does not play well with others." It follows that the population of New Europe must still be in nursery school, judging by polls.

Turkey was a particularly instructive case. The government resisted heavy pressure to prove its "democratic credentials" by following orders, overruling 95% of its population. Commentators were infuriated by this lesson in democracy, so much so that some even reported Turkey's crimes against the Kurds in the 1990s, previously a taboo topic because of the crucial US role—though that was still carefully concealed in the lamentations.

The crucial point was expressed by [Deputy Secretary of Defense] Paul Wolfowitz, who condemned the Turkish military because they "did not play the strong leadership role that we would have expected" and did not intervene to prevent the government from honoring near-unanimous public opinion. Turkey must therefore step up and say "We made a mistake . . . Let's figure out how we can be as helpful as possible to the Americans." Wolfowitz's stand is particularly informative because he is portrayed as the leading figure in the crusade to democratize the Middle East.

Anger at Old Europe has much deeper roots than contempt for democracy. The US has always regarded European unification with some ambivalence. In his "Year of Europe" address 30 years ago, [former secretary of state] Henry Kissinger advised Europeans to keep to their "regional responsibilities" within the "overall framework of order" managed by the United States. Europe must not pursue its own independent course, based on its Franco-German industrial and financial heartland. Concerns now extend as well to Northeast Asia, the world's most dynamic economic region, with ample resources and advanced industrial economies, a potentially integrated region that might also flirt with challenging the overall framework of order, which is to be maintained permanently, by force if necessary, Washington has declared.

Torturing Prisoners Is Sometimes Justifiable

by Henry Mark Holzer

About the author: *Henry Mark Holzer is an attorney and the author of* Why Not Call It Treason? Korea, Vietnam, Afghanistan and Today.

Recently [October 2002] we witnessed Chechen rebels taking over a Moscow theater, capturing hundreds of hostages, and threatening to kill them if the intruders' demands were not met. Let's assume the same thing happens in the United States, but with al-Qaeda terrorists. Assume further that we capture one of the terrorists who knows the plans of his comrades, but he won't talk. Should we use torture to force this crucial information out of him?

"Torture"—commonly defined as "the inflicting of severe pain to force information or confession"—comes principally in two varieties: physical (e.g., the "third degree") and psychological (e.g., sleep deprivation). The literature on torture is voluminous, most commentators concluding that torture is odious and unacceptable at *all* times and under *all* circumstances, especially in a democracy.

But is it?

The Ticking Time Bomb

Some of the commentators, in their analysis and discussion of the phenomenon of torture, admit being deeply troubled by how a democracy deals with the question of torture generally, let alone in the extreme example of the so-called "ticking time bomb" situation.

Until recently the question was hypothetical. It no longer is.

There are variations on the ticking time bomb situation, but the essence is in this plausible scenario: A known terrorist in FBI custody, whose information is credible, won't disclose where in Washington, DC, he has secreted a "weapon of mass destruction"—a nuclear bomb—set to detonate in two hours. The Bureau is certain that the terrorist will never voluntarily reveal the bomb's location. *In*

Henry Mark Holzer, "In Defense of Torture," *FrontPageMagazine.com,* November 29, 2002. Copyright © 2002 by Center for the Study of Popular Culture. Reproduced by permission.

two hours our nation's capital could be wiped from the face of the earth, our government decimated, surrounding areas irredeemably contaminated, and the United States laid defenseless to unimaginable predation by our enemies.
What to do?

The Realistic Choice

Accepting these facts for the sake of argument, we have only two choices. Do nothing, and suffer the unimaginable consequences, or torture the information out of the terrorist.

There are those among us—Jimmy Carter–like pacifists and Ramsey Clark–type America haters come to mind—who would probably stand by idly and endure an atomic holocaust. But most people would doubtless opt for torture, albeit reluctantly.

These realists would be correct. They would be entitled to be free of even a scintilla of moral guilt, because torture—of whatever kind, and no matter how brutal—in defense of legitimate self-preservation is not only *not* immoral, *it is a moral imperative.*

Unknown to most Americans, one case in two different courts in the United States—a state appellate court in Florida, and a federal Court of Appeals—have, albeit implicitly, endorsed such a use of physical force, and thus of torture, if necessary to save lives.

Jean Leon kidnapped one Louis Gachelin, who was held at gunpoint by Leon's accomplice. A ransom was arranged, a trap was sprung, and Leon was arrested.

Fearing that the accomplice would kill Gachelin if Leon didn't return promptly with the ransom money, the police demanded to know where the victim was being held. Leon wouldn't talk.

According to the Third District Court of Appeals of the State of Florida, when Leon "refused, he was set upon by several of the officers. They threatened and physically abused him by twisting his arm behind his back and choking him [and, allegedly, threatened to kill him] until he revealed where . . . [Gachelin] was being held. The officers went to the designated apartment, rescued . . . [Gachelin] and arrested . . . [the accomplice]."

While this was happening, Leon was taken "downtown," questioned by a different team of detectives, and informed of his Miranda rights. He signed a waiver and confessed to the kidnapping. But before Leon's trial, he sought to exclude his police station confession, arguing that it was the tainted product of the cops' literal arm-twisting, choking, and threats. (No self-incrimination issue arose from Leon having re-

> *"Torture—of whatever kind, and no matter how brutal—in defense of legitimate self-preservation is not only* not *immoral,* **it is a moral imperative."**

vealed the victim's location because that information was not sought to be used against him at his trial.)

The trial judge denied Leon's motion to suppress his confession on the ground that the force and threats used on him at the time of arrest *were not the reason for his confession.* In other words, the conceded coercion at the time of Leon's arrest had *dissipated* by the time of his confession, which the trial judge ruled had been given voluntarily.

> "It is neither immoral nor illegal **in principle** *to employ non-lethal torture in the name of saving thousands of innocent American lives."*

Leon appealed. The Florida appeals court affirmed, reaching the same conclusion as the trial judge: Whatever had happened at Leon's arrest, the coercion had dissipated by the time he'd confessed. Thus, it was proper to use Leon's confession against him at trial.

Using Force to Save a Life

That ruling should have been the end of Leon's first appeal because the only question in the case was the admissibility of Leon's confession. Yet the appeal court's opinion went further than the facts of the case required. In language lawyers call *dicta*—judicial reflections in no way necessary for a decision—the appellate judge added, gratuitously, that "*the force and threats asserted upon Leon in the parking lot were understandably motivated by the immediate necessity to find the victim and save his life.*"

Consider the implications. Even though the motive for using force, and the police's use of it, were irrelevant to the decision, the appellate court's 2-1 majority saw fit to give its *express* approval of physical and psychological coercion in this situation, so long as the product of that coercion (the confession) was not used against defendant Leon at his trial.

Lest anyone think that the *dicta* in this decision was an aberration, we need look only at the *unanimous* three-judge decision in Leon's further appeal to the United States Court of Appeals for the Eleventh Circuit.

The facts were not in dispute. Once again, the only issue on appeal was whether the physical and psychological coercion at the time of arrest tainted the confession, or whether the coercion had, by then, sufficiently dissipated to make Leon's confession voluntary.

First, the federal appeals court dealt with self-incrimination. As to Leon's arrest statement concerning where his accomplice was holding Gachelin, there was no issue since the prosecution, properly, had never tried to introduce that statement at the trial. Next, whatever coercion had been used, it did not taint Leon's later confession because, according to the court, "the totality of the circumstances . . . clearly confirms . . . that the second statement was voluntary." Therefore, that statement was both voluntary and admissible.

The federal appeals court's ruling concerning the voluntariness of Leon's confession *completely disposed of the case*. But, as with the earlier appeal, this court took the unnecessary step of including *dicta* to the effect that the use of coercion at Leon's arrest was "motivated by the immediate necessity of finding the victim and saving his life," and that "[t]his was a group of concerned officers acting in a reasonable manner to obtain information they needed in order to protect another individual from bodily harm or death."

All true. But, again, irrelevant to the sole question before the court as to whether the coercion used at the arrest had dissipated by the time of the confession.

Federal Acceptance of Coercion

Since the appellate courts, both state and federal, went out of their way to express their approval of coercion in a life-threatening situation, their *dicta* is noteworthy because it signals their acceptance of coercion *in principle*—a legitimization, as it were.

It is but a short step from arm-twisting, choking, and death threats to the use of torture.

If, without objection from a state and a federal appeals court (indeed, with their apparent approval), the Florida police could employ a relatively benign form of coercion to save the life of a kidnap victim, it follows that the same rationale would support actual torture (physical and/or psychological) in a ticking time bomb situation.

Once *that* threshold is crossed—once the principle is accepted that torture legitimately can be employed to save lives—all that remains is the *application* of that principle to concrete cases. While that application could be difficult—requiring some form of probable cause, judicial oversight, and the like—the need to create such important procedural safeguards does not negate the argument that, in this country, where killers are routinely put to death for the commission of a single murder, it is neither immoral nor illegal *in principle* to employ nonlethal torture in the name of saving thousands of innocent American lives.

Torturing Prisoners Is Not Justifiable

by Patrick Leahy

About the author: *Patrick Leahy is a U.S. senator from Maine.*

In the weeks since the [2004] abuses at Abu Ghraib prison [in Iraq] were re-vealed, evidence continues to seep out of similar mistreatment of prisoners in other US military detention centers in Iraq, Afghanistan, and Guantanamo Bay [in Cuba]. Top White House and Pentagon officials have sought to deny any pattern of illegality in the interrogation and treatment of prisoners in US cus-tody. They insist that members of [the terrorist organization] Al Qaeda and the Taliban [former rulers of Afghanistan] fall outside the protections of the Geneva Conventions.

The reach of the Geneva Conventions is debatable. What is not debatable is that the Convention Against Torture and Other Cruel, Inhuman, or Degrading Treatment or Punishment, which the United States signed and ratified, makes no distinction between American citizens, Iraqis, or anyone else. It unequivo-cally forbids the use of torture or cruel, inhuman, or degrading treatment, any-where, at any time, under any circumstances. So does US law. So does our mili-tary's manual for intelligence interrogation.

Circumventing the Law

Yet we now know that the White House and the Pentagon were actively work-ing to circumvent the law. Guidelines for interrogating prisoners were applied routinely in multiple locations in ways that were illegal.

It is also clear that US officials knew the law was being violated and for months, possibly years, did virtually nothing about it.

I first wrote to the White House, the Pentagon, and the CIA last June [2003] about the reported torture of Afghan prisoners by US interrogators.

Two prisoners had died during interrogation. Others described being forced to stand naked in a cold room for days without interruption, with their arms raised and chained to the ceiling and their swollen ankles shackled. They said they were denied sleep and forced to wear hoods that cut off the supply of oxygen.

My letter, and subsequent letters, were either ignored or received responses which, in retrospect, bore no resemblance to the facts. Sixteen months later, the investigations of those deaths, ruled homicides, remain incomplete.

Prisoners who are suspected of having killed or attempted to kill Americans do not deserve comforts. But the use of torture undermines our global efforts against terrorism and is beneath our nation.

> *"The law makes no exception for torture."*

There are many victims of this policy. First are the Iraqis, Afghans, and other detainees, some innocent of any crime who were tortured or subjected to cruel treatment. We now know that many other Iraqis and Afghans died in US custody, and many of those deaths were never investigated.

Second are our own soldiers, who overwhelmingly perform their duties with honor and courage, and who now have been unfairly tarnished.

Damage to America

And then there is America itself. The damage this administration has caused to our credibility will take years to repair.

The individuals who committed those acts are being punished, as they must be. But what of those who gave the orders or set the tone or looked the other way? What of the White House and Pentagon lawyers who tried to justify the use of torture? And what of the president? Last March [2003], referring to the capture of US soldiers by Iraqi forces, President [George W.] Bush said, "We expect them to be treated humanely, just like we'll treat any prisoner of theirs that we capture humanely. If not, the people who mistreat the prisoners will be treated as war criminals." At the same time, the president's lawyer called the Geneva Conventions "obsolete."

The law makes no exception for torture. The torture of criminal suspects flagrantly violates the presumption of innocence on which our criminal jurisprudence is based, and confessions extracted through torture are notoriously unreliable.

Once exceptions are made for torture it is impossible to draw the line, and more troubling is who would be in charge of drawing it. If torture is justified in Afghanistan, why is it not justified in China, or Syria, or Argentina, or Miami? If torture is justified to obtain information from a suspected terrorist, why not from his wife or children? Some argue it is a new world since the attacks of Sept. 11 [2001]. To some degree, they are right, which is why we have reacted with tougher laws and better tools to fight this war. But do we really want to usher in a new world that justifies inhumane, immoral and cruel treatment as any means to an end? We must reject the dangerous notion that torture can be legally justified.

The Use of Nuclear Weapons May Be Justified

by William Conrad

About the author: *William Conrad is a contributor to* Air & Space Power Chronicles, *the professional journal of the U.S. Air Force.*

For decades now, it has been taken for granted that nuclear weapons were, in some sense, useless. However, the argument has generally been that this was because of politics: the mammoth bombs were so powerful that only a relative handful of them needed to be dropped to destroy the world, rendering the presumably major conflict which led to their being dropped in the first place meaningless. (This, of course, may be a moot point since nuclear proliferation is putting many small arsenals into the hands of third-rank powers, though it still applies to the major ones.) Indeed, consciousness of this fact helped to foster what I call the "nuclear taboo", a belief that nuclear weapons are qualitatively different from other weapons, and that their use represents the crossing of some special threshhold, the commitment of a particularly inhuman act likely to lead to the destruction of humankind.

However, military history shows that the distinction between "acceptable" and "unacceptable" weapons exists solely in man's mind, a convention like any other, not necessarily logical and probably not permanent. Dynamite, after all, had once been thought such a weapon, not only inhumane, but certain to make war impossible by virtue of its destructiveness, or bring civilisation crashing down if it fell into "the wrong hands". The absurdity of such predictions is not only clear in hindsight, but indicates that the extent to which these conventions survive contact with the real world depends in large part on the characteristics of specific nuclear devices, rather than a general aversion to weapons based on the principles of fission and fusion. And while there may be little comparison in the potential destructive power of nuclear weapons to that of dynamite, the truth is that the uselessness of nuclear weapons may have stemmed as much from practicality as politics.

William Conrad, "The Future of Tactical Nuclear Weapons," *Air & Space Power Chronicles*, June 26, 2001.

Besides being very powerful, [early] nuclear weapons were highly radioactive and delivered with extreme inaccuracy, for which the sheer size of their blast was meant to compensate. There was no hope of employing them tactically against, say, troop concentrations; the "dirty" bombs of the early nuclear era left battlefields so hopelessly irradiated that soldiers could not fight on them. (The use of atomic bombs anywhere near friendly troops in the planned invasion of Japan was ruled out for that very reason.) Furthermore, the inaccuracy of the delivery systems meant that the yields of the weapons had to be fairly large, and the weapons used copiously, which only worsened matters.

> *"Military history shows that the distinction between 'acceptable' and 'unacceptable' weapons exists solely in man's mind."*

There may have been no paucity of schemes for getting around these problems, such as the use of smaller, more mobile units, but none of them was ever proven feasible. Consequently, the nuclear weapons of the era could only be employed strategically, and it was understood even then that strategic bombing, even on the grand scale on which it had been practiced, was of uncertain effectiveness in breaking a state's warmaking capacity. Even Hiroshima, after being atom-bombed, survived the damage inflicted upon it, and was functioning again within days. Additionally, it was considered highly questionable, at least with the weapons available in the forties, that nuclear attacks could bring Russia to its knees, much less stop the Red Army from overrunning Western Europe.

The Power of Conventional Weapons

Further, while no quantity of conventional munitions can equal a superpower's nuclear arsenal for sheer megatonnage, the effects of anything short of the nuclear exchange the superpowers were capable of launching by the early nineteen sixties could be replicated with non-nuclear munitions. The validity of the concept having been proven for the American high command by the firebombing of Tokyo, in which 16.7 square miles of the city were burned to the ground in a single night, General Curtis LeMay

> laid on firebombings night after night against city after city until his supply depots ran out of bombs; resupplied, he pursued the fire-bombing campaign . . . until the end of the war, by which time sixty-three Japanese cities had been totally or partially burned out . . . Hiroshima and Nagasaki survived to be atomic-bombed only because Washington had removed them from Curtis LeMay's target list.

For the purposes of demolishing one city at a time, atomic bombs were no more destructive than TNT, only less expensive logistically in that one plane could do the work of hundreds, which in turn meant that nuclear weapons were only useful insofar as it was desirable to destroy hundreds of cities at once.

Moreover, particularly in the later Cold War years, this was also a matter of self-annihilation, since even were it possible for one of the superpowers to destroy its adversary's nuclear forces in a first strike, the Earth's climate system would retaliate against it, so to speak. The environmental damage entailed by nuclear winter would not only have made it impossible to fight a war (for instance, the resulting clouds of dust and smoke would "degrade" the performance of jet engines), but made existence impossible, producing famine and epidemics on a hitherto unknown scale.

At the same time, it might be said that LeMay's fire-bombing of Japan constituted a quasi-nuclear campaign, which is why it should be surprising that despite the Cold War context in which the limited Korean War was fought, another, equally massive fire-bombing campaign was conducted against North Korea. Again, something resembling the effects of a nuclear war was attained without the deployment of actual nuclear weapons, save, of course, for the fact that napalm had the virtue of not showering radioactive fallout across Northeast Asia. Certainly, not all nuclear weapons states possessed such resources, but even the smaller nations which acquired nuclear arsenals were generally the militarily predominant powers in their region, and therefore only too capable of ensuring their security through conventional means, as the Israelis did in the 1973 Arab-Israeli War when their possession of a nuclear arsenal failed to prevent an (albeit limited) Arab attack.

"For the purposes of demolishing one city at a time, atomic bombs were no more destructive than TNT."

All of this made nuclear weapons less an effective tool of strategy or tactics than of annihilation, helping to foster the association of nuclear weapons with apocalypse. However, it is likely that there will be entirely new types of nuclear weapons deployed in the future; indeed, some countries appear to be banking on it. Following NATO's [North Atlantic Treaty Organization] 1999 air campaign against Yugoslavia, Russia has begun to reorganize its arsenal for limited nuclear warfare, as a halfway measure between doing nothing at all and committing its strategic nuclear arsenal, to a world-shattering exchange.

Low-Yield Nuclear Weapons

Russian weapons designers (and, presumably, their counterparts in other countries) have been for years developing new classes of nuclear weapons, with yields as low as a few tens of tons and one hundred to one thousand times "cleaner" than the current generation of weapons. (This will be because they achieve fusion without a fission primary, which means that no radioactive fissile material is used, and that there is no need to achieve critical mass, so that very small nuclear explosions are possible.) Further, the Russian government is reportedly initiating a buildup of ten thousand tactical nuclear weapons, with yields of one tenth of a kiloton or less, to achieve a "pinpoint" nuclear capability (the ability to use small nuclear weapons the same way in which the United States uses smart bombs and cruise missiles), making "limited nuclear war" theoretically possible.

Nuclear weapons as small and as clean as those the Russian military intends to deploy will blur the lines between nuclear and conventional weapons, since the newest versions of the former will, in theory, be only marginally more contaminating, indiscriminate or destructive than the latter (though they will be more efficient, by some measures). This will make their usage more practical from a military standpoint, as well as undermine the argument that they represent a unique and impermissible type of weapon. Accordingly, Russian strategists believe that this will make their use unlikely to provoke an all-out war, and the threat of their employment therefore more credible than the saber-rattling which accompanied earlier Russian protests over NATO expansion, or American policy towards Iraq.

Practical Nukes

Of course, this is by no means the first attempt to formulate a plan to fight a nuclear war, and it is possible that this doctrine may be as quixotic as all those which preceded it. However, it differs from the schemes of the Cold War in one very important way: the scope of these plans is far less ambitious. Where a nuclear bomb once substituted for hundreds of strategic bombers loaded down with thousands of tons of incendiary bombs (or hundreds of bombers substituted for a single nuclear weapon), a mini-nuke may now be used in place of a squadron of tactical aircraft with only a few tons of laser-guided bombs apiece. Further, while Russia may be unlikely to actually employ such weapons in all but the gravest crisis, such a conception means greater leeway for Russia to substitute its nuclear arsenal for its long since dilapidated conventional strength.

Nonetheless, that the Russians will be able to transform their vision into reality in the immediate future is anything but a given. It may be that the Russian government, which intentionally leaked these plans, is overstating the degree to which the relevant technologies have been perfected. Further, while the new weapons have reportedly been on the drawing boards for years, and are to be manufactured from existing nuclear materials and mated to available delivery systems, greatly reducing the cost of the program, virtually any expense, however modest, seems at times to be beyond Russia's resources. Despite the priority it has been accorded in funding, the Russian nuclear arsenal

> *"Russia has begun to reorganize its arsenal for limited nuclear warfare."*

grows increasingly decrepit, the government having been unable to maintain the infrastructure of its nuclear forces or the nuclear weapons production cycle, much less successfully develop and deploy new weapons. The endless delays in the construction of the first Borey-class ballistic missile submarine aside, the production of the new Topol-M intercontinental ballistic missile has been proceeding at a much slower pace than was originally expected. The most recent expedition into Chechnya is likely to reduce the available funding even further in the short term.

> *"Nuclear weapons may be the sole weapons capable of attacking specific types of targets, such as certain underground facilities."*

Regardless, one may assume that the Russians are sincere in their intentions, even as Western countries appear to be proceeding in the opposite direction. Both the United States and Great Britain have been much quicker to abandon tactical weapons than strategic ones. The assertion by many experts that the Revolution in Military Affairs has made it possible for conventional weapons to perform missions that would previously have been executable only with nuclear weapons has rendered them irrelevant in many eyes. This is especially true because many observers, after living for so long in the Cold War's shadow, do not seem able to decouple tactical and strategic nuclear war. In this atmosphere, President [George W.] Bush unilaterally ordered the destruction of American tactical nuclear weapons, and Congress has "cast this decision into concrete" by passing legislation forbidding the testing, development, and stockpiling of nuclear warheads having yields of less than five kilotons, so that the tactical nuclear option is, for now, off the table.[1] England's Royal Navy, at the same time, retains its only nuclear capability in its Trident ballistic missile submarines. Nonetheless, research has not come to a halt in these countries, as is indicated by continuing work on electromagnetic pulse weapons in the United States, and experiments in "confinement fusion" conducted by the five first members of the nuclear club, as well as by several non-nuclear, but advanced, states such as Germany and Japan.

A Weakened U.S. Military

Further, whether accuracy, at present, compensates completely for recent reductions in mass is another matter. The payload of a modern-day anti-ship missile packs only a fraction of the punch of a single shell fired from the main guns of an Iowa-class battleship of the Second World War era, four of which were called back into service in the nineteen eighties in the U.S. Navy because there was as yet no substitute for them. It is also often stated by observers that today's American military, while more technologically advanced in certain respects than it was in 1991, is still "not the force that won the Gulf War", and has seen its size slashed too deeply for it to repeat the feat.

One way of getting around this problem would be to increase the firepower, as well as the precision, of present systems, to mate the new nuclear weapons with the more precise delivery systems now available. Nuclear weapons of the

1. In 2004 Congress approved research on the development of low-yield nuclear weapons.

sort that the Russians have declared an intent to deploy would be one way of going about this. At present, for example, work is being done to turn cruise missiles into genuine unmanned bombers, capable of attacking multiple targets. Should appropriate low-yield nuclear submunitions, each with the power of a large conventional bomb, be developed to this end, they would drastically multiply the effectiveness of the Tomahawk's thousand-pound payload, which at present pales next to that of even a single attack plane. It stands to reason that one such cruise missile could do the work of several, perhaps even scores of Tomahawk missiles, greatly increasing the potency of what has become the preferred American response to provocations by rogue states. Conceivably, an aerial campaign could be executed without sending a single pilot into enemy airspace, and should cruise missiles flexible enough to make a tactical difference be developed, they could execute even more ambitious operations, such as slowing down an Iraqi reinvasion of Kuwait. More modestly, however, small expeditionary forces would be able to offset the superior numbers of local opponents with similar weapons fired from artillery or dropped from aircraft. (Such an approach would be of particular use to a country like Britain or France, which have nuclear arsenals and worldwide networks of bases, but are incapable of sending militarily significant forces very far away from home.)

Weapons of Last Resort

Politically, however, such an action may be untenable for some time (particularly in light of the admittedly reduced, but nonetheless extant, risk of radioactive contamination), and it is more likely that these weapons will initially be used in circumstances which offer no alternative to nuclear strikes. Nuclear weapons may be the sole weapons capable of attacking specific types of targets, such as certain underground facilities. (The latest addition to the American nuclear arsenal is the B 61-11, which is designed as an earth penetrator.) Furthermore, many of the current designs for space-based weapons, such as X-ray lasers; missile defense systems, like plasma weapons which ionize the atmosphere; and even

> *"Nuclear weapons will in the future be less contaminating, more discriminate, and more versatile."*

"non-lethal weapons", like the electromagnetic pulse (EMP) weapon, have a basis in nuclear weapons technology. (The development of these weapons, incidentally, may be legal under the Comprehensive Test Ban Treaty.) There may also be circumstances in which, for one reason or another, precision-guided munitions (or their command and control systems) may not be available in the necessary numbers.

Whether such a scenario will actually appear in the near future, however, is anything but certain. Many would point that this entire line of reasoning is moot due to the decline of conventional warfare in general which, it is pointed out correctly, is at least one reason why militaries have been shrinking in the first place. The Soviet Union, for all its military commitments, did not fight a conventional war after 1945, and nor did the United States after Korea until Desert Storm. In the kinds of wars that were usually fought, as in Vietnam, Lebanon and Afghanistan, even tactical nuclear weapons would have been, even assuming a willingness to contaminate friendly territory, of only occasional utility at best, the enemy generally being dispersed, concealed among the civilian population, prone to hit and run and possessing little infrastructure.

Certainly, most states today have no great fear of external invasion, the conventional wisdom holding that most wars will be internal affairs, waged between guerrillas or terrorists and the forces of domestic order. Regardless, no one would argue with the assertion that for at least the next few decades, marginal, underdeveloped states, like Ethiopia and Eritrea, may wage conventional, interstate warfare on a modest scale. Few would totally discount the possibility of war between larger states, such as India and Pakistan, or sporadic, asymmetrical conflict between the United States and rogue states like Iraq.

> *"The taboo will likely break down to some extent, applying only to particular categories of nuclear weapons rather than nuclear weapons generally."*

Even were that not the case, the rise of the guerrilla did not so much spell the end of conventional warfare as consign it to an end game, and then only because of the clear superiority of states in conventional military power, which they survive principally by avoiding. Guerrillas using hit and run tactics may be able to tie down massive resources, sap the will and strength of a larger opponent, exacerbate social tensions and even deny the enemy effective control over its own territory, but they can not occupy ground as they eventually must to win, next to which all is mere preparation. Saigon, after all, fell not to guerrillas, but to North Vietnamese armor, and the same logic holds true today; in Colombia, the FARC (Revolutionary Armed Forces of Colombia) insurgency is working towards attaining a level of strength that will allow it to openly challenge the government's forces in the field.

At the same time, it is probably incorrect to assume that "the forces of order" will remain centered upon the state. The monopoly of the state on violence has always been somewhat theoretical, and will likely become more so in the future. (Even in the United States, much of the population considers arming itself a constitutional right, and state governors have some authority to call on their own military units, namely the National Guard.) The decline of welfare systems, the emergence of a world market increasingly less unencumbered by borders or regulation, and the decline of interstate warfare in much of the world have deprived even the most successful of states of much of their reason for being. Other states, lacking political legitimacy in the eyes of their people, or economic viability, have simply ceased to exist, as has been the case in Somalia and Afghanistan, and could be the case in a great many other places in the foreseeable future.

In either case, the services that governments once provided are increasingly privatised, from health care to physical security, and even military power is increasingly dispersed. The end of the Cold War has seen the rise of private military companies, like Sandline International, which do everything from train one's soldiers to put down rebellions for a fee, and just as the condottieri have returned to the world stage, so to speak, so might lords and dukes. In Colombia, the central government has allied itself with the right-wing paramilitary forces which are in de facto control of ten percent of the country, in order to combat a seemingly intractable leftist insurgency. In Russia, there has even been talk of restoring the Cossacks as part of the military establishment.

Failing states, of which Colombia and Russia are two examples, moreover, will not always possess the preponderance of power that has forced guerrillas to hit and run. Instead, the breakdown of order will force them to accommodate themselves to the diffusion of armed force, even concluding alliances with some factions, which will brandish their military power more openly under the circumstances. Like the feudal lords who preceded them, they will probably have the modern-day equivalent of castles, and their armies might possess considerable heavy equipment, and the infrastructure which goes along with that. The Chechen insurgents, notably, had possessed an air force with over two hundred and fifty aircraft when Russia invaded the republic in 1994, as well as hundreds of armored vehicles and artillery pieces. The Bosnian Serb forces which laid siege to Sarajevo were similarly equipped. In any case, conventional wars will more likely change form or shrink in scope than disappear, just as it seems that some sort of central authority will survive in most places, even if the power of today's states will in many cases be parceled out to other players. These forces could all be targets of such weapons as are described here, or, perhaps, depending on how widely the technology proliferates, users of them.

Removing the Taboo

Regardless of the exact form that conflict will take in the future, however, nuclear weapons will in the future be less contaminating, more discriminate, and more versatile, which, with the decline of conventional forces and the splintering of international conflict, will strengthen the temptation to use them. Indeed, there may be situations in which tactical nuclear weapons will appear to be not only a choice, but the only choice, and it would not be the first time someone argued that nuclear weapons had to be used in order to save lives. The taboo will likely break down to some extent, applying only to particular categories of nuclear weapons rather than nuclear weapons generally, or the use of the weapons against specific targets, freeing decision makers to use them. The use of these weapons, in turn, will undermine the taboo, setting a precedent for others. In any case, what would have been condemned in one period, much as had been the case with dynamite, will come to be not merely accepted, but even praised in another, the early prohibition as anachronistic to future observers as the horror with which the Church had regarded crossbows seems to people of our time.

The Use of Nuclear Weapons Cannot Be Justified

by Gerard Donnelly Smith

About the author: *Gerard Donnelly Smith is a poet, musician, and creative writing instructor.*

In an age of "frighteningly normal" and mundanely average political leaders who conscientiously do their jobs, we must understand that the distinction between right and wrong, between evil and good, too often becomes a matter of perspective, of political expediency or "national security." To paraphrase Bosmajian: Euphemistic terms by making tolerable the intolerable, and justifiable the unjustifiable, also make manifest an ugly truth about human nature—humans are gullible folk whom the unscrupulous manipulate happily. In the name of national security, our leaders justify "pre-emptive strikes" upon, and "regime change" in whichever country they deem "evil" or part of the "axis of evil." Now, humanity faces a new threat: The use of a weapon of mass destruction in response to the use of any other type of weapon of mass destruction: chemical, biological or nuclear. But this time, the enemy isn't the USSR. Wish it were that simple and predictable. This time, the enemy can be anyone who harbours terrorists, anyone who threatens the security of the United States or any of its allies. As we have witnessed in Iraq, even with the slimmest evidence, or no evidence at all, [U.S. president George W.] Bush will attack. Now that we have witnessed the flagrant violation of UN [United Nations] principles by the United States, citizens everywhere must demand that nuclear weapons use be banned. That any world leader who uses any type of nuclear device as a weapon be charged with a crime against humanity and be brought to justice before the World Court.

Must one ask if the use of nuclear weapons or any other weapon is a "crime against humanity?" Terrorism has been defined as a crime against humanity.

Death by stoning has been called a crime against humanity. Rape, abortion, electro-convulsive shock, and the slave trade have been defined as crimes against humanity. Using weapons of mass destruction should certainly be added to this list. But has any nation or international body clearly defined any use of nuclear weapons as a crime against humanity?

In Colombo, Sri Lanka, the South Asian Association for Regional Cooperation [SAARC] on July 28, 1998 released the following statement:

> We, the peoples of South Asia, are dismayed and alarmed at the Indian and Pakistan nuclear tests of May 1998. The decision of the two traditional rivals, India and Pakistan, to build and deploy nuclear weapons has put at risk the survival of not only the peoples of India and Pakistan, but also the peoples of all the countries of South Asia.

> We believe that nuclearisation of the subcontinent is a betrayal of the sacred trust of the peoples reposed in their governments. There can be no justification either for the initial nuclear tests by India or the retaliatory tests by Pakistan. No amount of provocation or perceived threat legitimizes the development, testing, proliferation or use of nuclear weapons.

> Nuclear weapons are immoral weapons of mass destruction. It is a crime against humanity even to consider the use of nuclear weapons as an option.

Does the United States of America or any other nuclear power have such a statement?

In contrast, the Pentagon and the Bush administration resolve to develop "mini-nukes" or "bunker busters" in order to fight terrorism: the catch-phrase to replace the "cold war." On 10 January 2003, the Stockpile Stewardship Conference Planning Meeting for the Pentagon discussed the feasibility of low-yield tactical nukes. In their Future Arsenal Plan they listed the following "major" topic:

> What are the warhead characteristics and advanced concepts we will need in the post-NPR (Nuclear Posture Review) environment?

> (a) Establish methodology for making choices

> (b) Strategy for selecting first "small builds"

> (c) Requirements for low-yield weapons, EPWs [earth-penetrating weapons], enhanced radiation weapons, agent defeat weapons

> (d) Effects modeling capabilities to effectively plan for these weapons

> (e) What forms of testing will these new designs require?

> (f) What obvious weaknesses exist in our ability to attack targets and assess target damage for present and future targets and weapon systems?

Nuclear Weapons Are Different

Nuclear weapons have never been fully certified as non-lethal to civilians, nuclear physicists have not developed a nuclear weapon that does not spew radioactive material, have not ensured that ground water will not become contaminated, that dust particles will not ride the winds to cause mutation in future children. Despite scientific evidence to the contrary, Pentagon officials claim bunker busters with a nuclear warhead pose no threat to civilians because the devices explode underground. However, Princeton University physicist Robert Nelson concludes,

> [. . .] the use of any nuclear weapon capable of destroying a buried target that is otherwise immune to conventional attack will necessarily produce enormous numbers of civilian casualties. No earth-burrowing missile can penetrate deep enough into the earth to contain an explosion with a nuclear yield even as small as 1 percent of the 15 kiloton Hiroshima weapon. The explosion simply blows out a massive crater of radioactive dirt, which rains down on the local region with an especially intense and deadly fallout.

Despite the warnings of scientists that such weapons will cause "collateral damage," the Bush Administration and the Pentagon—using federal tax dollars—are morphing [former president] Bill Clinton's bunker buster program into a mini-nuke bunker buster.

> *"Citizens everywhere must demand that nuclear weapons use be banned."*

The "National Strategy to Combat Weapons of Mass Destruction," a joint report from [former] National Security Adviser Condoleezza Rice and [former] Homeland Security Director Tom Ridge clearly spells out George W. Bush's plan to keep "all our options on the table":

> The United States will continue to make clear that it reserves the right to respond with overwhelming force—including through resort to all of our options—to the use of WMD [weapons of mass destruction] against the United States, our forces abroad, and friends and allies[. . .]. In addition to our conventional and nuclear response and defense capabilities, our overall deterrent posture against WMD threats, is reinforced by reflective intelligence, surveillance, and interdiction, and domestic law enforcement capabilities[. . .]. (p 2. col. 1)

In defense of such position Bush declares: "We are at war to keep the peace." He further reiterates his administration's determination to keep the world safe: "We've got all our options on the table because we want to make it very clear to nations that you will not threaten the United States or use weapons of mass destruction against us or our allies or friends."

The Hypocrisy of the Bush Administration

Hasn't George Walker Bush been going to church? He says the Pledge of Allegiance, and swears this is one nation under god. He's even against abortion. In calling abortion murder, he defends the rights of unborn children. Abortion is genocide claims Justice for All, a national organization with charters on most American college campuses. Christian and staunchly pro-life, Justice for All might wonder at George Walker's hypocrisy. Clearly nuclear weapons will harm unborn children. Radiation creates mutations. In Hiroshima and Nagasaki [the two Japanese cities attacked with nuclear weapons in 1945], to this day, children are born with mutations caused by nuclear radiation. To this day, downwind from nuclear test sites incidents of cancer, leukemia, and birth defects are exponentially higher than national averages. If George Walker wants to protect unborn children from abortion, then he should oppose the use of nuclear weapons for any purpose. If abortion can be considered genocide, by any stretch of the imagination, certainly the use of nuclear weapons is a crime against humanity.

> *"Must one ask if the use of nuclear weapons or any other weapon is a 'crime against humanity?'"*

The World Council of Churches agrees with the aforementioned conclusion. Konrad Raiser, WCC General Secretary, clearly stated:

> We know that true security is never to be found in arms of any sort, and certainly not in these most terrible weapons ever devised by human beings. Nuclear weapons are sinful, and their production, possession and deployment, and the very threat of their use in an extreme case constitute crimes against God and humanity. (WCC Leaflet)

Sinful, says Secretary Raiser. Last time I went to Sunday School sinful meant evil, inspired by Satan; most definitely something Christians or members of any other faith should avoid if they want to get to heaven. Perhaps George Walker's god isn't the merciful one who loves all children, but that more ancient and fiery god who thrived on burnt babies. What was his name, Moloch [the biblical god of the Canaanites and Phoenicians to whom children were sacrificed]?

But aren't a few starving, mutated or burnt babies the price Americans will have to pay for national security, so their children can sleep safe at night, free from worries about terrorists who have weapons of mass destruction? Shouldn't we spend as much money as necessary to build those mini-nuke bunker busters? Is any price too high for that type of security?

Oscar Arias, former President of Costa Rica and Nobel Peace Laureate, believes that such defense money could be better spent:

> The existence of nuclear weapons presents a clear and present danger to life on Earth. Nuclear arms cannot bolster the security of any nation because they represent a threat to the security of the human race. These incredibly destructive weapons are an affront to our common humanity, and the tens of billions of dollars that are dedicated to their development and maintenance should be used instead to alleviate human need and suffering. (WCC Leaflet)

Tactical Nuclear Weapons

Instead, the Bush Administration plans to spend billions of dollars developing tactical nukes to fight world terrorism, naming seven nations as prime targets for "regime change." Rather than limit nuclear proliferation, threats of "regime change" via "bunker busting" with "mini-nukes" threaten to cause another arms race. Not an arms race between super powers. To the contrary, third-world countries may seek to arm themselves to defend against the big stick being waved by this administration or any future administration. Such brinkmanship supposedly helped [former president] Ronald Reagan bring down the Berlin Wall. But is that George Walker's game plan? Or is he circling the wagons, get ready to drop one for the Gipper?

What price for security? What will the United Nations be willing to allow? In an Advisory Opinion, the International Court of Justice (ICJ) said that,

> [. . .] the threat or use of nuclear weapons would generally be contrary to the rules of international law applicable in armed conflict, and in particular the principles and rules of humanitarian law;

> However, in view of the current state of international law, and of the elements of fact at its disposal, the Court cannot conclude definitively whether the threat or use of nuclear weapons would be lawful or unlawful in an extreme circumstance of self-defence, in which the very survival of a State would be at stake. (*ICJ Advisory Opinion*, par. 105, subsection 2 E)

A Legal Loophole

In this opinion the ICJ may have left George Walker a crucial loophole. This logic seems to protect nuclear weapons as lawful for self-defense purposes (UN Charter, Article 51) as long such use adheres to the principle of proportionality. In *Nicaragua v. United States of America*, the ICJ ruled "there is a specific rule whereby self-defence would warrant only measures which are proportional to the armed attack and necessary to respond to it, a rule well established in customary international law" (*ICJ Reports 1986*, p. 94, par. 176). Ergo, the ICJ concludes "The proportionality principle may thus not in itself exclude the use of nuclear weapons in self-defence in all circumstances." (*ICJ Advisory Opinion 1986*, par. 41).

"In Hiroshima and Nagasaki, to this day, children are born with mutations caused by nuclear radiation."

Perhaps in deference to Israel's "Samson Option" [the suggestion that Israel would launch worldwide nuclear war to defend itself], the ICJ has let the matter hang in judicial limbo. But limbo—the proverbial purgatory—is only few steps from the inferno. But does self-defense legitimize vaporizing an entire city? How proportional? Could the Bush Administration have legitimized the use of a tactical nuke in retaliation for the destruction of the World Trade Center? However, this loophole does not render the issue moot.

Convention on Genocide

All members of The United Nations by becoming Contracting Parties to the 1948 Convention on Genocide accept the following statement: Genocide is a crime against humanity. If Genocide is a crime against humanity, then the precalculated, pre-meditative use of nuclear weapons—even in self-defense—must also be a crime against humanity.

Article 1

The Contracting Parties confirm that genocide, whether committed in time of peace or in time of war, is a crime under international law which they undertake to prevent and to punish.

Article 2

In the present Convention, genocide means any of the following acts committed with intent to destroy, in whole or in part, a national, ethnic, racial or religious group, as such:

(a) Killing members of the group;
(b) Causing serious bodily or mental harm to members of the group;
(c) Deliberately inflicting on the group conditions of life calculated to bring about its physical destruction in whole or in part;
(d) Imposing measures intended to prevent births within the group;
(e) Forcibly transferring children of the group to another group.

Let's consider the articles point by point:

(a) Killing members of the group;

How many individual members of the group must be killed? 3,000, 50,000, 100,000? Perhaps 500,000. A one-megaton bomb detonated over any major city would easily vaporize 100,000 people. Yet one must ask whether any weapon that causes "mass" destruction violates this principle. Certainly a nuclear weapon causes "mass" destruction and loss of life. But how much "mass" in terms of human flesh must be destroyed? Would a "massive" aerial bombardment cause enough "mass destruction" to violate this principle?

> *"The Bush administration plans to spend billions of dollars developing tactical nukes to fight world terrorism."*

(b) Causing serious bodily or mental harm to members of the group;

Besides the serious bodily harm of being vaporized, the remaining members of the group would suffer radiation sickness, would suffer from serious burns, and those who survived would be traumatized by the event. The effects of conventional war certainly meet this criterion, so certainly nuclear weapon use does also.

(c) Deliberately inflicting on the group conditions of life calculated to bring about its physical destruction in whole or in part;

Even in self-defense, the use of a nuclear weapon is pre-meditated. The consequences of such a weapon are clearly documented. The leader who orders such an action would inflict upon the target population "conditions of life" that would cause immediate "physical destruction" and would lead to long-term consequences that would produce increased birth defects and increase the incidence of terminal illness. The effect of one nuclear warhead has been "calculated" so precisely that we know an airborne explosion is more deadly than a ground explosion, that any humans within 200 miles of the epicenter will die either immediately or shortly thereafter, that individuals down wind of the blast will suffer from radiation sickness which will significantly shorten their lives.

(d) Imposing measures intended to prevent births within the group;

Birth defects and sterilization caused by radiation can continue for generations after the nuclear event.

(e) Forcibly transferring children of the group to another group.

Of course, the last test of genocide is a moot point: most of the children directly affected by the nuclear blast will be killed immediately, or will die

> *"If George W. Bush, or any other leader, uses nuclear weapons, they will be guilty of genocide."*

from radiation sickness. They will have been transferred into their god's hands. Clearly the use of nuclear weapons, whether low-yield or high-yield, strategic or tactical, violates these principles of genocide. If this is so, then why do groups opposed to nuclear weapons not clearly and persistently make this argument. Why are not the terms genocide and nuclear weapons use synonymous?

Because the International Court of Justice has already found that nuclear weapon use violates the principles of international law in regards to armed conflict, any leader who uses then will:

1. fail to discriminate between military and civilian personnel (Principle of Discrimination);
2. cause harm disproportionate to their preceding provocation's and/or to legitimate objectives (Principles of Proportionality and Necessity);
3. cause unnecessary or superfluous suffering (Principle of Humanity);
4. affect neutral States (Principal of Neutrality);
5. cause widespread, long-lasting and severe damage to the environment (Principle of Environmental Security);
6. use asphyxiating, poisonous or other gases, and all analogous liquids, materials or substances (Principal of Toxicity). (WCP)

Violations of International Law

Each of these actions—even in self-defense—violates these principles of international law, and when violated, especially using weapons of mass destruction, are considered "war crimes." If we accept this logic, then nuclear weapons use equals genocide. Furthermore, if George W. Bush, or any other leader, uses nuclear weapons, they will be guilty of genocide. According to *Article 4* of the Convention on Genocide:

Persons committing genocide or any of the other acts enumerated in article III shall be punished, whether they are constitutionally responsible rulers, public officials or private individuals.

The loophole that allows the use of nuclear weapons in self-defense or as a pre-emptive measure to protect national security is clearly illegal. Even understanding this, we must be very clear in our conclusion, so that George W. Bush, and any other leader, cannot claim he/she misread, or misunderstood the consequences.

1. Nuclear weapons are a weapon of mass destruction.

2. Weapons of mass destruction when used equal a crime against humanity.

3. Nuclear weapon use brings about all of the effects that define genocide.

Remember the law clearly states that those in power who do not oppose genocide are complicit, are accessories to the crime. So what is the punishment for genocide Mr. Prime Minister, Mr. President, Mr. Vice President and Mr. Secretary of State?

Rape as a Tactic of War Must Be Stopped

by Jan Goodwin

About the author: *Jan Goodwin is an award-winning journalist and the author of* Price of Honor.

Last May [2003], 6-year-old Shashir was playing outside her home near Goma, in the Democratic Republic of the Congo (DRC), when armed militia appeared. The terrified child was carried kicking and screaming into the bush. There, she was pinned down and gang-raped. Sexually savaged and bleeding from multiple wounds, she lay there after the attack, how long no one knows, but she was close to starving when finally found. Her attackers, who'd disappeared back into the bush, wiped out her village as effectively as a biblical plague of locusts.

"This little girl couldn't walk, couldn't talk when she arrived here. Shashir had to be surgically repaired. I don't know if she can be mentally repaired," says Faida Veronique, a 47-year-old cook at Doctors on Call for Service (DOCS), a tented hospital in the eastern city of Goma, who took in the brutalized child.

"Why do they rape a child?" asks Marie-Madeleine Kisoni, a Congolese counselor who works with raped women and children. "We don't understand. There's a spirit of bestiality here now. I've seen 2- and 3-year-olds raped. The rebels want to kill us, but it's more painful to kill the spirit instead."

Age Is No Protection

In the Congo today, age is clearly no protection from rape. A woman named Maria was 70 when the Interahamwe, the Hutu militia that led Rwanda's 1994 genocide and now number between 20,000 and 30,000 of the estimated 140,000 rebels in the DRC, came to her home. "They grabbed me, tied my legs apart like a goat before slaughter, and then raped me, one after the other," she told me.

"Then they stuck sticks inside me until I fainted." During the attack Maria's entire family—five sons, three daughters and her husband—were murdered. "War came. I just saw smoke and fire. Then my life and my health were taken away," she says. The tiny septuagenarian with the sunken eyes was left with a massive fistula [injury] where her bladder was torn, causing permanent incontinence. She hid in the bush for three years out of fear that the rebels might return, and out of shame over her constantly soiled clothes. Yet Maria was one of the more fortunate ones. She'd finally made it to a hospital. Two months before we met, she had undergone reconstructive surgery. The outcome is uncertain, however, and she still requires a catheter.

> *"In the Congo today, age is clearly no protection from rape."*

Rape has become a defining characteristic of the five-year war in the DRC, says Anneke Van Woudenberg, the Congo specialist for Human Rights Watch. So, too, has mutilation of the victims. "Last year, I was stunned when a 30-year-old woman in North Kivu had her lips and ears cut off and eyes gouged out after she was raped, so she couldn't identify or testify against her atttackers. Now, we are seeing more and more such cases," she says. As the rebels constantly seek new ways to terrorize, their barbarity becomes more frenzied.

Sexual Sadism

I, too, was sickened by what I saw and heard. In three decades of covering war, I had never before come across the cases described to me by Congolese doctors, such as gang-rape victims having their labia pierced and then padlocked. "They usually die of massive infection," I was told.

Based on personal testimonies collected by Human Rights Watch, it is estimated that as many as 30 percent of rape victims are sexually tortured and mutilated during the assaults, usually with spears, machetes, sticks or gun barrels thrust into their vaginas. Increasingly, the trigger is being pulled. About 40 percent of rape victims, usually the younger ones, aged 8 to 19, are abducted and forced to become sex slaves. "The country is in an utter state of lawlessness; it's complete anarchy," says Woudenberg. "In this culture of impunity, people know they can get away with anything. Every armed group is equally culpable."

Cheaper than Bullets

In the Congo, rape is a cheaper weapon of war than bullets. Experts estimate that some 60 percent of all combatants in the DRC are infected with HIV/AIDS. As women rarely have access to expensive antiretroviral drugs, sexual assaults all too often become automatic death sentences. Médecins Sans Frontières ["Doctors Without Borders"] operates five health clinics offering antiretrovirals in the conflict zone of northeastern DRC, but many women don't know about the drugs and cannot travel safely to the centers. Moreover, according to Helen O'Neill, a nurse who set up MSF's sexual-violence treatment program, such drugs must be taken within forty-eight to seventy-two hours of the rape to prevent infection. If a woman has been exposed to the virus, the treatment is 80 percent effective. But in the Congo, rape victims who are not captive sex slaves must walk for days or weeks, often with massive injuries, and risk new capture by roving rebel bands, before reaching assistance.

"So far, 30 percent of rape victims being treated at our hospital are infected with HIV/AIDS," says Dr. Denis Mukwege, the French-trained medical director of the Panzi Hospital in Bukavu. "And nearly 50 percent are infected with venereal diseases like syphilis that greatly increase their chances of contracting HIV."

Rape as a Weapon

Rape as a weapon of war is as old as war itself. What has changed recently is that sexual violence is no longer considered just a byproduct of conflict but is being viewed as a war crime, says Jessica Neuwirth, president of Equality Now, a New York–based international women's human rights organization. "Rape as a violation of war was codified in the Geneva Convention, but only now is it being taken seriously. But it is still not effectively prosecuted, not proportional to the extent that sexual violence takes place," she says. Armed forces now have a legal obligation to stop rape and hold the offenders accountable. "This is a major shift in consciousness. But it needs to be followed by a major shift in conduct," says Neuwirth.

> *"In the Congo, rape is a cheaper weapon of war than bullets."*

In the DRC, rape is used to terrorize, humiliate and punish the enemy. Frequently husbands, fathers and children are forced to watch and even participate. Women sexually assaulted by members of one rebel organization are accused of being the wives of that group and raped again as punishment when a new militia takes over the area. "It's happened repeatedly to the women of Shabunda in the far east of the Congo, every time the region has changed hands," says Woudenberg.

Even the camps for internally displaced people are not safe. The barbed-wire encampment in Bunia is home to more than 14,000 people, but enemy militia infiltrate at night. Shortly before I arrived, an 11-year-old girl was dragged off and gang-raped, a not uncommon occurrence. There are more than 3 million internally displaced people made homeless by the war, many of whom have been forced to flee over and over again. UN [United Nations] officers admit they have nowhere near the numbers they need to be effective, or even to stay safe themselves.

"The rebels are all around us here. We don't feel secure and we've seen what these guys do to people, especially to women and girls. Our own people have been killed, after they were horribly tortured," a European UN major told me.

"The DRC is the size of Western Europe. We're supposed to have 8,500 troops here, but we've only got 5,000! I was in Bosnia, which is a fraction of the size of the Congo, and we had 68,000 NATO [North Atlantic Treaty Organization] troops, and even that wasn't enough." Patrols of MONUC, the UN's peacekeeping force in the DRC, have refused to pick up wounded rape victims and escort them to medical care when they were afraid they would be outnumbered by nearby rebels.

"People denounce the rapes but do nothing to bring the rebels to justice," says Woudenberg. "There isn't the political will, domestically or internationally, to make it happen. I've never seen anything like this, when war has become this horrible, and human life so undervalued."

Trevor Lowe, spokesperson for the UN World Food Program, echoes this view. "The nature of sexual violence in the DRC conflict is grotesque, completely abnormal," he says. "Babies, children, women—nobody is being spared. For every woman speaking out, there are hundreds who've not yet emerged from the hell. Rape is so stigmatized in the DRC, and people are afraid of reprisals from rebels. It's a complete and utter breakdown of norms. Like Rwanda, only worse." Adds his colleague Christiane Berthiaume, "Never before have we found as many victims of rape in conflict situations as we are discovering in the DRC."

Where Is the Outrage?

Yet where is the international media coverage? The outrage? The demand for justice?

During the Rwanda genocide [1994], rape as a war crime received extensive international media coverage. Despite initial reports of 250,000 women being sexually assaulted (a third more than there were Tutsi women living in the country at the time), evidence later suggested the total number was closer to one-fifth of that.

In Bosnia, where the European Community Investigative Mission concluded there were some 20,000 victims, reports of systematic rape by the Serbs first made international headlines one year into the war, and remained a major news focus for the remaining three years of the conflict. It was only after the Bosnia war, at the International Criminal Tribunal for the former Yugoslavia in The Hague in 1997, that rape was first prosecuted as a crime against humanity. A year later, at the Rwanda tribunal, rape was found to be a form of genocide.

"Rape as a weapon of war is as old as war itself."

Everyone I spoke with in the DRC and in the international UN, NGO [nongovernmental organization] and human rights community said they believe the incidence of rape there greatly exceeds that in both Bosnia and Rwanda, although it will be years before precise figures are available. The systematic nature of the assaults has been amply documented by the UN, humanitarian agencies and human rights organizations. Yet for the most part the media look the other way. As one editor of a national newspaper told me, "It's just another horror in the horror that is Africa." One has to ask, Does this kind of cynicism merely reflect public opinion or help create it?

Africa Slighted Again

Says Lowe, "Look at the square footage of Bosnia, a country that is dwarfed by the Congo, and look at the enormous number of reporters who covered Bosnia compared to the DRC. Clearly, Africa doesn't get the same coverage as Europe. The reasons are racial, geopolitical interests, ease of access, etc. The DRC conflict is an extremely dangerous one, which is one reason the press is not there. Selling Africa, and being part of an agency that does it all the time, is difficult. Africa is clearly not a place where the major powers have a lot of interest. The Congo is not on the geopolitical map. And the major-league press follows that geopolitical map." There is also media faddishness, what Lowe refers to as the CNN factor. "If CNN shows up, then other reporters become interested," he says.

> *"Armed forces now have a legal obligation to stop rape and hold the offenders accountable."*

Another factor is the complexity of the Congo conflict. In Rwanda, the media were able to present the issues as clear-cut, with the good guys and the bad clearly defined. "People consider the Congo conflict confusing; they label it tribal or ethnic, which is totally wrong," says Woudenberg. "The war in the DRC has been an international war, involving a number of different countries."

Conduct a straw poll among Americans who are usually well informed and few know of the vicious campaign of sexual violence against women in the DRC. Many are even unaware that the country is six years into a brutal conflict, in which up to 4.7 million people have died—the highest number of fatalities in any conflict since World War II. Or that six countries—Rwanda, Burundi, Uganda, Zimbabwe, Angola and Namibia—have been fighting proxy wars in the DRC, and helping to plunder the country's tremendous mineral wealth to fill their coffers.

The indifference, according to Woudenberg, extends to the arms of government that should be most deeply concerned with the DRC's crisis. "In November I tried to raise the issue with the US Mission to the UN in New York, and they told me fairly point-blank that they were aware rape was going on in the Congo, and it was just not high on their priorities," she says. "I had a similar response from the US State Department."

Meanwhile, a UN Security Council panel has cited eighty-five multinational corporations, including some of the largest US companies in their fields, for their involvement in the illegal exploitation of natural resources from the DRC. The commerce in these "blood" minerals, such as coltan, used in cell phones and laptops, cobalt, copper, gold, diamonds and uranium (Congolese uranium was used in the atomic bombs dropped on Hiroshima and Nagasaki [by the United States in 1945]), drives the conflict. The brutality of the militias—the sexual slavery, transmission of HIV/AIDS through rape, cannibalism, slaughter and starvation, forced recruitment of child soldiers— has routinely been employed to secure access to mining sites or insure a supply of captive labor.

> *"The systematic nature of the assaults has been amply documented by the UN, humanitarian agencies and human rights organizations."*

If that isn't enough to awaken the international community's interest, one would think it would be of concern that "blood" business practices also fund terrorism. Lebanese diamond traders benefiting from illegal concessions in the Congo have been tied to the Islamic extremist groups Amal and Hezbollah. According to a UN report, the Lebanese traders, who operate licensed diamond businesses in Antwerp, purchased diamonds from the DRC worth $150 million in 2001 alone. Such linkage between African rebel groups and global terrorist movements is not new. Sierra Leone's Revolutionary United Front reportedly sold diamonds to Al Qaeda, thus helping to finance both organizations.

Greed Fuels Rape

The lobbies of the two luxury hotels in Kinshasa, the DRC's capital, are full of elegant, $5,000-a-day corporate lawyers from New York, London and Geneva, and scruffier diamond dealers from Tel Aviv and Antwerp, as they while away the hours waiting for government ministers and senior representatives of armed groups to smooth their way. These institutional fortune-makers are 1,800 miles away from the nightmares of northeastern Congo. Yet they are not so far removed from the atrocities perpetrated there. Rape is a crime of the war they are fueling with their greed.

Today's conflict profiteers are not the first to sponsor a campaign to ransack, rape, pillage and plunder in the Congo. A century ago, Belgium's King Leopold II amassed a fabulous fortune this way. During the monarch's genocidal reign of terror, when villagers couldn't meet his impossibly high quotas harvesting rubber or mining ore, their hands were amputated and women were taken as slaves. By the time he was finished, an estimated 10 million Congolese, half the population, were dead.

Kinshasa's policy-makers, who serve in a government with four vice presidents in a misguided attempt to appease various factions, now claim a new political beginning after the so-called peace accord last year. But there is a "huge and dangerous gap" between what is happening in Kinshasa and what is going on in the northeast, says Irene Khan, Amnesty International's secretary general. "In Kinshasa there is talk of peace and political progress, of regional harmony and democratic elections. But while the newly appointed members of government are wrangling for power and privilege in Kinshasa, in the Kivus and Ituri people are confronted daily with death, plunder and carnage. Mutilations and massacres continue. Rape of women and girls has become a standard tactic of warfare. It is absolutely outrageous that many of the senior members of the government and the political parties they represent are closely linked to the armed groups who are committing these abuses."

At the time of King Leopold's predatory rule, an international Congo reform movement was formed with the support of [famous authors] Mark Twain, Arthur Conan Doyle and Joseph Conrad. It was Conrad who described what was being done as "the vilest scramble for loot that ever disfigured the history of human conscience." He would recognize what is happening now.

For the sake of 6-year-old Shashir and tens of thousands of girls and women who have been infected with HIV/AIDS, forcibly impregnated or so badly damaged internally they will never be able to have children, and who are so psychologically traumatized they may never recover, we can only hope that a similarly prominent group of today's social commentators will find its conscience and its voice soon.

Chapter 4

Can War Be Prevented?

Current
CONTROVERSIES

Chapter Preface

The question of whether or not war can be prevented has been debated for centuries. Some claim that people are naturally inclined to be violent and thus warlike, while others believe that armed conflict is a modern invention produced by political and religious social constructs.

Extended periods of peace have been rare in recorded history. War is and has been so common, in fact, that many have argued that it is inevitable because of the aggression inherent in human nature. English political philosopher Thomas Hobbes wrote that man's natural state is to be at war, with "every man . . . [and] enemy to every man." The French writer Voltaire was even more pessimistic in his evaluation of human nature. He wrote: "Famine, plague, and war are the three most famous ingredients of this wretched world. . . . All animals are perpetually at war with each other. . . . Air, earth and water are arenas of destruction."

Others suggest that war is neither natural nor inevitable. Author William Ury claims that the argument that mankind has always been warlike is mistaken: "Archaeologists have found little evidence of organized violence during the first ninety-nine percent of human history. We have been maligning our ancestors." The psychologist and philosopher Erich Fromm argued that primitive people are not warlike, and that "warlikeness grows in proportion to civilization." These beliefs led to the concept of the "noble savage," the peaceful, primitive human whose nature has been corrupted by modern society. As evidence of humans' natural peacefulness anthropology professor Robert W. Sussman points to the behavior of primates. Fighting and competing is rare among them, he claims: "We find that aggressive behavior is extremely rare, even in baboons, [which are] thought to be among the most aggressive primates."

But others contend that the noble savage is a myth. Evolutionary biologist Steven Pinker says that stories of peaceful, primitive tribes are urban legends. "Careful studies show that hunter-gatherers are dead serious about war. They make weapons as destructive as their ingenuity permits. And if they can get away with it, they massacre every man, woman, and child."

For thousands of years, many Western religious leaders have espoused the biblical view of man as fallen, inherently sinful, and with a propensity for violence. Conversely, eastern spiritual leaders often take a more positive view of humanity. The fourteenth Dalai Lama, for example, notes that "peaceful animals, such as deer, which are completely vegetarian, are more gentle and have smaller teeth and no claws. From that viewpoint we human beings [who have similar characteristics] have a nonviolent nature. As to the question of human survival, human beings have a nonviolent nature. In order to survive we need companions."

151

The question of whether or not humans are inherently violent informs all arguments concerning the prevention of war. The authors in the following viewpoints explore this controversial topic in depth. While some believe that humans' violent nature makes war an inevitable part of human existence, others reject the idea that people are naturally warlike and argue for particular approaches to preventing war.

War Can Be Prevented

by Jonathan Power

About the author: *Jonathan Power is the author of* Like Water on Stone: The Story of Amnesty International.

Is our aim to prevent war or to pre-empt apparent threats? There is an important difference; not just in the semantics. In Bush-speak pre-emption may mean taking military action in order to avoid some presumed catastrophe looming over the political horizon. Preventing war means taking some bold, resolute action, short of war, to try and remove the probable cause of belligerency. Actually the U.S. can and does do both, despite the presumption by critics that it is obsessed with the second to the exclusion of the first. In Liberia, where it has just withdrawn its forces [on August 25, 2003], the U.S., by putting some ships with marines off shore and a mere 200 peacekeepers on the ground, shored up the morale—and expertise—of a West African peace keeping force that so far has done a remarkable job in quieting the country and forestalling a likely new round of internecine strife.

The U.S., it may be forgotten, did the same thing in Macedonia in ex-Yugoslavia in 1992. Whilst war was boiling in Bosnia, Croatia and Serbia the U.S sent troops into still peaceful Macedonia and, working under the UN flag, reminded the local antagonists that they were being watched and at the same time bolstered those politicians inclined to compromise with the knowledge that the world was on their side.

UN Successes

The problems we now face are legion. Few pretend that rooting out [the terrorist group] Al Qaeda, putting Iraq on its feet or de-fanging Iran and North Korea are easy tasks. On the other hand if we cast our eye back to the way the world has changed since 1945—decolonization, the emergence of new regional powers, the rapid spread of highly sophisticated military technology and the collapse of the Soviet empire, it is striking how many of these developments, all of which could have triggered major wars, progressed to a peaceful conclusion. A great amount of radical change has been negotiated and parlayed into a peaceful transition—and a good part of that through the UN and other international institutions.

One good example is when the Baltic states finally broke away from the Soviet Union. Unsurprisingly they tried to refuse citizenship to the large numbers of native Russians that over the years had settled there. Moscow was highly angered and threatened to stop the withdrawals of Russian forces. Many on both sides talked of war. The multilateral East-West body, the Organization for Security and Cooperation in Europe, led by Sweden, sent in high powered teams of negotiators and although the questions of troop withdrawals and citizen-

> *"Preventing war means taking some bold, resolute action, short of war, to try and remove the probable cause of belligerency."*

ship for Russians living in the Baltic states were never formally linked a deal was arranged, not least because the western allies, infused with their own principles on the rights of minorities, could see the point of the Russian argument.

Anticipating Crises

Good leadership can anticipate crises building up a military head of steam not only by the deft use of peacekeepers or international mediation but by taking a dispute to the World Court. Nigeria and Cameroon recently did this, avoiding a border dispute that risked seriously destabilizing the oil rich region of the Gulf of Guinea which provides a sizeable 15% of U.S. crude oil imports. There had been military skirmishes between the two neighbors and, as the Nigerian president, Olusegun Obasanjo, told me in a recent interview, he faced strong pressure from his minister of defense to go to war. Obasanjo overruled the military and insisted that the dispute be taken to the International Court of Justice in The Hague. Last October [2002] the Court upheld the Cameroonian claim. There was much champing at the bit in Nigeria, but Obasanjo faced his critics down and a year later the issue is mute.

What has now become undeniably clear in retrospect—although many reformed and sober people have been making the point for years—is that the preventive work the UN arms inspectors did after the 1991 Gulf War was so successful it should have avoided, in a normal, more self-disciplined, political atmosphere, the need for [the 2003 Iraq war]. If it hadn't been for [the September 11, 2001, terrorist attacks] it is highly doubtful that the U.S. and British governments would have ever convinced themselves (for sure, their intelligence services would not have bent so much with the political wind) that war was necessary.

Prevention Versus Pre-Emption

Prevention has a lot more going for it than pre-emption. We don't have to choose between intervention and inaction. Why should we be forced to choose between two types of failure when there is a good alternative? "The problem" as Pierre Sane, a former secretary general of Amnesty International once said, "is not lack of early warning, but lack of early action".

Many diplomats, aid workers and human rights activists with an ear to the ground know where the problems are building up to seismic proportions. Since 1945 the world has developed many tools for dealing with them. Contrary to the defeatist spirit of our current malaise there have been plenty of successes which should inspire us to face down the clarion calls for pre-emptive war and instead encourage us to step up the pace of preventive action.

Globalization Can Prevent War

by Erich Weede

About the author: *Erich Weede is a professor of sociology at the University of Bonn in Germany.*

Although neither "realist" theorizing about interstate politics nor critical treatments of globalization recognize it, a strong and beneficial link exists between globalization and the avoidance of war. In my view, the economic benefits of globalization and free trade are much less important than the international security benefits. The quantitative literature comes fairly close to general agreement on the following four propositions from economics, political sociology, and international relations.

Democracies Coexist Peacefully

First, democracies rarely fight each other. This finding does not necessarily imply that democracies fight fewer wars than do other regimes. It is even compatible with the view widely shared until recently that the risk of war between democracies and autocracies might be even higher than the risk of war between autocracies. I agree with critics of the democratic peace that we do not yet understand fully *why* democracies rarely fight each other and whether normative or institutional characteristics of democracies matter most. Explaining the democratic peace between Western democracies as "an imperial peace based on American power" [according to Rosato] is not justified, however. Admittedly, I held this view thirty years ago. Then I explained peace among U.S. allies by their common ties or even by their subordination to the United States. Later, however, I discovered that autocratic U.S. allies, in contrast to democratic U.S. allies, fought each other or against democratic U.S. allies, as the football war in Central America [the four-day war between El Salvador and Honduras in 1969] and the Falklands War illustrate. Thus, I became a convert to the democratic-

Erich Weede, "The Diffusion of Prosperity and Peace by Globalization," *Independent Review,* vol. ix, Fall 2004, pp. 168–71, 81. Copyright © 2004 by The Independent Institute, 100 Swan Way, Oakland, CA 94621-1428. www.independent.org, info@independent.org. Reproduced by permission.

peace proposition. John Oneal, in unpublished analyses carried out in Bonn in 2003, found that although the democratic-peace proposition consistently calls the imperial-peace proposition into question, controlling for an imperial peace does not subvert the democratic-peace proposition.

Second, prosperity, or high income per capita, promotes democracy.

Third, export orientation in poor countries and open markets in rich countries (that is, trade between rich and poor countries) promote growth and prosperity where they are needed most, in poor countries.

Fourth, bilateral trade reduces the risk of war between dyads of nations. As to *why* trade contributes to the prevention of war, two ideas come to mind. First, war is likely to disrupt trade. The higher the level of trade in a pair (dyad) of nations is, the greater the costs of trade disruption are likely to be. Second, commerce might contribute to the establishment or maintenance of moral capital, which has a civilizing and pacifying effect on citizens and statesmen. In the context of this article, however, answering the question of why trade affects conflict-proneness or providing the answer with some microfoundation is less important than establishing the effect itself in empirical research.

Unconvincing Criticism

Although some writers have questioned or even rejected the "peace by trade" proposition, their criticisms are not convincing. Beck, Katz, and Tucker raised the serious technical issue of time dependence in the time-series cross-section data, but Russett and Oneal responded to the objections raised against their earlier work and demonstrated that those objections do not affect their substantive conclusions. For a while, Hegre's study seemed to necessitate a qualification of the "peace by trade" proposition. He found that the pacifying effect of trade is stronger among developed countries than among less-developed countries. More recently, however, Mousseau, Hegre, and Oneal corrected this earlier finding and reported: "Whereas economically important trade has important pacifying benefits for all dyads, the conflict-reducing effect of democracy is conditional on states' economic development." Gelpi and Grieco suggested another qualification. In their view, trade no longer pacifies relations between autocratic states. According to Mansfield and Pevehouse, another modification of the "peace by trade" proposition might be required. The institutional setting, such as preferential trade agreements, matters. It is

> *"Although some writers have questioned or even rejected the 'peace by trade' proposition, their criticisms are not convincing."*

even conceivable that other forms of economic interdependence, such as cross-border investments, exercise some pacifying impact. Foreign direct investment (FDI) certainly promotes prosperity, growth, and democracy, but the conceivable pacifying impact of FDI still lacks sufficient empirical investigation.

The most radical criticism comes from Barbieri, according to whom bilateral trade *increases* the risk of conflict. As outlined by Oneal and Russett, her conclusion results from disregarding the military power of nations—that is, their different capabilities to wage war across considerable distances. Should we really proceed on the presumption that war between Argentina and Iraq is as conceivable as between the United States and Iraq or between Iran and Iraq? Of course, trade has no pacifying effect on international relations wherever the risk of conflict is extremely close to zero to begin with. Even this inadequate handling of the power and distance issue by itself does *not* suffice to support her conclusions. If the military-conflict variable is restricted to those conflicts that resulted in at least one fatality, then trade is pacifying, whether power and distance are adequately controlled or not. Moreover, Barbieri herself found some pacifying effect of economic freedom and openness to trade on the war involvement of nations. In spite of the attempted criticism of Russett and Oneal's findings, the "peace by trade" proposition stands and enjoys powerful empirical support.

Another issue also must be considered. Barbieri's measures are based on dyadic trade shares relative to national trade, whereas Russett and Oneal's measures are based on dyadic trade shares relative to the size of national economies. Gartzke and Li have demonstrated—arithmetically as well as empirically—that trade shares relative to national trade may rise when nations are *dis*connected from world trade. Nations may concentrate most of their trade on a few partners and remain rather closed economies. If Barbieri's and Oneal and Russett's measures of bilateral

> "The pacifying effect of trade might be even stronger than the pacifying effect of democracy."

trade and their effects are simultaneously considered, then Barbieri's trade shares exert a conflict-enhancing effect and Oneal and Russett's trade dependence exerts a conflict-reducing effect. This finding of Gartzke and Li's study not only replicates the substantive findings of both main contenders in the debate about trade and conflict, but it remains robust whether one relies on the Oneal and Russett data or on the Barbieri data, whether one includes all dyads or only dyads for which there is some risk of military conflict to begin with. If one is interested in finding out whether more trade is better or worse for the avoidance of military conflict, then it seems more meaningful to focus on a measure that is related to openness at the national level of analysis, as Oneal and Russett have done, than on a measure that may be high for fairly closed economies, as Barbieri has done.

The Pacifying Effect of Trade

Actually, the pacifying effect of trade might be even stronger than the pacifying effect of democracy, especially among contiguous pairs of nations, where conflict-proneness is greater than elsewhere. Moreover, trade seems to play a pivotal role in the prevention of war because it exerts direct and indirect pacifying effects. In addition to the direct effect, there is the indirect effect of free trade as the consequent growth, prosperity, and democracy reduce the risk of militarized disputes and war. Because the exploitation of gains from trade is the essence or purpose of capitalism and free markets, I label the sum of the direct and indirect international security benefits "the capitalist peace," of which "the democratic peace" is merely a component.

> *"By promoting capitalism, economic freedom, trade, and prosperity, we simultaneously promote peace."*

Even if the direct "peace by trade" effect were discredited by future research, economic freedom and globalization would still retain their crucial role in overcoming mass poverty and in establishing the prerequisites of the democratic peace. For that reason, I advocated a capitalist-peace strategy even before Oneal and Russett convinced me of the existence of a directly pacifying effect of trade. An Asian statesman understood the capitalist peace intuitively even before it was scientifically documented and established. According to Lee Kuan Yew, "The most enduring lesson of history is that ambitious growing countries can expand either by grabbing territory, people or resources, or by trading with other countries. The alternative to free trade is not just poverty, it is war.". . .

Globalization Leads to Peace

On the one hand, globalization promises to enlarge the market and therefore to increase the division of labor and to speed productivity gains and economic growth. On the other hand, it remains under attack from special-interest groups and misguided political activists. Critics of globalization not only forget both the benefits of free trade and globalization for developing countries and for their poor and under-employed workers and the benefits of free trade to consumers everywhere, but they know almost nothing about the international-security benefits of free trade. Quantitative research has established the viability and prospect of a capitalist peace based on the following causal links between free trade and the avoidance of war: first, there is an indirect link running from free trade or economic openness to prosperity and democracy and ultimately to the democratic peace; second, trade and economic interdependence by themselves reduce the risk of military conflict. By promoting capitalism, economic freedom, trade, and prosperity, we simultaneously promote peace.

Conceivable instruments to promote capitalism, economic freedom, free trade, and prosperity include advice about the institutional and legal foundations of capitalism and economic policies. Such advice is more likely to be persuasive if Western societies provide models for emulation to poor and conflict-prone countries. Open markets in rich countries for exports from poor countries generate credibility for free-market institutions and policies. They complement export-oriented growth strategies in poor countries. FDI by private enterprises and even donations from private Western sources to poor countries are more likely to have a positive effect on the growth path of poor countries than will official development aid, which tends to strengthen the state at the expense of free markets. The more capitalist the rich counties become, the more they provide an effective model for emulation to poor countries as well as a market and a source of technology and investment. By resistance to protectionism and to the creeping socialism of the welfare state, Western nations may simultaneously strengthen their own economies, improve the lot of the poor in the Third World, and contribute to the avoidance of conflict and war.

Democracy Can Prevent War

by George W. Bush

About the author: *George W. Bush is the forty-third president of the United States.*

Editor's Note: This viewpoint was excerpted from an address by President George W. Bush to the United Nations on September 21, 2004.

Thank you for the honor of addressing this General Assembly. The American people respect the idealism that gave life to this organization. And we respect the men and women of the U.N. [United Nations], who stand for peace and human rights in every part of the world.

Welcome to New York City. And welcome to the United States of America. During the past three years, I've addressed this General Assembly in a time of tragedy for our country, and in times of decision for all of us. Now we gather at a time of tremendous opportunity for the U.N., and for all peaceful nations. For decades the circle of liberty and security and development has been expanding in our world. This progress has brought unity to Europe, self-government to Latin America and Asia and new hope to Africa. Now we have the historic chance to widen the circle even further, to fight radicalism and terror with justice and dignity, to achieve a true peace, founded on human freedom.

The United Nations and my country share the deepest commitments. Both the American Declaration of Independence and the Universal Declaration of Human Rights proclaim the equal value and dignity of every human life. That dignity is honored by the rule of law, limits on the power of the state, respect for women, protection of private property, free speech, equal justice and religious tolerance. That dignity is dishonored by oppression, corruption, tyranny, bigotry, terrorism and all violence against the innocent. And both of our founding documents affirm that this bright line between justice and injustice, between right and wrong, is the same in every age and every culture and every nation.

George W. Bush, address to the United Nations, September 21, 2004.

Free Nations Choose Peace

Wise governments also stand for these principles for very practical and realistic reasons. We know that dictators are quick to choose aggression, while free nations strive to resolve differences in peace. We know that oppressive governments support terror, while free governments fight the terrorists in their midst. We know that free peoples embrace progress and life instead of becoming the recruits for murderous ideologies.

Every nation that wants peace will share the benefits of a freer world. And every nation that seeks peace has an obligation to help build that world. Eventually there is no safe isolation from terror networks or failed states that shelter them or outlaw regimes or weapons of mass destruction. Eventually there is no safety in looking away, seeking the quiet life by ignoring the struggles and oppression of others. In this young century, our world needs a new definition of security. Our security is not merely found in spheres of influence or some balance of power, the security of our world is found in the advancing rights of mankind.

These rights are advancing across the world. And across the world, the enemies of human rights are responding with violence. Terrorists and their allies believe the Universal Declaration of Human Rights and the American Bill of Rights and every charter of liberty ever written are lies to be burned and destroyed and forgotten. They believe the dictators should control every mind and tongue in the Middle East and beyond.

Enemies of Freedom

They believe that suicide and torture and murder are fully justified to serve any goal they declare. And they act on their beliefs. In the last year alone [2004], terrorists have attacked police stations and banks and commuter trains and synagogues and a school filled with children. This month [September] in Beslan, we saw once again how the terrorists measure their success: in the death of the innocent and in the pain of grieving families. Svetlana Deibesov (ph) was held hostage, along with her son and her nephew. Her nephew did not survive. She recently visited the cemetery and saw what she called the little graves. She said, I understand that there is evil in the world, but what have these little creatures done?

Members of the United Nations, the Russian children did nothing to de-

> *"Free nations strive to resolve differences in peace."*

serve such awful suffering and fright and death. The people of Madrid and Jerusalem and Istanbul and Baghdad have done nothing to deserve sudden and random murder. These acts violate the standards of justice in all cultures and the principles of all religions. All civilized nations are in this struggle together, and all must fight the murderers. We're determined to destroy terror networks wherever they operate, and the United States is grateful to every nation that is helping to seize terrorist assets, track down their operatives and disrupt their plans.

Ending State-Sponsored Terror

We're determined to end the state sponsorship of terror, and my nation is grateful to all that participated in the liberation of Afghanistan [in 2001]. We're determined to prevent proliferation and to enforce the demands of the world, and my nation is grateful to the soldiers of many nations who have helped to deliver the Iraqi people from an outlaw dictator [in 2003]. The dictator agreed in 1991 as a condition of a cease-fire to fully comply with all Security Council resolutions, then ignored more than a decade of those resolutions.

Finally, the Security Council promised serious consequences for his defiance. And the commitments we make must have meaning. When we say serious consequences, for the sake of peace there must be serious consequences. And so a coalition of nations enforced the just demands of the world. Defending our ideals is vital, but it is not enough. Our broader mission as U.N. members is to apply these ideals to the great issues of our time. . . .

Advancing Democracy

At this hour, the world is witnessing terrible suffering and horrible crimes in the Darfur region of Sudan, crimes my government has concluded are genocide. The United States played a key role in efforts to broker a cease-fire, and we're providing humanitarian assistance to the Sudanese people. Rwanda and Nigeria have deployed forces in Sudan to help improve security so aid can be delivered. The Security Council adopted a resolution that supports an expanded African Union force to

> *"Because we believe in human dignity, peaceful nations must stand for the advance of democracy."*

help prevent further bloodshed and urges the government of Sudan to stop flights by military aircraft in Darfur. We congratulate the members of the council on this timely and necessary action.

I call on the government of Sudan to honor the cease-fire it signed and to stop the killing in Darfur. Because we believe in human dignity, peaceful nations must stand for the advance of democracy. No other system of government has done more to protect minorities, to secure the rights of labor, to raise the status of women or to channel human energy to the pursuits of peace. We've witnessed the rise of democratic governments in predominantly Hindu and Muslim, Buddhist, Jewish and Christian cultures.

Democratic institutions have taken root in modern societies and in traditional societies. When it comes to the desire for liberty and justice, there is no clash of civilizations. People everywhere are capable of freedom and worthy of freedom. Finding the full promise of representative government takes time, as America has found in two centuries of debate and struggle. Nor is there only one form of representative government because democracies, by definition, take on the unique character of the peoples that create them.

Universal Desire for Freedom

Yet this much we know with certainty: The desire for freedom resides in every human heart. And that desire cannot be contained forever by prison walls or martial laws or secret police; over time and across the Earth, freedom will find a way. Freedom is finding a way in Iraq and Afghanistan, and we must continue to show our commitment to democracies in those nations. The liberty that many have won at a cost must be secured.

As members of the United Nations, we all have a stake in the success of the world's newest democracies. Not long ago, outlaw regimes in Baghdad and Kabul threatened the peace and sponsored terrorists. These regimes destabilized one of the world's most vital and most volatile regions. They brutalized their peoples in defiance of all civilized norms.

Afghanistan and Iraq

Today the Iraqi and Afghan people are on the path to democracy and freedom. The governments that are rising will pose no threat to others. Instead of harboring terrorists, they're fighting terrorist groups. And this progress is good for the long-term security of all of us. The Afghan people are showing extraordinary courage under difficult conditions.

They're fighting to defend their nation from [former ruling regime] Taliban holdouts and helping to strike against the terrorist killers. They're reviving their economy. They've adopted a constitution that protects the rights of all, while honoring their nation's most cherished traditions. More than 10 million Afghan citizens, over 4 million of them women, are now registered to vote in next month's [October 2004] presidential election. To any who still would question whether Muslim societies can be democratic societies, the Afghan people are giving their answer.

Since the last meeting of this General Assembly, the people of Iraq have regained sovereignty. Today in this hall, the prime minister of Iraq and his delegation represent a country that has rejoined the community of nations. The government of Prime Minister Allawi has earned the support of every nation that believes in self-determination and desires peace. And under Security Council Resolutions 1511 and 1546, the world is providing that support.

The U.N. and its member nations must respond to Prime Minister Allawi's request and do more to help build an Iraq that is secure, democratic, federal and free. A democratic Iraq has ruthless enemies because terrorists know the stakes in that country. They know that a free Iraq in the heart of the Middle East will be a decisive blow against their ambitions for that region.

So a terrorist group associated with Al Qaida is now one of the main groups killing the innocent in Iraq today, conducting a campaign of bombings against civilians and the beheadings of bound men. Coalition forces now serving in Iraq are confronting the terrorists and foreign fighters so peaceful nations around the world will never have to face them within our own borders. Our coalition is standing beside a growing Iraqi security force.

The NATO [North Atlantic Treaty Organization] alliance is providing vital training to that force. More than 35 nations have contributed money and expertise to help rebuild Iraq's infrastructure. And as the Iraqi interim government moves toward national elections, officials from the United Nations are helping Iraqis build the infrastructure of democracy.

These selfless people are doing heroic work and are carrying on the great legacy of Sergio de Mello [UN representative to Iraq who was killed in August 2003]. As we've seen in other countries, one of the main terrorist goals is to undermine, disrupt and influence election outcomes. We can expect terrorist attacks to escalate as Afghanistan and Iraq approach national elections.

A Future of Liberty

The work ahead is demanding, but these difficulties will not shake our conviction that the future of Afghanistan and Iraq is a future of liberty. The proper response to difficulty is not to retreat; it is to prevail. The advance of freedom always carries a cost paid by the bravest among us. America mourns the losses to our nation and to many others.

And today I assure every friend of Afghanistan and Iraq and every enemy of liberty, we will stand with the people of Afghanistan and Iraq until their hopes of freedom and security are fulfilled. These two nations will be a model for the broader Middle East, a region where millions have been denied basic human rights and simple justice.

For too long, many nations, including my own, tolerated, even excused oppression in the Middle East in the name of stability. The oppression became common, but stability never arrived. We must take a different approach. We must help the reformers of the Middle East as they work for freedom and strive to build a community of peaceful, democratic nations.

> *"The desire for freedom resides in every human heart."*

This commitment to democratic reform is essential to resolving the Arab-Israeli conflict. Peace will not be achieved by Palestinian rulers who intimidate opposition, tolerate corruption and maintain ties to terrorist groups.

The long-suffering Palestinian people deserve better. They deserve true leaders capable of creating and governing a free and peaceful Palestinian state. Goodwill and hard effort can achieve the promise of the road map to peace. Those who would lead a new Palestinian state should adopt peaceful means to achieve the rights of their people and create the reformed institutions of a stable democracy.

Arab states should end incitement in their own media, cut off public and private funding for terrorism, and establish normal relations with Israel. Israel should impose a settlement freeze, dismantle unauthorized outposts, end the daily humiliation of the Palestinian people and avoid any actions that prejudice final negotiations. And world leaders should withdraw all favor and support from any Palestinian ruler who fails his people and betrays their cause.

Democracy Is Not Only for the West

The democratic hopes we see growing in the Middle East are growing everywhere. In the words of the Burmese democracy advocate Aung San Suu Kyi, We do not accept the notion that democracy is a Western value. To the contrary, democracy simply means good government rooted in responsibility, transparency and accountability.

Here at the United Nations, you know this to be true. In recent years, this organization has helped to create a new democracy in East Timor and the U.N. has aided other nations in making the transition to self-rule.

Because I believe the advance of liberty is the path to both a safer and better world, today I propose establishing a democracy fund within the United Nations. This is a great calling for this great organization. The fund would help countries lay the foundations of democracy by instituting the rule of law and independent courts, a free press, political parties and trade unions.

Money from the fund would also help set up voter precincts in polling places and support the work of election monitors. To show our commitment to the new democracy fund, the United States will make an initial contribution. I urge all other nations to contribute as well.

International Cooperation

I have outlined a broad agenda to advance human dignity and enhance the security of all of us. The defeat of terror, the protection of human rights, the spread of prosperity, the advance of democracy: These causes, these ideals call us to great work in the world. Each of us alone can only do so much. Together we can accomplish so much more.

History will honor the high ideals of this organization. The Charter states them with clarity: to save succeeding generations from the scourge of war, to reaffirm faith in fundamental human rights, to promote social progress and better standards of life and larger freedom. Let history also record that our generation of leaders followed through on these ideals, even in adversity. Let history show that in a decisive decade, members of the United Nations did not grow weary in our duties or waver in meeting them.

I'm confident that this young century will be liberty's century. I believe we will rise to this moment because I know the character of so many nations and leaders represented here today, and I have faith in the transforming power of freedom. May God bless you.

The Use of Nonviolent Force Can Prevent War

by Gabriel Moran

About the author: *Gabriel Moran is the author of* Both Sides: The Story of Revelation.

On April 6, 1927, Foreign Minister Aristide Briand of France communicated the following message to the United States: "France would be willing to subscribe publicly with the United States to any mutual engagement tending to outlaw war, to use an American expression, as between these two countries." After some discussions about enlarging the agreement to include other nations, the treaty was signed in Paris on Aug. 27, 1928. It was ratified in 1929 by the United States Senate with only one dissenting vote. There were 15 other signatories.

This agreement was the fruit of 10 years of effort by a committee for the "outlawry of war." In light of World War II and subsequent decades, this movement has been dismissed as an embarrassingly naive episode. Or more contemptuously, the attitude reflected in the "outlawry of war" is seen as emblematic of the weakness that led to Hitler's rise.

Undeniably, the movement was afflicted with naivete, although perhaps not so much as is usually assumed. The movement began while World War I was still being fought. The leaders of the movement realized that simply passing a law would not eliminate war. Nonetheless, they thought that making all wars illegal could be a step in the right direction. They proposed an international criminal court, recognizing a need that is only beginning to be fulfilled eight decades later. Surely it is a strange fact that terrorism, assassination and torture are illegal but war is not.

John Dewey [American philosopher], agonizing over whether to support United States entry into World War I, tried in several essays to distinguish force and violence, force and war. Dewey never carried through consistently on his distinctions. His efforts were dismissed by commentators who pointed out that

Gabriel Moran, "Outlawing War: Reforming the Language of War Is the First Step Toward Ending It," *National Catholic Reporter,* vol. 40, November 7, 2003, p. 14. Copyright © 2003 by *National Catholic Reporter*, www.NCRonline.org. Reproduced by permission.

in international conflicts, "force" and "war" are used interchangeably. That criticism is true, but it is a statement of the problem, not a reason for dismissing the question. Until the language of power, force and war is reformed, discussion of war will always be between "realists" who are certain that war is an inevitable fact of human life and "idealists" who think that the use of force is immoral.

World War I

The First World War had changed the nature of warfare or the very meaning of the word "war." The entire populace of nations was mobilized for the war effort. War was no longer a battle between competing armies. The line between combatant and noncombatant could never again be clearly drawn. The people who wished to outlaw war recognized the potential for horror that had been brought on by the "Great War." Whatever justification for war had been advanced in the past, all wars henceforth were stupid, criminal and immoral.

The 1920s and 1930s proved to be inept in developing the means to stop war. By the end of the 1930s, Europe was faced with a horrendous situation; there seemed no alternative to war. As a result, World War II, despite the slaughter of 50 million people, is widely hailed as a "good war," one that was justified by the evils of Nazism.

The Committee for Outlawry of War at first acknowledged the need for "organized force" to control violators of international law. However, after 1921 the group's position was that reliance should be solely on organized moral sentiment. They claimed it was a false analogy to compare a domestic police force and an international use of force. Although it is the nature of analogy to "limp," the comparison of domestic and international policing functions seems quite appropriate.

In the 21st century, organized moral sentiment is a powerful force but it is still insufficient to restrain all criminal activity. At the same time, the nature of war has shifted again. The technology that changed the nature of war in 1914–1918 has now reached dizzying levels of sophistication. The potential for violence has escalated immeasurably. But used wisely, the technology could be used to lessen the violence in international conflict. Few people are so naive as to think that technology itself can reduce violence. But if the technology were under wise international control, it could serve that purpose.

Where the 21st century does show a possible advance is in the existence of a body of international law, the activities of the United Nations and the beginning of a permanent international court.

> *"Surely it is a strange fact that terrorism, assassination and torture are illegal but war is not."*

Unfortunately, the language to discuss power, force and war remains as confused and unimaginative as it was in the 1920s. Developing a better language is only one step, but we cannot get an answer to a question if the language to ask the question is not available.

Force vs. Violence

What is needed is to change the use of the term "force" in international discussions of conflict. Can the term "force" be changed in meaning? Actually, the most common meaning of force is precisely the one that is needed. In practically all uses of the term, outside discussions of war, force is distinguishable from violence. While violence is thought to be a dangerous possibility when force is introduced, the term is not equated with explosions of obscene amounts of violence that destroys every living being in its path. Why then, in international discussions, do people say "force" when they mean war? It seems to be a euphemism, but one that has the unfortunate result of closing off imagination about how force and forces could be used to avoid war. When the European Union last February [2003] tried to dissuade the United States from war on Iraq, it stated: "War is not inevitable. The use of force should be the last resort." Wouldn't they have spoken more logically, realistically and effectively, if they had said: "Force is inevitable. But war should be the last resort."

Force is a pressure upon humans or nonhumans to get them to act in a desired way. For nearly everyone, the use of force is a daily occurrence, from forcing open a jar of pickles to forcing one's way through a crowd. As a one-directional action, force is always questionable. Especially in attempting to coerce human agreement to a certain way of acting, force is a restriction on the freedom of another. Force may indeed slide into violence. But where a

> *"Between humans, force is a sign that human power has failed."*

human being is incompetent or is criminally dangerous, force of restraint is necessary. Force may be needed to keep a child from running into the street, or force may have to be used to stop a would-be rapist. Less obvious uses of force are present in the business and political world, and even religious and educational institutions. Force allows for innumerable degrees of exercise from psychological intimidation to a swift blow to the midsection.

Force is constantly used against the physical environment. Since there is no resistance by another's will, the moral issue is less ambiguous. Nonetheless, human beings have slowly been learning that they cannot be cavalier in the use of force against the environment. Force has to be carefully rationed because a human being can never grasp all the effects of any action in trying to make the world suit his or her desires.

The misuse of the term "force" in international conflicts is not likely to be corrected unless a deeper linguistic confusion in using "power" is unearthed. "Power" stands on one side of "force" as "violence" does on the other. Linguistically, force collapses into violence because power has already collapsed into force. Unless the term power is used in ways that do not inevitably lead to force, then a nation's use of force becomes equated with war.

"Power," like so many important words, has two almost opposite meanings.

When people who call themselves "realists" talk about power, they have one very clear meaning of power in mind. Power means the exercise of force; power in this context is the means to coerce and dominate. One of the most discussed essays on international affairs in 2002 was Robert Kagan's essay, "Power and Weakness." Slightly expanded, it was published as a book with the title *Of Paradise and Power.* There is no question in Kagan's mind that power is the opposite of weakness, that the United States represents power and Europe represents

> *"Showing love to one's enemies and deliberately refusing to offer violence for violence requires courage, determination and an understanding of power."*

weakness. The reference to paradise in the book's title might suggest something positive about Europe but, for Kagan, Europe's living in a paradise is a delusion made possible by United States (military) power. Kagan would probably acknowledge other kinds of power than military power but his standard use of the term is to equate power and military power. Therefore, countries that do not spend a sizeable part of their budget on military power are "weak."

Liberal commentators in the United States were skeptical of Kagan's crude stereotypes. But a book they did praise was Joseph Nye's *The Paradox of American Power: Why the World's Only Superpower Cannot Go It Alone.* Nye distinguished between "hard power and soft power"; this distinction was widely hailed as a breakthrough in thinking about U.S. power. Many people were therefore surprised when Nye supported the United States war on Iraq. Where did soft power go? The answer, I think, is that a distinction between hard and soft is only a minor issue of degrees in the exercise of power. Nye never gets to the real paradox of power. His hard and soft powers still refer to coercing people in a one-way exercise of force. If manipulation with soft power does not get us what we want, there is hard power (bombs) as a backup.

The Potentiality of Power

The real paradox of power is that power can be almost the exact opposite of force. In addition to meaning active coercion, power can also mean passive receptiveness. In fact, this latter meaning is the root from which all power springs. Power belongs to the same linguistic family as possible, potential, passive. In classical and medieval philosophy, power is the lowest and weakest form of being—mere possibility that has yet to be realized or actualized. Power is capacity for action but needs to be brought to act.

When one comes to the human as the paradoxical union of matter and spirit, what was weakness can be turned into strength. The fact that humans, in contrast to other animals, are mostly unformed at birth can be turned to advantage. Humans are born with capacity, the power that is receptiveness. They are not born with wings, but they can invent an airplane. Among the other animals, they are on the weak side in "brute strength," but the human strength of intelligence gives them an advantage far beyond the other animals.

The paradox of power is that power begins as weakness or passivity, an undesirable condition in the material world. But humans have a passiveness or receptiveness that is their strength. They are able to exercise control of their surroundings by ideas and language. True, elements of force are mixed in with the human efforts of control. When threatened, humans may mistakenly equate their power with force. For defending themselves against hostile animals or dangerous weather, force may be an appropriate defense. But with other human beings, human power resides in listening and responding. Between humans, force is a sign that human power has failed.

When human beings enter into mutual exchanges, then the power of each is enhanced. Human life becomes richer the more that receptivity to others is exercised. Of course, not all human encounters are mutually affirming. Some people, for whatever the cause, never grasp the paradox of human power. For them, the world has a top and a bottom; they are willing to do whatever is necessary to get on top. Other people who are on the receiving end of this kind of force are tempted to act the same in return. Worse, they are pressed to accept this picture of the world with a top and a bottom. One of the worst aspects of being a slave is that it can make you desire to be a slave owner.

Passive Resistance as Action

The most human response to a force that has turned violent is to act asymmetrically. That is, human power resides in not returning violence for violence, whatever is done, it must be action to break a cycle of violence so that a degree of mutuality can be restored. Doing good to one's enemies is not a form of weakness but of human strength. What is sometimes called "passive resistance" can be misunderstood as doing nothing. But "passive resistance" is an action, the most intensely human action. The Sermon on the Mount is often cited as an advocacy of doing nothing in the face of evil. But showing love to one's enemies and deliberately refusing to offer violence for violence requires courage, determination and an understanding of power.

> *"War should be made illegal, although policing action by a legitimate international body is still a necessity."*

In "realist" literature, the Sermon on the Mount is often praised as an ideal that individuals should try to live by. But to protect these good and innocent people the government has to be amoral; it cannot be naive and idealistic in a world of predators. The assumption is that the only thing that counts in international affairs is "self-interest." However, the question for a nation is the same as for the individual: what kind of self are you becoming? That is, what are your interests? The nation-state has a proclivity to feel threatened and therefore to use the crudest

171

forms of force. One nation cannot change this long history, but it is possible that the world's nation-states might establish a system that allows for nations to have "interests" other than that of being more militarily powerful than their neighbors.

The United Nations

The United Nations is the present fragile structure for international cooperation. The right wing in the United States contemptuously dismisses the United Nations as a debating society, but that is precisely what it should be. As a forum for discussion, it needs the help of other international or transnational bodies to facilitate numerous forms of national exchanges, such as business, athletic or religious dealings. It also needs a legal and judicial structure to be a restraint on the misuses of force that continue to be part of human experience.

War should be made illegal, although policing action by a legitimate international body is still a necessity. Terrible conflicts are not likely to disappear soon, but it is time to start speaking a language of power, force and war that will reduce human violence and unlock human power. A country that equates power and military power is on the way to self-destruction. The alternative is to use the human power of mutual pacts that provide as much security as human beings are likely to have in this world.

War Cannot Be Prevented

by Victor Davis Hanson

About the author: *Victor Davis Hanson is a military historian and a senior fellow at the Hoover Institution at Stanford University.*

Unfortunately, wars are not as rare as lasting periods of peace. More people have perished in conflict since the Second World War than the 60 million who died during that horrific bloodletting. Americans should remember that even in the last two decades of "peace" we have still fought small wars in Grenada, Libya, Panama, the Gulf, Serbia, and Afghanistan. The democratic Athenians in the fifth century—the greatest hundred years of their culture—fought three out of every four years against Persians, Aegean Islanders, Cypriots, Egyptians, Spartans, Syracusans, and a host of other smaller city-states. Plato, who saw firsthand the last two decades of it all, summed up the depressing truth best when he said peace was but "a parenthesis"—as every state was always in an undeclared state of war with another.

About the only prolonged period of real peace in civilization's history occurred during the second century A.D., when for nearly a hundred years, under the so-called "Five Good Emperors," Rome's government defeated most of its enemies, ran the Mediterranean world, and pretty much treated its own people humanely. Unfortunately, we can be assured that war will never be eliminated or outlawed—only that it can be delayed or, in some cases and for long periods, prevented. In the context of the Middle East, we are on the verge of War No. 5 of the last 55 years (1947, 1956, 1967, 1973, 2002). Afghanistan has not really been at peace for a quarter-century. Iraq in a single decade has invaded Iran and Kuwait, sent missiles into Israel, and killed thousands of Kurds and Shiites.

If Wars Are So Frequent, What Causes Them?

A number of great philosophers, political scientists, and historians have written vast treatises on the subject. While there is no general agreement, few believe that they arise simply out of real material "grievances"—the inequity and oppression that leave thousands of innocents poor, sick, and hungry. Make everyone literate and well fed, and war might become less common—but it would not go away. Hannibal as a child swore eternal enmity toward Rome not because of an impoverished Carthage, but to restore the pride of his clan and country after the humiliation of the First Punic War.

North Korea and North Vietnam invaded the southern halves of their peninsulas neither because their respective peoples were under attack by non-Communist, nor because their own resources and land were being stolen. Rather, they knew that only with absolute conquest of a nearby antithetical—and more attractive—alternative to their own rule could their hold on

> *"We can be assured that war will never be eliminated or outlawed."*

power be preserved. Kim Il Sung [founder of North Korea] and Ho Chi Minh [founder of North Vietnam] had no illusions that Marxism or totalitarianism would make the Koreans or Vietnamese freer, wealthier, or happier. In fact, they had good reason to think just the opposite. But both did trust that they could invade and win, or at least achieve stalemate—and so both attacked, were proved right, and thus held onto or expanded their power.

Saddam Hussein [former Iraqi president] wanted land from Iran, oil from Kuwait, and obeisance from the Kurds, and sought allies by attacking Israel. Yet his own people had plenty of territory and resources well before he went to war. He was stopped not by U.N. envoys or the Arab League, but only by the guns of the United States. And he is a threat today not as a result of our determination to rid the world of him, but because of a misguided forbearance that spared him.[1] Sadly, the careers of the real war-makers—Alexander, Caesar, Cortés, Hitler, or Tojo—confirm that the Greeks had it right after all: States often fight for irrational reasons like "honor, fear, and self-interest," and ambitious men regard restraint as weakness, not mercy.

Why Do Wars Actually Break Out?

Yet an aggressive state's desire to go to war does not necessarily mean that wars need follow. The causes and origins of conflict are *not* the same as the immediate circumstances that lead to the actual fighting and killing.

Unfortunately, conflict-resolution arbitration, international accords, or world policing bodies—while helpful in diffusing some minor crises and valuable in enforcing accords—rarely prevent wars. Otherwise the Italians would have never entered Ethiopia [1935], or the Japanese Nanking [1937] or the Russians Afghanistan [1979]. Deterrence alone can stop bullies. The astute Theban general Pagondas once reminded his unsure troops that the only way they could live safely next to Athens was by projecting an air of strength, since peoples

---

1. In 2003 the United States invaded Iraq and deposed Hussein.

such as the Athenians attacked, rather than admired, neighbors who were docile. His hoplites then defeated the Athenians and the latter never again invaded Boeotia.

So states that seek to start wars can be dissuaded from attacking when they realize there is a very good chance that the ensuing calamity will be worse for them than for their enemies—or, if irrational, they can be summarily defeated only through superior military force.

We cannot fathom exactly the state of mind of autocratic leaders in Iran, North Korea, or China. We know only two things about them: Given the state of America's current defenses these countries will not attack us; and should they be so foolish, they would lose quickly. Should we reduce our arms and begin relying on our NATO [North Atlantic Treaty Organization] allies, the U.N. [United Nations], or the goodwill of authoritarian states to leave us alone, it is more—rather than less—likely that we would find ourselves at war with all of them.

How Do Wars Cease?

The actual misery of killing ends in a variety of ways, but the longest periods of peace usually follow from decisive victories which prove aggression to be suicidal. The German army in 1918 surrendered in France, *not* Germany—and was back on French soil in 22 years. The German army in 1945 was ruined at home—and has been nowhere else in 57 years.

No wonder we often hear not of "war" but of plural "wars"—the Persian Wars, the Peloponnesian Wars, the Punic Wars, the Roman and English Civil Wars—in which armed conflicts are punctuated by shaky armistices until the ultimate victory of one of the two combatants. What ends particular wars for good is the defeat and exhaustion—and humiliation—of one side, often followed by a change of government or attitude among the defeated. After Plataea (479) no Persian king ever again thought his troops could defeat Greeks in pitched battle—or tried. There was a Roman Carthage in North Africa, but after 146 B.C. not a

> *"The longest periods of peace usually follow from decisive victories which prove aggression to be suicidal."*

Punic one—and so lasting peace on both sides of the Mediterranean. Once a series of elected governments in the United States decided it was not worth the loss of lives and treasure in Vietnam, we ceased to fight and win, and so the war tragically was lost and will probably not be renewed.

The Middle East will have peace when the Arabs either destroy the state of Israel, or learn that the costs of their failed attempts are so dreadful that no Arab leader will again dare try. Again, we should remember that the latest round of fighting followed *not* from Israeli aggression, but from the rushed and failed Israeli peace initiatives prompted by President [Bill] Clinton—coupled with the earlier unilateral Israeli withdrawal from Lebanon—all of which suggested to [former Palestinian leader Yasir] Arafat a new weakening in, rather than the old preponderance of, Israeli strength. In that regard, our prior demand that Israel not reply to dozens of Iraqi Scuds probably did far more damage than good: in establishing the precedent that either Israel could not answer the bombing of its cities, or the United States would not let them.

> *"Military force has a great power of clarity."*

Pundits shout on television that there is no hope in sight in the Middle East. In fact, we have come a long way from the last war of 1973 [between Israel and Egypt and Syria]. No Arab government will ever again invade Israel with conventional weapons—unless there is such a change in the Israel defenses that they believe they can defeat the Jewish state. Instead, there is a growing realization in Syria, Jordan, and Egypt that attacking Israel means the death and destruction of far more Arabs than Jews—especially when there is no longer a patron Soviet Union around for them to threaten and barter for what they cannot themselves obtain on the battlefield.

Even during this most disheartening current crisis, few Palestinian leaders believe they can any longer rally the Arab world en masse to invade Israel. And as they begin to realize that the continuance of suicide bombing results not in returned land, but in the systematic destruction of the homes and offices of the Palestinian elite, they seem more, not less, anxious to seek the intervention of the United States. The bellicose rhetoric of the Palestinian autocracy grew much more muted—and their calls for peace, conciliation, international peace-keepers, and outside intervention more frequent—once Israelis stopped talking of reprisals against murderers and simply took them.

Does War Serve Any Purpose?

Military force has a great power of clarity. With the Israeli reply, the world has seen at last that terrorists with explosives strapped to their bodies prefer to blow up small children rather than roll under tanks. There are plenty of militarily significant targets now for the Palestinian "soldiers," but apparently none that offer the specter of terror, publicity, fame—and money—to be found in blowing up civilians at Passover dinners.

Instead of seeing soldiers, we witness bombers who dismember women and children on holy days; outlaws who shoot and then run for sanctuary into sacred Christian shrines; poor suspects who are summarily executed without trial on suspicion of helping the Israelis. So far, Palestinians have executed more of their own bound and unarmed civilians than they have killed Israeli soldiers in combat. "General" Arafat now nearly has the "war" he threatened and the chance for "martyrdom" he promised. The bombers have the enemy targets they desire right in their backyards. The Arab world is "united" in its furor and can easily join in to attack Israel.

War, in other words, destroys pretense.

As we have seen in the current crisis, those who are the most educated, the most removed from the often humiliating rat race of daily life (what [writer Thomas] Hobbes called the *bellum omnium contra omnes*), and the most inexperienced with thugs and bullies, are the likeliest to advocate utopian solutions and to ridicule those who would remind them of the tragic nature of mankind and the timeless nature of war. Ironically, they are also the most likely to get others less fortunate than themselves killed—as we saw in World War II, and most recently during the last decade in Iraq, Serbia, and in our ongoing experience with the Middle Eastern terrorists. . . .

The pacifists and utopians who believe war never solved anything should recall the words of the firebrand, slave-owning, and utterly lethal Nathan Bedford Forrest upon learning that many of his fellow Confederates were promising years of guerrilla warfare after 1865. "Men, you may all do as you please, but I'm a-going home. Any man who is in favor of a further prosecution of this war is a fit subject for a lunatic asylum, and ought to be sent there immediately."

Mr. Forrest was a brave man and formidable fighter—indeed, he had personally killed 29 Union soldiers in battle and had 30 horses shot from under him. But what made him give up the fight was neither Abolitionist rhetoric nor a sudden change of heart, but the likes of William Tecumseh Sherman—who tore through Georgia and the Carolinas—and the thousands of Union cavalrymen that overran Forrest's beloved Tennessee.

And, remember, Mr. Arafat is no Nathan Bedford Forrest.

Globalization Cannot Prevent War

by Gerald Cavanaugh

About the author: *Gerald Cavanaugh is an activist who taught at Columbia, Princeton, and the University of California–Berkeley.*

"The notion of globalization as it is commonly used to describe some natural and inexorable force, the 'telos' of capitalism as it were, is misleading and ideologically loaded. A superior term would be 'neoliberalism.' This refers to a set of national and international policies that call for business domination of all social affairs with minimal countervailing force. Governments are to remain large so as to better serve the corporate interests, while minimizing any activity that might undermine the rule of business and the wealthy. Neoliberalism is almost always intertwined with a deep belief in the ability of markets to use new technologies to solve social problems far better than any alternative course. The centerpiece of neoliberalism is invariably a call for commercial media and communication markets to be deregulated. What this means in practice is that they are 're-regulated' to serve corporate interests. [So understood, what we have] is the newest stage of class struggle under capitalism and the antidemocratic implications of neoliberalism move to the front and center of the debate. . . .

"Neoliberalism is more than an economic theory, however. It is also a political theory. It posits that business domination of society proceeds most effectively when there is a representative democracy, but only when it is a weak and ineffectual polity typified by high degrees of depoliticization, especially among the poor and working class. It is here that one can see why the existing commercial media system is so important to the neoliberal project, for it is singularly brilliant at generating the precise sort of bogus political culture that permits business domination to proceed without using a police state or facing effective popular resistance."

—Robert W. McChesney, "Global Media, Neoliberalism, and Imperialism," *Monthly Review*, March 2001

As the epigraph indicates, we must be clear about the phenomenon of so-called "globalization" or, better, "neoliberalism." In the first place, it is not entirely new. Rather we are living through a continuation of a historical trend toward "a world market that gives a cosmopolitan character to production and consumption in every country." The words are those of [Karl] Marx (and [Friedrich] Engels), in the *Communist Manifesto*, written in 1847.

In that *Manifesto*, Marx presciently, and at that time uniquely, pointed out that the logic of capital entails the expansion of its markets globally.

There is no magic bullet, no technological fix, no instant success, but citizen activism, protests, and politicking can make a difference. Here are some thoughts on what everyone can do to see that the changes so many of us realize are necessary do take place.

What You Can Do

- Get active. Do some research first—unless you see and understand the problem(s), you cannot be effective in action.
- Join with others. As [consumer advocate] Ralph Nader says, we know what the solutions are; we must get them off of the shelves and implement them. But it takes political activism. Help get the vote out, there are good Democrats running. Or participate in the Green Party, which is offering a real and feasible alternative.
- Join/volunteer/participate in NGOs [nongovernmental organizations] that are doing the best, necessary work—Health Care For All-Oregon; Physicians for a National Health Plan; Anti-nuke groups; Friends of the Earth; Headwaters; S.O. ANSWER; etc. Coalitions are crucial.
- Encourage your church group to take public stands.
- Write letters to editors, bombard them; shame them; complain to the network and local TV moguls: threaten to turn them off. Support the alternative or progressive media.
- Communicate with your "representatives" constantly, as individuals and as groups.
- Attend public forums and show you are involved and paying attention.
- Shake up the allegedly "progressive" groups.
- Give money to the groups you support—everything costs.

"Two hundred years of globalization have moved the gap between rich and poor countries from 3-1 up to 19-1 in 1998."

"Capitalism, by the rapid improvement of all instruments of production, by the immensely facilitated means of communication, draws all, even the most barbarian nations into [modernization]. It batters down all Chinese walls, it compels all nations under pain of extinction to adopt the capitalist mode of production; it compels them to introduce what it calls civilization into its midst, that is, become capitalist themselves. In a word, it creates a world after its own image." [from the *Communist Manifesto*]

Transnational Corporations

But there are changes along with continuities. The most dramatic and influential of these changes is the massive growth of the Transnational Corporations (TNCs). The 500 largest TNCs account for one-third of all manufacturing exports, 75 percent of all commodity trade, and 80 percent of the trade in technology and management services, and these trends are accelerating.

With production and sales in every profitable place on the globe, over the decades since 1945 the TNCs have gradually cut themselves loose from any necessary connection to a "homeland," thus their watch-word is "Capitalists have no country." The CEO of Colgate-Palmolive has proclaimed: "The United States does not have an automatic call on our resources. There is no mind-set which puts this country first."

The TNCs have in practice escaped most of the controls and directions sovereign states once applied to them. Technological developments have, of

> *"Global corporate power has engaged in the destruction of trade union power by weakening unions."*

course, enabled and accelerated this escape; computerization of both manufacturing and services operations (especially financial services and speculation); robotization and numerically coordinated machinery have released capitalists from most reliance on skilled workers; transportation and communications advances have facilitated the explosion of coordinated global production, and have allowed "wage arbitrage" to beat down the wages and benefits of all workers.

These corporate/economic potentialities were all exploited and made fully operational by means of political interventions. Beyond being what Marx described as "the executive board" of the capitalists, political leaders are today themselves the capitalists, as the Enron infiltration of the Bush administration (one of many) demonstrates. Thus, the quite anti-democratic "Fast Track" phenomena of NAFTA [North American Free Trade Agreement], the WTO [World Trade Organization], the World Bank, the International Monetary Fund, and many other multilateral and bilateral agreements, all the result of ostensibly "democratic" political decisions, are in fact representative only of the needs and wishes of corporate hegemons, the official rhetoric of "free trade" and "democracy" notwithstanding. As the Archbishop of Mexico City said in regard to NAFTA, "It was passed behind the backs of the Mexican People," so, too, was it and all such agreements, passed behind the backs of the American people.

The Globalization Connection to War

So, what is the connection between the "neoliberal globalization" and war and civil conflict? A list will suffice to sketch out the pathologies:

Increasing and accelerating division globally between the few rich and the many poor. Two hundred years of globalization have moved the gap between rich and poor countries from 3-1 up to 19-1 in 1998. Within the richest countries, in 1960 the top 20 percent had 30 times the income of the poorest 20 percent. By 1997, the top 20 percent received 74 times the income of the bottom 20 percent. In the mid-nineties, the income gap between the rich and the poor in New York City was greater than in Guatemala. And this trend of increasing inequality is clearly manifest in the great majority of "developing nations." Merrill Lynch's World Health Report 2001 finds that an exclusive club of 7.2 million "high net worth individuals" had financial assets valued at $27 trillion in 2000, almost the size of the world's total GDP. And the income of the richest 10 percent of the US population (25 million people) is equal to the total income of the poorest 43 percent (almost a billion people) of the rest of the world.

Having suborned or otherwise taken over governments, global corporate power has engaged in the destruction of trade union power by weakening unions, stripping away legal labor rights and laying off workers, who are replaced by automation and cheap foreign labor. The use of non-lethal means is the usual method in places like America and Great Britain; in the rest of the world more direct brutal and lethal means are used against those who would dare to organize. What we are seeing is both the feminization of the labor force and the reintroduction of easy acceptance of child labor in the developing world. In Europe, 35 million are unemployed and another 15 million are unwillingly in part-time work or have given up the job search. In the "developing world," there are more than two billion un- and underemployed workers. And there will be more than 700 million people entering the labor market between now and the year 2110.

"Poverty is the greatest single source of underlying cause of death, disease and suffering worldwide." (WHO [World Health Organization] 1995) And poverty is increasing despite the claims, and because of the consequences, of neoliberal globalization.

> *"What we are seeing is both the feminization of the labor force and the . . . acceptance of child labor in the developing world."*

Environmental degradation, global warming, destruction of habitat, and species extinction are all accelerating despite the claims of those who say that the reverse is the case or that a technological "fix" is at hand. It must be emphasized that this irreversible destruction has enormous economic costs as well as enormously disruptive social consequences.

Structural adjustment programs forced upon the developing nations include forcing open their markets to foreign goods, thus destroying the local industries and farms; coercive and corrupt selling off, at bargain prices, of public goods such as water systems, electrical grids, and telecommunication systems to TNCs, leading to higher prices and unequal access; slashing funding for education, health care, and social security; implementing measures to protect foreign investment and interest rates. All this leads to loss of democratic sovereignty in relation to social, environmental, and economic decisions.

Integrated World Economy

The 20th century system of aggressive and expansive nationalist imperialistic states and alliances has been superseded by an integrated world economy in which there are shared material interests, but not, yet, shared equitable returns, by the reality both of American military hegemony and equally important shared ecological and resource constraint interests. In terms of war we are unlikely ever to see the return of "world wars." This makes even more obscene our present military budget and structure, as if the Cold War were still a factor or as if China were a rational replacement for the USSR as a meaningful threat. What we are seeing and will continue to see, if we do not address their causes in a non-military fashion, are "low intensity Third World conflicts manifesting themselves as insurgencies, paramilitary crime, sabotage, terrorism and other forms of intrastate violence" (Report of the U.S. Commission on Integrated Long-Term Strategy, 1988). Every one of these types of conflict are intimately related to distinct local conditions and causes, most but not all of which pre-existed the advent of globalization, but which have been exacerbated and inflamed by the socially and politically disruptive consequences of that neoliberal intrusion.

> *"Every one of [today's conflicts has] . . . been exacerbated and inflamed by the socially and politically disruptive consequences of [globalization]."*

Destroying Cultures

Before the TNCs moved into the developing world, most peoples there lived mainly in rural settings, in extended families in settled communities, poor, perhaps, but stable, traditional, and mutually supportive. Once their undemocratic military and oligarchic regimes allowed the TNCs to "invest" in their lands, these powerless peoples were pitch-forked directly into the 20th century and, as if to facilitate their transition, these people, now dispossessed of their lands and livelihoods, were driven by brute force and necessity into the massive, unplanned "free Trade Zones" of the developing world. There they were converted into a proletariat experiencing the worst sweatshop excesses, a stopover on the way to "modernization" that threatens to be a permanent hell-hole.

With entire cultures being destroyed, with all traditional values and belief systems overwhelmed, with anomic misery in place of their previous collectively-shared poverty, with incessant social and economic changes confronting them, all within an imported pop culture emphasizing materialism, selfishness, and violence, with repressive regimes and their own political and economic impotence staring them in the face, it is small wonder that, given the ready availability of "small arms" with massive firepower, "low intensity conflicts" are endemic in so many of these lands.

The solution, of course, cannot be more fire power, more tactical nuclear weapons, more "special forces" and anti-terrorist brigades parachuted into exotic lands or into our own urban and rural ghettos. The solution must be economic justice; it must be social justice and an end to outright and brutal exploitation; the solution is in making sure that all peoples have access to enough food, water, shelter, education, health care and the opportunity to fully develop their unique potentials within stable societies, cultures, and families in peaceful and constructive ways.

The solution lies in rejecting the ideology and mechanisms of "neo-liberal globalization," replacing it with the philosophy and mechanism of social goods, of truly democratic decision-making instead of rigged "market imperatives," of an ethic of cooperation rather than competition.

The False Utopia of the Market

It seemed once that democratic societies had learned the lesson of how foolish and destructive it had been to rely upon the utopia of the market to provide for all human and social needs and that henceforth the market must be consciously subordinated. The catastrophes of wars and depressions of the early 20th century, which were intimately related to such wholesale reliance on market mechanisms, ought to have brought home that lesson for good.

I am calling here for a revolution in both consciousness and in our economic structures and mechanisms. This may at first seem like too much to ask, but in my view, it is the minimum required of us if all peoples are to live lives of peace and dignity.

Democracy Cannot Prevent War

by James Ostrowski

About the author: *James Ostrowski is an attorney and the author of* Political Class Dismissed: Essays Against Politics.

I never thought I would end up as a presidential translator since I am fluent only in one language. Yet, here I am, serving as your translator for President [George W.] Bush's [January 2005 State of the Union] speech. That speech was written in a dialect that I do not speak but can, with great effort, read: purple English. My natural dialect is plain English.

Why didn't the President's programmers have him speak in plain English? A couple of plain reasons. First, many pseudo-intellectuals confuse ineffability with profundity. The more obscure the meaning, the greater must be the minds that confuse us. Second, this speech is part of realpolitik. Its practitioners think you need to spend a zillion years getting a Ph.D. at a prestigious institution to understand it, but it's a game children play all the time. Speak with forked tongue to keep your opponents off balance. Don't say what you really mean and no one will hold you accountable.

But I believe in puncturing pretension and holding people accountable, so here is my translation of the speech from purple to plain English.

The Translation

President Bush('s speechwriters):

"America was attacked on [September 11, 2001] because people who live in undemocratic countries resent their lack of freedom and come under the spell of ideologies that blame the United States for their plight and urge the murder of Americans as a response.

("I define freedom as being able to vote. I do not mean personal freedom: doing what you want with what you own. That freedom can be taken away by

James Ostrowski, "Bush's Speech: A Translation," www.LewRockwell.com, January 27, 2005.

elected governments as in the United States.")

"These angry people can cross our highly defended borders and attack us.

"The only way to stop them is for their countries to become democratic.

"The United States will now pressure and/or coerce non-democratic states to become democratic. If necessary, the U.S. will invade them and force them to hold elections.

"As for Iraq, we are staying to the bitter end, regardless of the cost in American or foreign lives or dollars. I will accept no set of facts as evidence that the Iraq War has failed. I will not let a beautiful theory be killed by ugly facts.

"Americans have and will die in wars to force other countries to have elections. That's okay since forcing foreign countries to have elections is more important than these soldiers' lives. Lots more disposable Americans will die in this cause. Get ready.

"Now, let me talk about domestic policy. . . ."

The Myth of Democratic Peace

Now that the speech, at least the foreign policy part, has been translated, its merits can be debated. Let's think long and hard about whether any of this makes any sense. Time's up. No, it doesn't. Nor is it profound. It's the old myth of democratic peace. Too bad Bush missed my Mises Scholars Conference lecture. Democracy may not make people peaceful but it sure makes them dumber. It's frightening to compare this aristocratic-republican fellow's thought processes to Bush's.

A myriad of domestic political concerns have led democracies into war. Modern democracies tend to extensively intervene in the free market by means of high taxes, welfare, and subsidies in order to buy the votes that keep the politicians in power. As [economist and social philosopher] Ludwig von Mises demonstrated, each intervention into the economy causes problems that lead to the demand for ever further interventions. Government thereby creates its own demand. Eventually, the economic problems become intractable, leading to the inevitable temptation to create a foreign policy distraction. Combine that with the fact that war, while undeniably harming the economy, gives the appearance of stimulating the economy, and we have a formula for why democratic governments would have a motive for war.

> *"Domestic political concerns have led democracies into war."*

Private Agendas

Special interest group politics is another flaw of democracy that can lead to war. By focusing their efforts, votes, and campaign contributions, small segments of the population can exercise influence on policy all out of proportion to their numbers. This is frequently seen in domestic policy. What is rarely remarked, however, is that this special interest group analysis applies to foreign policy as well. For example, there are over 150 hundred million Arabs in the Middle East, mostly Moslems, and they have one billion coreligionists around the world. Arab countries have vast oil reserves. Yet, for over fifty years, United States foreign policy has favored the tiny state of Israel, much to the chagrin of these Arab and Islamic millions. This is a foreign policy most decidedly not in the interests of the average American. This policy has dragged the United States into every aspect of the running fifty-year-old war over the Middle East. In addition to supplying massive military aide to Israel, American troops have shed blood nearby in Lebanon in a related conflict. Further, there is reason to believe that the terrorist attacks on September 11th were in part in retaliation for American support for Israel. As a result of those attacks, the United States is now at war in Afghanistan and Iraq. President Bush himself admitted that a major cause of the Iraq War was concern that [Iraqi leader Saddam Hussein] would strike Israel.

There are other examples of countries getting into wars to advance discrete private agendas. Historian Ralph Raico has written that most Americans wanted the United States to stay out of World War I, except for the East Coast economic and social elite which had close business and social ties to England. The United States has engaged in numerous military actions at the behest of private corporations that were foolish enough to invest in countries where property rights were not secure. The

> *"Democracies are vulnerable to messianic crusades."*

United States fought a major war in Kuwait and Iraq the only apparent reason for which was to preserve an oriental despotism. Surely, the actual reason was to protect certain discrete private interests in oil in Kuwait and Saudi Arabia. From any rational point of view, the dispute did not concern the average American in the slightest. They would buy their gasoline as usual at the pump, at prices set by the vagaries of the world oil market, regardless of which crooked Middle East politician sold the rights to oil (he had previously stolen) to some private company. Thus, once again, war was fought by a democracy to advance a special interest.

Messianic Crusades

Democracies are vulnerable to messianic crusades. Democratic politicians have a sense of moral superiority which impels them to reform other nations just as they seek to reform their own citizens and societies. [Former president] Woodrow Wilson is the foremost example of this spirit: "America is henceforth to stand for the assertion of the right of one nation to serve the other nations of the world." The temptation to add, ". . . whether they like it or not," is irresistible. Thus, the messianic impulse (or rationalization) would launch America into the disastrous World War I, and later wars such as Viet Nam, the Gulf War, and the bombing of Serbia.

Oftentimes, democracies end up in wars that were seemingly started by non-democracies. For example, the United States got involved in World War II because of the Japanese attack on Pearl Harbor. The reality is more complex. What was in dispute was which nation would be the dominant power in East Asia. America had staked its imperial claim in Asia forty-three years earlier by going to war with Spain.

> *"Democracies also have the means to fight wars."*

Subsequently, in a bloody war, America seized the Philippines from the natives. Japan invaded China in 1937. America applied diplomatic and economic pressure on Japan and demanded that Japan leave China. An oil embargo was imposed. Japan responded by seizing the oil fields of Malaysia and, anticipating American opposition, struck Pearl Harbor. The genesis of the conflict, however, was America's (democratic) imperial designs on East Asia. See, John V. Denson, "Roosevelt and the First Shot: A Study in Deception," in *Reassessing the Presidency*.

Democracy and War

Democracies also have the means to fight wars. Analysts of war spend too much time thinking about why wars are fought and far too little time contemplating the means of war. The resources for war are acquired by conscription, taxation, confiscation, and inflation. Without cannon and cannon fodder, there are no wars. In modern times, politicians neither fight nor pay for the wars they start or join. With their aura of legitimacy, democracies are particularly adept at utilizing all these means. Since citizens tend to identify with the democratic state, there is usually little trouble conscripting troops and confiscating the economic resources required for war. Perhaps this is why democracies tend to win the wars they fight. War is the health of the state, but the democratic state is also the health of war.

The history and evidence of democratic bellicosity is thoroughly explained by a theoretical examination of democracies' motives for war and means to wage them. In spite of their advantages over dictatorships, democracies in fact tend to be aggressive, imperialistic, and warlike. These tendencies provoke terrorism, which in turn provokes further foreign intervention, and more terrorism, in an endless circle of violence. While they tend to be aggressive abroad, they continually grow domestically, in power, scope and size. They ever-increase the property and liberty they confiscate. They stir up ethnic and religious hostilities by pushing towards one way of life for all groups, whether the politically weaker groups like it or not.

Two of the most important wars in modern history were fought in part for the express purpose of advancing democratic principles. President [Abraham] Lincoln explicitly justified the bloody Civil War as a war to save majority rule. Woodrow Wilson called World War I the war "to make the world safe for democracy." We have heard this refrain over and over again as the rationalization for war: in Korea, Viet Nam, and the Balkans.

The modus operandi of democracies is closer to that of dictatorships than is commonly thought. Though these regimes differ in the manner leaders are selected (force v. elections), they differ little in the manner in which they relate to their subjects on a daily basis: both regimes impose their will by force! True, most democracies have in storage pieces of paper with words printed on them (constitutions) which supposedly limit the amount of force they can use. Alas, as [novelist George] Orwell taught us, words can mean virtually whatever we want them to mean. At the end of the day, the democratic state has the most powerful dictionary: the army.

Democratic Pacifism

Ultimately, the theory of democratic pacifism contains a dangerous contradiction:

Democracies do not fight each other

If all states were democracies, there would be no war

War is bad; peace is good

Not all states are democracies

Dictatorships are resistant to internal change

The goal of world peace requires that democracies go to war with dictatorships to make them peaceful.

Proponents of the theory, of course, will reject the last premise, but cannot deny that the last premise is an accurate description of democratic behavior in the last 100 years and currently.

Thus, the paradox is that the theory of democratic pacifism causes war as it has in Iraq [when the United States invaded that nation in 2003] and, if we take Bush at his word, may soon in Iran, North Korea, Saudi Arabia, China, Egypt, Cuba. . . .

First, let me note the dishonest absurdity of Bush's claim that the U.S. is vulnerable even though we have well-defended borders. While we have troops, ships and planes all over the world, our own borders are quite open to our enemies. We do have well-defended constituencies supportive of massive illegal immigration that can deliver votes on election day.

> *"The paradox is that the theory of democratic pacifism causes war."*

Second, Bush commits the horror of horrors sin for any neocon. By attempting to explain [the September 11, 2001, terrorist attacks], isn't he "justifying" it? After all, the folks at LewRockwell.com and Antiwar.com and elsewhere have been accused of the same transgression: justifying 9/11 because we tried to explain its antecedents.

But it's worse than blatant hypocrisy. Bush not only "justifies" 9/11, he appears to at least partially blame the United States itself. Most of the hijackers came from states with dictatorships or authoritarian regimes that have been subsidized, supported and/or protected by the democratic United States for many years, including Saudi Arabia and Egypt. To summarize Bush's cockamamie theory: democracy is the solution to democracies being attacked by dictatorships that have been propped up by other democracies.

Imposing Democracy

Now for the really bad news. Let's juxtapose Bush's theory of preemptive strikes with Bush's theory of imposing democracy on dictatorships. Bush invaded Iraq even though Saddam never explicitly threatened the U.S. Bush has now strongly implied that he will attack and invade dictatorships when he deems them a threat to the U. S. Has he not then invited them to attack first under his own preemptive strike theory? Thus, instead of staying out of foreign countries' business, as advised by Washington, he has announced aggressive intentions toward numerous states and left us all vulnerable to a preemptive strike from any of them at any time. That's why preemption is a self-refuting theory.

Bush promises a Wilsonian-messianic crusade for democracy oblivious to how Wilson's crusade pretty much ruined a century, and created the artificial country of Iraq that Bush is now trying to keep together by brute force.

God bless us, Mr. Bush? God help us!

The United Nations Cannot Prevent War

by Ryan Malone

About the author: *Ryan Malone is assistant managing editor of the* Trumpet, *a monthly publication of the Philadelphia Church of God.*

Herbert Armstrong, termed by many world leaders an "unofficial ambassador for world peace," attended the inaugural session for the United Nations in San Francisco, April 1945. From San Francisco, Mr. Armstrong wrote that day: "Already I see the clouds of World War III gathering at this conference. . . . I do not see PEACE being germinated here, but the seeds of the next WAR! . . . The United Nations conference is producing nothing but strife and bickering, and is destined from its inception to end in total failure. Yet world leaders are pronouncing it THE WORLD'S LAST HOPE—with the only alternative ANNIHILATION OF HUMANITY!"

In a personal in the August/September *Plain Truth* some 25 years later, he wrote, "World War II was the 'war to END all wars.' The United Nations was the world 'peace effort' to prevent further wars. What are the results after a quarter-century? There have been more than 50 wars. The UN has contributed to the shortening of four wars—BUT—there is no evidence to show that the United Nations has PREVENTED any war!"

From Bad to Worse

In the January 1977 *Plain Truth*, Mr. Armstrong prophesied: "For the immediate future—the next five, ten or twenty-five years—the sobering revelation of Bible prophecy shows this world will go from bad to worse. World confusion, hatred, strife, warfare and terrible destruction will increase with rapid acceleration. It's the natural course to expect."

And indeed, we see these predictions verified. But notice the next paragraph! "The United Nations won't be able to bring peace. The aggressor nations—and we are so gullible we never recognize them until AFTER they plunge the world into another war—will go right on with their scheming and diabolical planning for world rule."

I think you get the picture. Mr. Armstrong KNEW that the United Nations would not—could not—bring peace to this world. How did he know? By looking into God's Word, which reveals the nature of man. "And the way of peace have they not known" (Rom. 3:17). He saw, through the Bible, that peace would never come on the Earth by mankind; it could only be possible by JESUS CHRIST upon His return with His world-ruling government to usher in a thousand years of utopian peace and harmony (Rev. 20:4–6; Isa. 2:2–4; 9:6–7; 11:1–9).

So was Mr. Armstrong correct? Was he—as God's messenger of specific prophecies concerning our time TODAY—accurate in his predictions?

The UN's Track Record

Let's take a brief look at the UN's track record. The 188-nation organization has been the center of growing cynicism. Sir Anthony Parsons, British Ambassador to the UN from 1979 to 1982, declared it "a disastrous failure." Jeanne Kirkpatrick, American ambassador to the UN in the early '80s, said it was "nothing more than a place for the nations to let off rhetorical steam." Karl Posche, appointed as an efficiency expert in 1995, said after seven months on the job, "The UN is a good example of waste and inefficiency."

From the inception of the UN in 1945 until 2000, there were 187 wars with over 45 million killed—nearly as many as in World War II itself! The UN was involved in 49 peacekeeping missions in that time, in 2000 maintaining 17 missions. And the number of worldwide conflicts in 2000 was 33—resulting in over 20 million refugees! Is the UN succeeding in "keeping peace"? Or have God's prophecies, as proclaimed by Mr. Armstrong, come to pass?

Headlines such as these are almost exact replicas of Mr. Armstrong's predictions over 50 years ago! "UN 'Triumph' Masks Waning of its Power" (*London Times*, Feb. 25, 1998). "Report Concludes UN Failed Rwanda" (AP [Associated Press] Online, Dec. 17, 1999). "UN Apologizes for Not Preventing E. Timor Violence" (Reuters, Dec. 30, 1999).

The stories under those last two headlines showed how top UN officials, according to several reports, are becoming good apologizers. The AP Online report described Secretary-General Kofi Annan's regrets for allowing the 1994 Rwandan genocide in which almost 800,000 minority

> *"There is no evidence to show that the United Nations has PREVENTED any war!"*

Tutsis were victims of a Hutu-sponsored genocide. Annan had similar feelings concerning the death of thousands of Bosnian Muslims in the UN-protected enclave of Srebrenica in 1995. To the people of East Timor, another apology was in order for not preventing the violence that engulfed the territory late last year

191

[1999], according to the head of UN Transitional Administration in East Timor, Sergio Vieira de Mello. "We have to acknowledge our mistakes and shortcomings," he said.

Minor Successes

The organization experienced some minor successes, however, when it "brokered a Russian withdrawal from Afghanistan, an end to the Iran-Iraq war, independence for Namibia and reconciliation in Cambodia, as well as the collective military response to Iraq's invasion of Kuwait" (*London Times*). But, according to this report, "since the heady days at the end of the Cold War . . . the organization has seen its powers whittled away." Yes, the world scene has changed dramatically since then, with the downfall of communism and the rapid rise of the European superstate. Is it coincidental that the UN would begin to be whittled away from that moment? Hardly!

> *"From the inception of the UN in 1945 until 2000, there were 187 wars with over 45 million [people] killed."*

Also, note how the UN was "initially sidestepped in the Kosovo conflict" (Reuters, Dec. 30, 1999). Instead, enter NATO [North Atlantic Treaty Organization]—with Germany pulling the strings!

Prophecy

Yes, Mr. Armstrong's predictions—some 55, some 25 years old—have come to pass. But the *Trumpet* magazine has made predictions on top of those. In our December 1995 issue, we stated—concerning the pope's visit to the UN during its Jubilee year: "Is it possible that the pope, whose rallying cry to the nation-states of Europe is to 'return to your [Catholic] roots,' sees that the ailing and divided voice of the UN is on the verge of needing replacement from a more vigorous 'peacemaker'? A peacemaker of beast-like proportions, mounted by a great whore who has dominated Europe in her previous historic guise as the 'holy' component in the Holy Roman Empire" (write for your free copy of *The History and Prophecy of Germany*).

Understand! The failure of the UN to keep peace in the world will be replaced, first by a united Europe under the umbrella of Catholicism, but ultimately by the RETURN OF JESUS CHRIST—the Prince of peace (Isa. 9:6), who will rule the Earth for 1000 years—making all nations united in His way of prosperity!

That is man's only hope for peace. That has been prophesied in the Bible. Mr. Armstrong restated it for many to hear. The *Trumpet* prophesies the same so more can hear it. And very shortly, that prophecy WILL thankfully come to pass!

Organizations to Contact

Amnesty International USA
322 Eighth Ave., New York, NY 10001
(212) 807-8400 • fax: (212) 627-1451
Web site: www.amnesty-usa.org

Amnesty International works to ensure that governments do not deny individuals their basic human rights as outlined in the United Nations Universal Declaration of Human Rights. It publishes numerous books; *Amnesty Now*, a quarterly magazine; an annual report; and reports on individual countries. Its Web site contains recent news, reports, and a searchable database of archived publications.

Brookings Institution
1775 Massachusetts Ave. NW, Washington, DC 20036
(202) 797-6000 • fax: (202) 797-6004
e-mail: brookinfo@brook.edu • Web site: www.brook.edu

Founded in 1927, the institution conducts research and analyzes global events and their impact on the United States and U.S. foreign policy. It publishes the quarterly *Brookings Review* and numerous books and research papers on foreign policy. Its Web site publishes editorials, papers, testimony, reports, and articles written by institution scholars, including "War, Profits, and the Vacuum of Law: Privatized Military Firms and International Law" and "An Alliance of Democracies."

Carnegie Endowment for International Peace (CEIP)
1779 Massachusetts Ave. NW, Washington, DC 20036
(202) 483-7600 • fax: (202) 483-1840
e-mail: info@ceip.org • Web site: www.ceip.org

CEIP is a private, nonprofit organization dedicated to advancing cooperation between nations and promoting active international engagement by the United States. Its work is nonpartisan and dedicated to achieving practical results. Through research, publishing, convening, and, on occasion, creating new institutions and international networks, endowment associates shape fresh policy approaches. Its quarterly journal *Foreign Policy*, a magazine of international politics and economics, is published in several languages and reaches readers in more than 120 countries.

Cato Institute
1000 Massachusetts Ave. NW, Washington, DC 20001-5403
(202) 842-0200 • fax: (202) 842-3490
Web site: www.cato.org

Cato is a libertarian public policy research foundation dedicated to peace and limited government intervention in foreign affairs. It publishes numerous reports and periodicals, including *Policy Analysis* and *Cato Policy Review*, both of which discuss U.S. policy in regional conflicts. Its Web site contains a searchable database of institute articles, news, and commentary, including "Congress and the Power of War and Peace" and "The Wages of War."

Center for Defense Information (CDI)
1779 Massachusetts Ave. NW, Suite 615, Washington, DC 20036
(202) 332 0600 • fax: (202) 462 4559
e-mail: cdi@igc.apc.org • Web site: www.cdi.org

CDI was founded by retired senior military officers to serve as an independent monitor of the military. It focuses on all matters relating to U.S. military, foreign policy, spending, and weapons. To encourage the intellectual freedom of its staff, the center does not hold organizational positions on public policy issues. It publishes the weekly journal *Defense Monitor.*

Center for Security Policy
1920 L St. NW, Suite 210, Washington, DC 20036
(202) 835-9077 • fax: (202) 835-9066
e-mail: info@centerforsecuritypolicy.org • Web site: www.centerforsecuritypolicy.org

The Center for Security Policy is a nonprofit, nonpartisan organization committed to the philosophy of promoting international peace through American strength. It accomplishes this goal by stimulating and informing national and international policy debates, in particular those involving regional, defense, economic, financial, and technology developments that bear upon the security of the United States. Its Web site features a wealth of papers related to military and defense matters.

Center for Strategic and International Studies (CSIS)
1800 K St. NW, Washington, DC 20006
(202) 887-0200 • fax: (202) 775-3199
Web site: www.csis.org

CSIS is a public policy research institution that specializes in the areas of U.S. domestic and foreign policy, national security, and economic policy. The center analyzes world crisis situations and recommends U.S. military and defense policies. Its publications report on issues of interest to the center. Its Web site has a searchable database of news, articles, testimony, and reports, including "Winning the War on Terror" and "The 'Post Conflict' Lessons of Iraq and Afghanistan."

Coalition for the International Criminal Court (CICC)
c/o WFM, 777 UN Plaza, New York, NY 10017
(212) 687-2176 • fax: (212) 599-1332
e-mail: cicc@iccnow.org • Web site: www.iccnow.org

CICC is a network of over two thousand nongovernmental organizations advocating for a fair, effective, and independent International Criminal Court (ICC). CICC publishes the semiannual *ICC Monitor*, recent issues of which are available on its Web site. The CICC Web site also makes available fact sheets and statements in support of the ICC.

Council on Foreign Relations (CFR)
58 E. Sixty-eighth St., New York, NY 10021
(212) 434-9400 • fax: (212) 434-9800
Web site: www.cfr.org

CFR specializes in foreign affairs and studies the international aspects of American political and economic policies and problems. Its journal *Foreign Affairs*, published five times a year, includes analyses of current conflicts around the world. Its Web site publishes editorials, interviews, and articles, including "The Humanitarian Transformation: Expanding Global Intervention Capacity" and "Is World Peace Through Conflict Prevention Possible?"

Foreign Policy Association (FPA)
470 Park Ave. South, 2nd Fl., New York, NY 10016
(212) 481-8100 • fax: (212) 481-9275
e-mail: info@fpa.org • Web site: www.fpa.org

FPA is a nonprofit organization that believes a concerned and informed public is the foundation for an effective foreign policy. Publications such as the annual *Great Decisions* briefing book and the newsletters *FPA Today* and *Global Views* cover foreign policy issues worldwide. FPA's Web site has an extensive searchable resource library of articles, reports, and speeches.

Global Exchange
2017 Mission St., #303, San Francisco, CA 94110
(415) 255-7296 • fax: (415) 255-7498
e-mail: info@globalexchange.org • Web site: www.globalexchange.org

Global Exchange is a human rights organization that exposes economic and political injustice around the world. In response to such injustices, the organization supports education, activism, and a noninterventionist U.S. foreign policy. It publishes the quarterly newsletter *Global Exchange.*

Heritage Foundation
214 Massachusetts Ave. NE, Washington, DC 20002-4999
(202) 546-4400 • fax: (202) 546-8328
e-mail: pubs@heritage.org • Web site: www.heritage.org

The foundation is a public policy research institute that advocates limited government and the free-market system. The foundation publishes the quarterly *Policy Review* as well as monographs, books, and papers supporting U.S. noninterventionism. Its Web site contains news and commentary and searchable databases on foundation issues.

Hoover Institution
Stanford University, Stanford, CA 94305-6010
(650) 723-1754 • fax: (650) 723-1687
e-mail: horaney@hoover.stanford.edu • Web site: www-hoover.stanford.edu

The Hoover Institution on War, Revolution, and Peace at Stanford University is a public policy research center devoted to advanced study of politics, economics, and political economy—both domestic and foreign—as well as international affairs. It publishes books on a wide range of national and international policy issues that may be purchased through the Hoover Press or read online.

Human Rights Watch
350 Fifth Ave., 34th Fl., New York, NY 10118-3299
(212) 290-4700 • (212) 736-1300
e-mail: hrwnyc@hrw.org • Web site: www.hrw.org

Founded in 1978, this nongovernmental organization conducts systematic investigations of human rights abuses in countries around the world. It publishes many books and reports on specific countries and issues as well as annual reports, recent selections of which are available on its Web site.

Joan B. Kroc Institute for International Peace Studies
PO Box 639, University of Notre Dame, Notre Dame, IN 46556
(219) 631 6970 • fax: (219) 631 6973
e-mail: krocinst@nd.edu • Web site: www.nd.edu

The institute follows the Catholic social tradition of promoting the prevention of violence and war. The institute pursues its aims through interdisciplinary educational programs on the graduate and undergraduate levels, peace research by its own faculty and visiting fellows, and public outreach aimed at bringing research to the public and to policy makers in the United States and throughout the world. It publishes the journal *Report* twice each year. A database of its research papers is available on its Web site.

Nuclear Age Peace Foundation
1187 Coast Village Rd., Suite 1, PMB 121, Santa Barbara, CA 93108-2794
(805) 965-3443 • fax: (805) 568-466
Web site: www.wagingpeace.org

Founded in 1982, the Nuclear Age Peace Foundation, a nonprofit, nonpartisan international education and advocacy organization, initiates and supports worldwide efforts to abolish nuclear weapons, to strengthen international law and institutions, to use technology responsibly and sustainably, and to empower youth to create a more peaceful world. Its Web site has a searchable database of news, editorials, and articles, including "Terrorism and Nonviolence" and "The Iraq War and the Future of International Law."

RAND Corporation
1700 Main St., Santa Monica, CA 90407-2138
(310) 393-0411 • fax: (310) 451-6960
Web site: www.rand.org

RAND is a nonprofit institution that attempts to improve public policy through research and analysis. It was created at the urging of its original sponsor, the U.S. Air Force (then the U.S. Army Air Forces), and from its inception has focused on the nation's most pressing policy problems. Objective research on national security became the institution's first hallmark. Its free journal *RAND Review* is published four times a year.

Reason Foundation
3415 S. Sepulveda Blvd., Suite 400, Los Angeles, CA 90034
(310) 391-2245 • fax: (310) 391-4395
Web site: www.reason.org

The foundation promotes individual freedoms and free-market principles, and opposes U.S. interventionism in foreign affairs. Its publications include the monthly *Reason* magazine, recent issues of which are available on its Web site.

United Nations Association of the United States of America
801 Second Ave., New York, NY 10017
(212) 907-1300 • fax: (212) 682-9185
e-mail: unahq@unausa.org • Web site: www.unausa.org

The association is a nonpartisan, nonprofit research organization dedicated to strengthening both the United Nations and U.S. participation in the UN Security Council. Its publications include *Interdependent*, a quarterly magazine. Its Web site publishes press releases, annual reports, fact sheets, surveys, and articles, including "A Beacon in the Dark: The International Criminal Court."

Bibliography

Books

Daniel Benjamin and Steven Simon — *The Age of Sacred Terror: Radical Islam's War Against America.* New York: Random House, 2003.

Mark Bowden — *Black Hawk Down: A Story of Modern War.* New York: Signet, 2002.

Carl Von Clausewitz — *On War.* Princeton, NJ: Princeton University Press, 1990.

Steve Coll — *Ghost Wars: The Secret History of the CIA, Afghanistan, and Bin Laden, from the Soviet Invasion to September 10, 2001.* New York: Penguin Group USA, 2005.

Mark Danner — *Torture and Truth: America, Abu Ghraib, and the War on Terror.* New York: New York Review of Books, 2004.

Michael DeLong and Noah Lukeman — *Inside CentCom: The Unvarnished Truth About the War in Afghanistan and Iraq.* Washington, DC: Regnery, 2004.

Thomas X. Hammes — *The Sling and the Stone: On War in the 21st Century.* Osceola, WI: MBI, 2004.

Victor Davis Hanson — *Ripples of Battle: How Wars of the Past Still Determine How We Fight, How We Live, and How We Think.* New York: Doubleday, 2003.

Chris Hedges — *War Is a Force That Gives Us Meaning.* New York: Bantam Doubleday Dell, 2003.

John Keegan — *The Iraq War.* New York: Alfred A. Knopf, 2004.

Gilles Kepel — *The War for Muslim Minds: Islam and the West.* Cambridge, MA: Harvard University Press, 2004.

Ronald Kessler — *The CIA at War: Inside the Secret Campaign Against Terror.* Irvine, CA: Griffin, 2004.

Michael T. Klare — *Resource Wars: The New Landscape of Global Conflict.* New York: Henry Holt, 2002.

Bernard-Henri Levy — *War, Evil, and the End of History.* Hoboken, NJ: Melville House, 2004.

| Bernard Lewis | *The Crisis of Islam: Holy War and Unholy Terror.* New York: Random House, 2003. |

| Chris Mackey and Greg Miller | *The Interrogators: Inside the Secret War Against al Qaeda.* New York: Little, Brown, 2004. |

| Walter Russell Mead | *Power, Terror, Peace, and War: America's Grand Strategy in a World at Risk.* New York: Knopf, 2004. |

| Richard Miniter | *Shadow War: The Untold Story of How Bush Is Winning the War on Terror.* Washington, DC: Regnery, 2004. |

| Natan Sharansky | *The Case for Democracy: The Power of Freedom to Overcome Tyranny and Terror.* New York: PublicAffairs, 2004. |

| Kenneth W. Waltz | *Man, the State, and War: A Theoretical Analysis.* New York: Columbia University Press, 2001. |

| Michael Walzer | *Arguing About War.* New Haven, CT: Yale University Press, 2004. |

Periodicals

| Correlli Barnett | "Why al-Qa'eda Is Winning," *Spectator*, December 13, 2003. |

| David Cortright | "Can the UN Battle Terrorism Effectively?" *USA Today Magazine*, January 2005. |

| *Economist* | "The Case for War Revisited," July 19, 2003. |

| *Economist* | "Is Torture Ever Justified?" January 19, 2003. |

| Bay Fang and Bruce B. Auster | "Iraq: A Magnet for Angry, Fervent Men," *U.S. News & World Report*, September 29, 2003. |

| William Greider | "Under the Banner of the 'War on Terror,'" *Nation*, June 21, 2004. |

| Husain Haqqani | "The Rage of Moderate Islam," *Foreign Policy*, January/February 2004. |

| Llewellyn D. Howell | "Terrorism's Violence Warp," *USA Today Magazine*, January 2005. |

| Walter Laqueur | "The Terrorism to Come," *Policy Review*, August/September 2004. |

| Maggie Ledford Lawson | "The Fatal Legend of Preemptive War," *National Catholic Reporter*, February 27, 2004. |

| Tom Lewis | "Why Attacking Iraq Made Strategic Sense," *Quadrant*, December 2004. |

| J.F.O. McAllister | "You Can't Kill Them All: Pre-Emptive Strikes Against Terror Will Win Some Battles but Lose the War," *Time International*, August 4, 2004. |

| Deroy Murdock | "Saddam Hussein's Philanthropy of Terror," *American Outlook*, Fall 2003. |

Bibliography

Caryle Murphy	"The War on Terrorism: Why It Really Will Be a Long One," *America*, April 28, 2003.
Andrew Natsios	"Fighting Terror with Aid: Underlying Conditions That Foster Terrorism," *Harvard International Review*, Fall 2004.
George Osborne	"While England Sleeps," *Spectator*, August 14, 2004.
Norman Podhoretz	"World War IV: How It Started, What It Means, and Why We Have to Win," *Commentary*, September 2004.
Paul Savoy	"The Moral Case Against the Iraq War," *Nation*, May 31, 2004.
James V. Schall	"When War Must Be the Answer," *Policy Review*, December 2004.
John L. Scherer	"The U.S.'s Befuddled Approach to the War on Terrorism," *USA Today Magazine*, November 2004.
P.W. Singer	"The War on Terrorism: The Big Picture," *Parameters*, Summer 2004.
Moeed Yusef	"The United States and Islamic Radicals: Conflict Unending?" *International Social Science Review*, Spring/Summer 2004.
Fareed Zakaria	"It's More than a War: To Defeat Terrorism We Must Think Beyond Bureaucratic Reform and Even Beyond Military Force," *Newsweek*, August 2, 2004.
Howard Zinn	"Our War on Terrorism," *Progressive*, November 2004.
Mortimer B. Zuckerman	"The Real Truth About Iraq," *U.S. News & World Report*, November 1, 2004.
Mortimer B. Zuckerman	"We Can Win—and We Must," *U.S. News & World Report*, September 13, 2004.

Index

Index